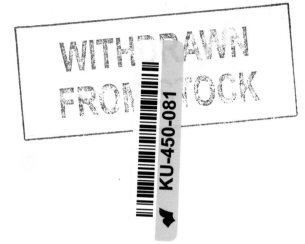

Solid Modelling
with DESIGNBASE
Theory and Implementation

Solid Modelling
with DESIGNBASE
Theory and Implementation

Hiroaki Chiyokura

Ricoh Company Limited, Tokyo
Ricoh Corporation, San Jose, CA

ADDISON-WESLEY PUBLISHING COMPANY

Singapore • Wokingham, England • Reading, Massachusetts
Menlo Park, California • New York • Don Mills, Ontario • Amsterdam
Sydney • Bonn • Tokyo • Madrid • San Juan

The publisher gratefully acknowledges the use of translated extracts from the book "Solid Modelling" by Hiroaki Chiyokura, originally published in Japanese, © Kogyo Chosakai Publishing Co. Ltd, Tokyo, 1985.

The programs presented in this book have been included for their instructional value. They have been tested with care but are not guaranteed for any particular purpose. The publisher does not offer any warranties or representations, nor does it accept any liabilities with respect to the programs.

Many of the designations used by manufacturers and sellers to distinguish their products are claimed as trademarks. Addison-Wesley has made every attempt to supply trademark information about manufacturers and their products mentioned in this book.

Jacket designed by Crayon Design of Henley-on-Thames and printed by The Riverside Printing Co. (Reading) Ltd.
Typeset by Times Graphics, Singapore.
Printed in Great Britain by T J Press (Padstow) Ltd, Cornwall.

First printed in 1988.

British Library Cataloguing in Publication Data
Chiyokura, Hiroaki
  Solid modelling with Designbase
  1. Products. Design & manufacture.
  Applications of computer systems
  I. Title
  670.42′7
  ISBN 0–201–19245–4

Library of Congress Cataloguing in Publication Data
Chiyokura, Hiroaki.
    [Soriddo moderingu. English]
    Solid modelling with Designbase : theory and implementation / Hiroaki Chiyokura.
      p. cm.
    Translation of: Soriddo moderingu.
    Bibliography: p.
    Includes index.
    ISBN 0–201–19245–4 (U.S.)
    1. Designbase (Computer program) 2. Computer graphics.
  3. CAD/CAM systems. I. Title.
  T385.C5213 1988
  670′.285′5369––dc19
                                 88–1930 0
                                   CIP

Foreword

Interactive CAD tools constitute one area where the ever increasing computing power of modern work stations is most welcome. While in the past the system designer had to make compromises and use approximations because of the limited amount of computing power available, the emerging trend is to use the increased power 'to do the task right' and to cater more to the needs of the user than to the shortcomings of the machine.

This trend is becoming quite visible in CAD/CAM modelling systems for the design of mechanical parts. Fast but ambiguous wireframe representations are giving way to full solid models with explicit topological information. Where speed of rendering was the major concern in the past, ease of use by the designer now starts to dominate. Where limited memory once forced the tersest representation, completeness and consistency of information is now more important.

While the desirable characteristics of a 'design-station' are well understood today, it is less clear how these features are best realized. For various aspects of a modelling system, there exist several possible choices, each offering a few special advantages, and none of them being perfect. One key choice concerns the underlying data representation.

Constructive Solid Geometry (CSG) is particularly well suited to provide a terse and consistent representation of the shapes of mechanical parts. Because the CSG representation reflects the original modelling process, it can easily be modified and parameterized. However, in this representation it is difficult to implement the local operations needed for rounding corners, inserting fillets, and fine-tuning free-form curved surfaces. A description of the surface of an object, on the other hand, can easily be modified locally, but it may not always represent a consistent solid object. It can readily be converted to a wire-frame display in which edges belonging to backfaces are dotted by localized tests, thus providing a very effective approximation to a rendering with hidden line elimination. The trade-offs between these two representations have intrigued designers of solid modelling systems for over a decade. Their aspiration is to find a way to combine the best features of both approaches in a symbiotic and yet efficient manner.

DESIGNBASE represents a fine example of a good engineering solution to this challenge. This modelling system allows the user to start with a hierarchical compositional CSG-view of a part and then to refine it with local but consistent operations on the boundary representation of the object. By basing all operations available to the user on well-defined, invertible Euler-operations, it is possible to keep a compact representation of the complete design history of a part, and thus to 'undo' and 're-do' any sequence of operations. This encourages the designer to try out ideas without fear of destroying a model in which several hours of design time have already been invested. It also makes it possible to store several alternative versions of a design in a natural and efficient manner.

Another task that a modelling system aimed at industrial mechanical applications must deal with is rounded edges and fillets. One of the significant contributions of DESIGNBASE is an elegant and very effective way to integrate these features with the representation of free-form surfaces. It offers a simple, elegant, and computationally efficient way of dealing with curved surfaces for mechanical parts. Convenient higher-level operations are provided to carry out rounding operations on edges and vertices that will cover a large percentage of the typical needs of industrial designs with some default settings. Dr Chiyokura's work in that area has been truly inspirational.

This book openly discusses the decision processes that led to various implementation choices made in DESIGNBASE. While different application areas may require different decisions in some of the trade-offs, seeing the trade-offs discussed objectively is very educational and broadens one's perspective. This book should prove stimulating or even inspirational to all people seriously interested in solid modelling.

Carlo H. Séquin,
Professor, U.C. Berkeley
February 1988

Preface

Solid modelling is the name given to a technique used to represent three-dimensional shapes in computers. Recently, the importance of solid modelling in computer-aided design and manufacturing has been increasing. A solid modelling system for creating and managing solid models is the kernel of any advanced CAD/CAM system, and as such supports many activities in CAD/CAM.

I first researched solid modelling technology through a Masters course at Keio University and then in the course of my Doctorate at the University of Tokyo, during which I developed an experimental solid modelling system, MODIF. Subsequently DESIGNBASE, a solid modelling system for practical use, has been developed at the Software Research Center of Ricoh. The advantage of DESIGNBASE is that a wide range of solid shapes from polyhedra to free-form surfaces can be designed in a unified manner. This book describes the theory and implementation techniques of solid modelling through the experience of developing DESIGNBASE.

I would like to thank Dr Hideko S. Kunii, a director of the Software Research Center, and Professor Tosiyasu L. Kunii, of the University of Tokyo, for their valuable contributions both to the development of DESIGNBASE and to this book. I also wish to thank Professor Fumihiko Kimura, Professor Toshio Sata, Professor Mamoru Hosaka and Dr Katsumori Matsushima for their contributions to my doctoral research; Professor Masakazu Nakanishi and Professor Yoshio Ohno for their advice during my research for my Masters. I acknowledge my colleagues at the Software Research Center for the implementation of DESIGN-BASE: Hiroshi Toriya and Toshiaki Satoh for Boolean operations; Teiji Takamura for ray tracing; Kenji Ueda for undo and redo operations; Masaaki Kagawa for scan-line shading; Takashi Hashimoto for reference functions; Kouichi Konno for two-dimensional input; Hung-tien Ting for numerical control programming; and Kenji Koori and Naoko Ichikawa for test programming of DESIGNBASE.

Lastly I thank my wife, Masako, and my son, Nagahide, for their support which helped me to finish this project.

Hiroaki Chiyokura
January 1988

Contents

Chapter 1

Solid Modelling in CAD/CAM

1.1 GEOMETRIC MODELLING IN CAD/CAM

CAD/CAM (computer-aided design and manufacturing) technology for supporting many computerized activities in design and manufacturing is now playing an increasingly important role in production industries. The importance of CAD/CAM has been widely recognized. Many people in engineering anticipate that CAD/CAM technologies will make it possible to shorten product development time and also lower the cost of development. Additionally, the reliability and the quality of the product can be improved. CAD/CAM systems have therefore been developed in various fields of industry including automobile and aircraft manufacture, architecture and shipbuilding, and there are currently many commercial CAD/CAM systems available.

The major problem in CAD/CAM is how to represent information on the product in a computer. In conventional design and manufacturing, product information is described in an engineering drawing. Because the information is described in this form, it can be interpreted only by trained engineers. In the case of CAD/CAM, information must be stored in a computer so that it can be manipulated by use of a computer. Thus the development of techniques for representing and utilizing product information in a computer is very important.

In mechanical engineering, one of the most important pieces of information in any drawing is the three-dimensional shape of the product. A designer will describe the shape of the product in the drawing so that it satisfies various engineering requirements. When the designed object is part of an assembled machine, its shape plays a functional role. On the other hand, when the object is the body of an electrical product or a car, for instance, its shape plays an aesthetic role. When using CAD for mechanical design, it is necessary to represent a three-dimensional shape in a computer and therefore techniques are required to construct the representation. The representation of three-dimensional shape is referred to as a **geometric model**; the technique of constructing the shape is called **geometric modelling**.

Broadly speaking, the techniques required in geometric modelling are divided into two groups: **solid modelling** (sometimes called **volume modelling**) and **curved surface modelling**. Solid modelling includes techniques for the construction of a designed object as a rigid solid, data structures to represent solids and computation of the intersection of two solids. Curved surface modelling includes techniques to represent curved surfaces, the interpolation of given points and curves and surface approximation.

The shapes of industrial products are represented by a great number of edges and faces and have a variety of curved surfaces, so both solid modelling and curved surface modelling are important design tools.

1.2   DESIGNING THREE-DIMENSIONAL SHAPES

In conventional design and manufacturing, information about three-dimensional (3-D) shapes is described in engineering drawings. However, drawing-based design presents several problems. This section discusses the problems involved in conventional 3-D design and then describes how geometric model-based design can solve these problems.

Figure 1.1 shows the process of using drawings to design aesthetic shapes. A designer begins by drawing rough sketches of the object. Then he or she will make a 3-D rough model to check the design. After the design is fixed, the designer produces a drawing representing the final shape. The next stage is for a modeller to make a 3-D model using soft materials such as wood or clay. The model will be refined several times, and the final one is then the master model. A die for making the product is produced from this master, using a machine tool.

This design process contains the following problems.

1.   Communication between the designer and the modeller

Although the designed object is 3-D, the information in the drawing is 2-D, so the information passed from the designer to the modeller is incomplete. Generally, the designer is not satisfied with the first model. When the shape includes **free-form surfaces** (sometimes called **sculptured surfaces**), the problem is particularly serious. These free-form surfaces

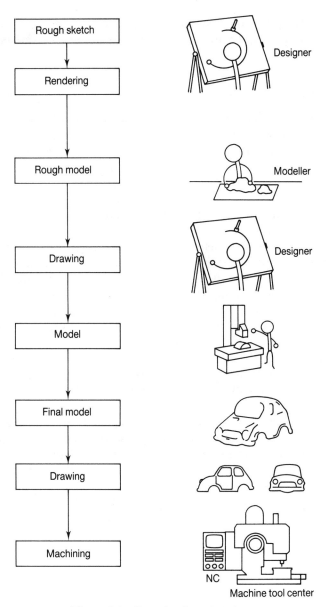

Figure 1.1 Drawing-based design.

are smooth surfaces which cannot be represented by geometrical surfaces such as the cylinder and cone. To define free-form surfaces, therefore, a designer will draw many cross-sections. However, the designer often cannot adequately express the shape that he envisions, so the first model may need many modifications. To satisfy these design requirements, the modeller will then make a new model and this process will be repeated as necessary. However, because both the finance and the time available for design are in general limited, the designer is not always satisfied by the final model.

2.   Time taken and costs incurred in the design process

After the designer has specified the modifications required, obviously he would like the new model made as quickly as possible, and for the modeller to make as many models as necessary. However, it takes several weeks to make each model, and they are expensive to produce. In developing a commercial product, it is desirable to shorten the time taken in designing it and to minimize expenditure. It is therefore difficult to allow the designer to produce as many models as he or she might wish.

To solve these problems, a system of design based on geometric modelling has been proposed. Figure 1.2 shows such a design process. In this method, the designer does not produce a finished drawing, but works interactively on a computer to refine the design and produce a geometric model. To enable the designer to understand the shapes represented in a computer, the system displays realistic colour images on a raster graphic display, and automatically makes true 3-D models using a 3-D plotter. If the shape of the model does not satisfy the designer, the geometric model in the computer is easily and quickly modified. A die for making the final product is automatically made using a numerically controlled machine tool.

This design method enables the designer to modify a 3-D shape until it fits his exact requirements. It is possible also to make a great number of 3-D models, since each one can be quickly made. This both raises the quality of design and shortens the total time-taken. However, this method has not been widely used in practical engineering fields. One of the main reasons for this is that conventional CAD systems do not make it easy for a designer to model a 3-D shape. In order to realize the design framework outlined above, it is necessary for a modelling system to be developed which enables a designer to make a geometric model easily and naturally.

1.3   GEOMETRIC MODELLING

Many methods have been used to represent 3-D shapes in scientific and engineering fields (Requicha, 1980; Besl and Jain, 1985). The most well-known are **spatial occupancy representations, generalized cone representations, wire-frame models, surface models, boundary representations**, and **constructive solid geometry representations**. Of spatial occupancy representations, **octree representations** are the most famous (Meagher,

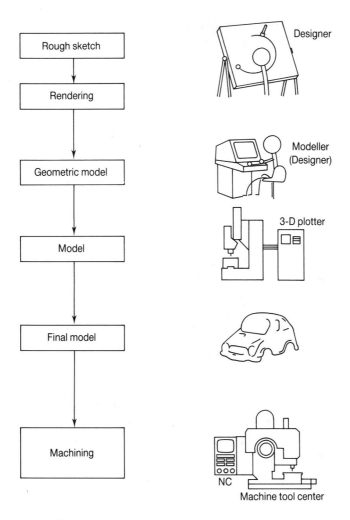

Figure 1.2   Geometric model-based design.

1981). An octree is a hierarchical representation of spatial occupancy. Volumes are broken down into cubes of various sizes. The cube size depends on the distance from the root node. Generalized cones are often called **sweep representations** (Agin and Binford, 1973). The object shape is represented by a 3-D space curve indicating the axis of the cone and by 2-D cross-sectional shapes. The sweeping rule defines how the cross-section is modified along the space curve. Octrees and generalized cones have been used in computer graphics applications and computer vision for recognizing 3-D shapes. However, because these representations cannot adequately describe the detail in 3-D shapes, they have not been used in mechanical CAD systems to represent internal structures.

In conventional mechanical CAD systems, wire-frame models, surface models, boundary representations (**B-reps**), and constructive solid geometry representations (**CSG-reps**) have been used as 3-D geometric models. Although a wire-frame model or surface model represents part of a designed object, B-reps and CSG-reps represent the complete shape of an object as a closed space in 3-D space. Here we will call B-reps and CSG-reps **solid models**. Only a solid model makes it possible to check whether or not any point in a space is included in the solid. The geometrical representations used in CAD systems are described below.

1. Wire-frame model

A wire-frame model is represented by tables defining edges and points. The start point and the end point of each edge are stored in the edge table. An edge may be a line or a curve. The coordinates (x, y, z values) of each point are stored in the point table. This representation is natural for a designer who is familiar with mechanical drawings, since it is the lines and curves in a drawing which define the 3-D shape. A wire-frame model is stored very simply in a computer as a data structure. The storage space is small and the access time very short. Most of the early 3-D CAD systems used wire-frame models. However, a wire-frame model is ambiguous when determining the surface area and volume of an object. Although several methods have been proposed for converting wire-frame models to solid models (Markowski and Wesley, 1980; Hanrahan, 1982; Courter and Brewer, 1986), many different solids can often be defined from a single wire-frame. Figure 1.3(a) shows an example of an ambiguous wire-frame model. Figures 1.3(b) and (c) show the different solids defined by this representation.

2. Surface model

A surface model is represented by tables of edges and points, as is a wire-frame model, plus a table of faces. The face table stores information on which edges are attached to each face. Figure 1.4 shows a surface model. In the face table, a record of face F_1 stores edges E_1, E_2, E_3 and E_4. In most conventional CAD systems for free-form surfaces, surface models have been used as internal representations. However, a surface model is a set of faces, and as such is ambiguous when determining the volume of an object.

3. Boundary representation (B-rep)

A boundary representation of a solid model has information on the faces, edges and vertices in a surface model, plus **topological information** which

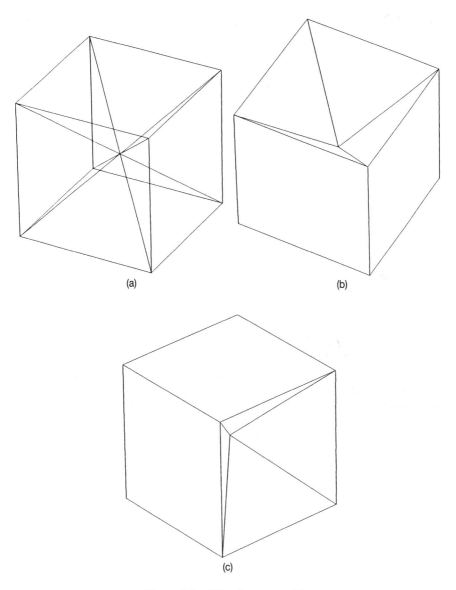

Figure 1.3 Wire-frame model.

defines the relationships between the faces, edges and vertices. Figure 1.5 shows an example of topological information. Edge E_1 runs between vertices V_1 and V_2, and meets faces F_1 and F_2. Vertex V_1 is connected to edges E_1, E_2 and E_3. Because boundary representations include such topological information, a solid is represented as a closed space in 3-D space.

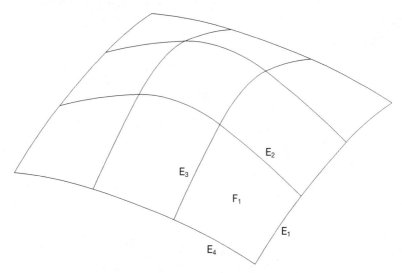

Figure 1.4   Surface model.

4.   Constructive solid geometry representation (CSG-rep)

One of the most useful tools for making a complex solid is a **Boolean operation** (sometimes called a **set operation**). Using a Boolean operation, a new solid is made from two intersecting solids. The operations consist of **union**, **intersection** and **difference**. Figure 1.6(a) shows two solids to which

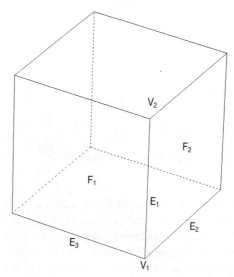

Figure 1.5   A boundary representation showing topological information.

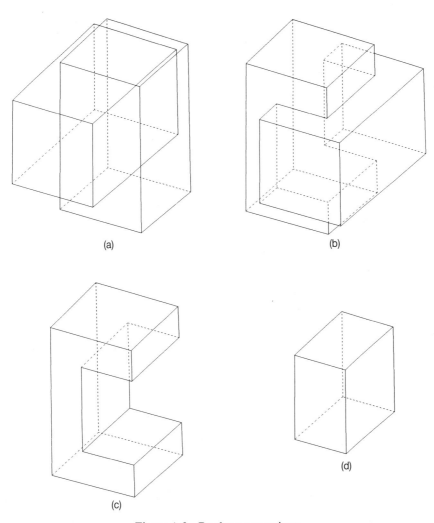

(a)

(b)

(c)

(d)

Figure 1.6   Boolean operations.

Boolean operations will be applied. Figures 1.6(b), (c) and (d) show the resulting solids generated by union, intersection and difference, respectively. The CSG-rep of a solid model is specified in terms of a set of Boolean operations and a set of 3-D primitive solids (e.g. blocks, cylinders and spheres). Figure 1.7 shows an example of a CSG-rep. In the figure, solid C is made from solids A and B using a union operation. Solid E is then made from solids C and D using a different operation. This type of modelling process is known as a CSG-rep, and is represented by a binary tree called a **CSG-tree**. Since a solid model may be either a B-rep or a CSG-rep, the advantages and disadvantages of each representation will be discussed in Chapter 3.

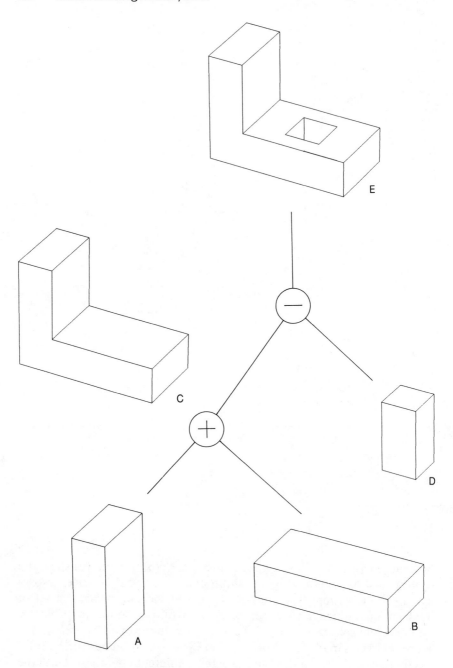

Figure 1.7 A constructive solid geometry representation.

1.4   APPLICATIONS OF SOLID MODELLING

Because there is no ambiguity in using a solid model to represent a 3-D shape, the importance of using solid modelling in CAD/CAM has been widely recognized. The solid model can support a wide range of activities, examples of which are described below.

1.   Interference checks

An assembled machine consists of a great number of mechanical parts. Therefore when designing a machine, the interference between the parts must be checked. In conventional design, 3-D models are made, and the interference between the models is then checked. This is a lengthy procedure. In CAD, on the other hand, where the parts are represented as solid models in a computer, interference checks can be done automatically (Boyse, 1979). It is also possible to compute and display the region of intersection of any two parts which interfere.

The same techniques have been applied to the modelling of industrial robots (Pickett *et al.*, 1984). Recently, computers have been used to control the movements of industrial robots. After they have been programmed, the interference between robots and workpieces must be examined. If there is any interference, the robots could cause havoc in the production line. By including a solid modelling system in a robot programming system, the relational movements of robot and workpieces can be easily examined, and the interference path of the robot can be automatically detected.

2.   Computation of volume and surface area

The volume of a designed solid and the area of the faces of that solid are conventionally calculated using a mechanical drawing and 3-D models. Using information derived from solid models, volume and area can be automatically computed (Lee and Requicha, 1982; Lien and Kajiya, 1984). One method of determining volume is to divide the volume of a model into cells, i.e. cubes of the same size, and to classify these as inside or outside the object. A count of cells inside the object yields the volume. Accuracy is determined by the size of the cells.

3.   Cutter path generation

In order to make a 3-D model or die using numerically controlled (NC) machine tools, the **cutter path** must first be computed. Since the solid model provides useful information for generating the cutter path, many automatic methods have been proposed for deriving NC information, although the range of shapes is limited (Grayer, 1977; Woo, 1977; Stacey and Middleditch, 1986). A solid modelling system also can be applied to the automatic verification of NC information (Wang and Wang, 1986). By modelling the trajectory of a cutter, we can examine the interference between a cutter and its environment.

4. Computer vision

Much research for determining the 3-D location and orientation of an object from digitized image data has been done (Besl and Jain, 1985). This research can be usefully applied in the development of robotic 'eyes'. If the object is represented as a solid model, several stable orientations of the object can be computed (Wesley *et al.*, 1980). Such information is useful in object recognition.

5. Finite element analysis

To simulate the stresses and strains on designed objects using finite element analysis, meshes of the objects are required. It is possible to derive these meshes from solid models and automatic generation methods have been proposed (Wördenweber, 1984).

1.5 SOLID MODELLING SYSTEMS

Nowadays, there are several commercial solid modelling system available (Johnson, 1986), among which are CATIA (Dassault Systems), EUCLID (Matra Datavision), GEOMOD (Structural Dynamic Research Corporation) and ROMULUS (Shape Data Ltd). These systems generate primitive solids such as the cube, cylinder, cone, torus and sphere. Specifying precise dimensions, complex solid shapes are modelled from the primitive solids using Boolean operations. The shapes are exactly represented so that the models can support many applications in design and manufacturing.

DESIGNBASE, on the other hand, has been developed to support the conceptual design of aesthetic shapes. In the early stages of such designs, it is often more important to model the characteristics of the final shape than to specificy dimensions. Designers require the system to respond quickly and to provide simple facilities for modelling complex free-form surfaces. DESIGNBASE satisfies these requirements. In our present system, the faces of solids are represented by either planes or free-form surfaces. This version of DESIGNBASE does not deal with quadric surfaces which are important in producing models of mechanical components.

Chapter 2

Interactive Solid Modelling Systems

2.1   History of solid modelling systems
2.2   Problems of solid modelling systems
2.3   Advanced solid modelling technology

2.1   HISTORY OF SOLID MODELLING SYSTEMS

The concept of a solid modelling system was first proposed independently by Okino *et al.* (1973) at Hokkaido University and by Braid and Lang (1973) at Cambridge. They implemented the systems TIPS and BUILD, respectively, and demonstrated the superiority of solid modelling over any other geometric modelling system. Both groups presented their research at the PRORAMAT international conference, held in Budapest in 1973 (Hatvany, 1973).

In both their methods for defining a solid, primitive solids (e.g. blocks and cylinders) are first positioned in 3-D space by translation and rotation. Using Boolean operations, a complex solid shape is then generated from primitive solids. Although in both systems the methods for defining a solid are almost the same, their methods of representing solids in a computer are completely different. In TIPS, Boolean operations and primitive solids used to define a solid are used in the representation. Nowaday, such a representation is called a **CSG (constructive solid geometry)** representation. On the other hand, in BUILD, a solid is represented by a set of all the faces of the solid, plus topological information on how its faces, edges and vertices are connected. This representation is called a **B-rep (boundary representation)**. Since these systems were developed, many solid modelling systems have been devised (Baer *et al.*, 1980; Requicha and Voelcker, 1982, 1983). Most systems have used either a CSG-rep or B-rep or both, thus demonstrating the importance of both TIPS and BUILD in solid modelling research.

After TIPS and BUILD, many people discussed which of the two representations, the CSG-rep or the B-rep, was the better. Considering the wide variety of applications of solid models, each representation had its advantages and drawbacks, neither one could be said to be superior. At about the same period as this discussion, an important solid modelling system, PADL-1, was developed by Voelcker and Requicha (1977) at the University of Rochester. In PADL-1, although the **internal representation** of a system is a CSG-rep, a B-rep is generated from a CSG-rep when a B-rep is required (i.e. when a wire-frame picture is drawn). PADL-1 can provide both representations for different applications, and is therefore a **dual representation** method. When PADL-1 appeared the debate on the two representations changed emphasis to become a discussion on which is better as an internal representation of a solid modelling system. If a CSG-rep is used as an internal representation, the system can provide both representations because it is possible to convert a CSG-rep to a B-rep. On the other hand, a system using a B-rep as an internal representation does not provide a CSG-rep because it is generally difficult to convert a B-rep to a CSG-rep. However, the B-rep based system has the advantage that a great variety of operations can be used to change the shape of a solid (see Section 3.1).

2.1.1 CSG-rep based systems

As mentioned above, TIPS and PADL-1 were the earliest CSG-based systems. However, there are differences in the CSG-reps of the two systems. Although the leaves in PADL-1's CSG-tree are always primitive solids, TIPS can use **half-spaces** as leaves in its CSG-trees. Half-spaces are infinite surfaces which divide a 3-D space into two regions. For example, a cube composed of six faces is represented by six half-spaces.

TIPS has been improved upon at Hokkaido University, up to the present, and is available through CAM-I, Inc. (a non-profit consortium in Arlington, Texas) (CAM-I, 1981). PADL-2, an updated version of PADL-1, has been developed by the Rochester University group (Brown, 1982). While PADL-1 was an experimental system whose only primitive solids were the block and the cylinder, PADL-2 was designed for industrial use and has quadric surface objects as primitives. General Motors has developed GMSolid (Boyse and Gilchrist, 1982) (a system for internal use) which was strongly influenced by the concepts behind PADL-1.

2.1.2 B-rep based systems

At Stanford University Baumgart (1974) developed GEOMED, a system for computer vision, independently of BUILD. In GEOMED, solids were represented by use of a **winged-edge structure**. This method has since influenced many B-rep based systems. At Cambridge University, BUILD2 (Braid, 1979) was developed using this method. A B-rep based system ROMULUS (Veenman, 1979), which inherits the concept of BUILD and GEOMED, has been released as a commercial product by Shape Data Ltd of Cambridge, England.

In the early 1970s, other B-rep based solid modelling systems appeared, examples of which are GEOMAP (Hosaka *et al.*, 1974; Hosaka and Kimura, 1977) at the University of Tokyo, COMPAC (Spur and Gausemeier, 1975) at the Technical University of Berlin and GLIDE (Eastman and Henrion, 1977) at Carnegie-Mellon University. These systems provided the basis for contemporary industrial systems.

2.2 PROBLEMS OF SOLID MODELLING SYSTEMS

Although the usefulness of solid modelling has been widely recognized, most CAD systems for mechanical design use wire-frame and surface models as internal representations of 3-D shapes. However, there is only a small number of solid modelling systems used in industry, since several problems are encountered when conventional solid modelling systems are used to design industrial products. The following four problems are especially significant.

1. Response time

For a system to be an interactive design tool, it must have a fast response time. Because the design process is one of trial and error, a designer expects the response to all the commands in the system to be rapid. However, response times in most conventional solid modelling systems are slow, since Boolean operations mainly are used to construct complex solid shapes. In a Boolean operation to combine two solids, the interference between all the faces of one solid and all the faces of the other solid must be checked. So although a Boolean operation has the advantage that a valid solid is always generated, it requires much computation time. In addition, the computation time depends on the complexity of the solids being modified.

2. The range of solid shapes generated

Conventional solid modelling systems were designed to generate poly-hedra and solids with simple surfaces, such as cylinders and cones. However, the shapes of industrial products involve a great variety of complex surfaces. It is therefore necessary to be able to model a wide range of shapes in a single solid modelling system.

The design of aesthetic objects particularly requires that free-form surfaces can be easily modelled. Systems for modelling free-form surfaces generally use a surface model in internal representations and have been developed independently of solid modelling systems. Thus a technique to integrate solid modelling and free-form surface modelling is required.

3. Ease of use

A variety of facilities are required for a designer easily to create complex shapes using a solid modelling system as a design tool. First, the input method should be considered. Many designers are used to drawing engineering drawings to define product shapes, so the input methods in conventional CAD systems are not familiar to them. In addition, the design process is one of trial and error, so the system should structure it in such a way that any previous shape can be quickly regenerated. However, conventional systems are inadequate in these respects.

4. System reliability

Because a CSG-tree is represented by a binary tree, the data structure of a CSG-rep is simple, and the operations to create and modify a CSG-rep are easily implemented. On the other hand, a B-rep consists of tables of faces, edges and vertices, and elements of their tables are connected by pointers to represent topological information. Thus the implementation of operations to create and modify a B-rep is complex. If the operater makes even a small mistake, the system can destroy the structure of solid models which a designer has laboured long and hard to create. System reliability is therefore of vital importance.

2.3   ADVANCED SOLID MODELLING TECHNOLOGY

Happily, the problems described in the previous section have been resolved, and we will now describe these solutions.

1. Response time

Two methods have been proposed to shorten the response time of a solid modelling system: one is to develop a fast algorithm of a Boolean operation; the other is to devise an efficient operation, other than a Boolean operation, to create and modify solid shapes. In the Boolean operations to combine two solids, the search procedure to establish which part of a solid intersects with the other requires much computational time. Several methods have been suggested in which spatial occupancy representations are created and each cell stores information

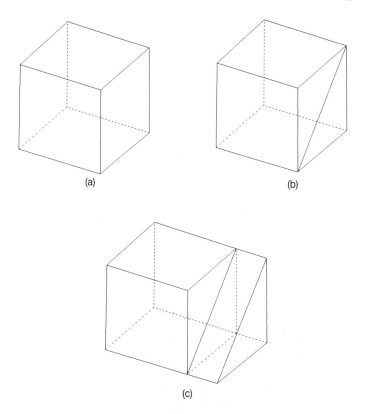

(a)

(b)

(c)

Figure 2.1   Local operations.

on which edges and vertices of the solid are included in the cell (Mäntylä and Tamminen, 1983; Carlbom, 1987; Thibault and Naylor, 1987), i.e. the spatial occupancy is used as the spatial directory of a solid. As a result, geometric intersections can be efficiently discovered. There has also been research undertaken to develop special hardware for Boolean operations (Yamaguchi and Tokieda, 1984).

Local operations are alternative methods of efficiently constructing the shape of a solid. Local operations can locally create or modify B-reps of solids, for example, by making edges and sweeping a face, as shown in Figure 2.1. It is cheap to use local operations to construct solids, because their use does not require global interference checks, as do Boolean operations. In addition, the computation time of local operations is usually independent of the complexity of the solids being modelled. However, local operations have the disadvantage that **self-intersecting** or **self-touching solids** are easily created. Figure 2.2 shows an example of a self-intersecting solid. If local operations are used in the construction of a solid, the geometric consistency of the designed object must therefore be checked.

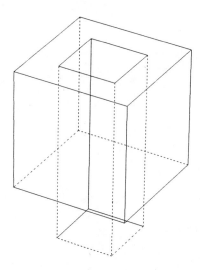

Figure 2.2 A self-intersecting solid.

Local operations originate from **Euler operations**, which were developed by Baumgart (1975). Such operations add or delete faces, edges and vertices according to Euler's formula for solid objects. Later, Braid *et al.* (1980) developed the **stepwise construction** method as an extension of Baumgart's method. Nowadays, these operations are called local operations. Because they are dependent on the B-reps of solids, most operations can not be applied to CSG-reps.

While a CSG-based system can provide both a CSG-rep and a B-rep to support a wide range of applications, it is difficult to implement local operations in the system. When designing our solid modelling system, we considered it most important to enable the user to employ a great variety of operations. We therefore adopted a B-rep as the internal representation. In DESIGNBASE, a user can employ these local operations and a rounding operation, which is a new local operation, to construct solids with free-form surfaces (Chiyokura and Kimura, 1983).

2. The range of solid shapes generated

There has recently been much research into expanding the range of shapes which solid modelling systems can generate. Broadly speaking, these methods form three groups. The first is the expansion of Boolean operations so that they can be applied to solids with free-form surfaces. The technique essential in implementing the Boolean operation is the computation of intersecting curves between two different free-form surfaces. Several methods have been proposed (Houghton *et al.*, 1985; Barnhill *et al.*, 1987; Farouki, 1987). In addition, several systems have been developed applying Boolean operations to free-form surfaces (Riesenfeld, 1983; Sarraga and Waters, 1984; Thomas, 1985).

The second group comprises methods of constructing fillets which blend between two different surfaces (Rossignac and Requicha, 1984; Hoffmann and Hopcroft, 1985; Middleditch and Sears, 1985; Rockwood and Owen, 1987). These methods are limited to the modelling of smooth surfaces between implicit surfaces such as quadrics.

The third group is that of methods to generate free-form surfaces from polyhedra. This method was first proposed by Doo and Sabin (1978), Catmull and Clark (1978). Chiyokura and Kimura (1983) then proposed a local operation, the rounding of a polyhedron, to integrate solid modelling and free-form surface modelling. The method of rounding a polyhedron has recently been expanded (Beeker, 1986; Fjällström, 1986; Séquin, 1986; Tan and Chan, 1986; Wijk, 1986; Nastri, 1987). As complex calculations are not usually necessary, computation time and reliability are not adversely affected. However, there are several restrictions in the range of shapes generated.

In DESIGNBASE, free-form surfaces are generated by rounding operations. The edges and vertices of polyhedra can be locally rounded, and the user can specify the radii of curves to be generated (Chiyokura, 1987).

3. *Ease of use*

Although solid modelling systems provide both Boolean and local operations with which to construct complex solids, designers may often wish to use 2-D pictures to define 3-D shapes, since they are familiar with engineering drawing methods. Thus various methods have been proposed for constructing solids from orthographic views (Idesawa, 1973; Wesley and Markowsky, 1981; Sakurai and Gossard, 1983). Some commercial solid modelling systems, including MEDUSA (Cambridge Interactive Systems Ltd), provide graphic windows which correspond to different views in 2-D drawings. In these systems, solid models can be constructed in a manner akin to drafting.

In interactive systems, recovery facilities for users are important, because data may be accidentally destroyed. In order for systems to be more user-friendly, several methods of user recovery have been proposed (Archer *et al.*, 1984; Vitter, 1984). In DESIGNBASE, the process of constructing a solid is represented by a tree data structure. In addition, all operations are implemented so that their inverse can be executed. These facilities enable the user to choose quick **undo** and **redo** operations to regenerate any previously designed solid (Toriya *et al.*, 1986).

4. *System reliability*

In conventional B-rep based solid modelling systems, the user implementing operations and applications must fully understand solid data structures. However, because the structure of a B-rep is complex, the programmer may make mistakes. This reduces the reliability of the system.

Recent B-rep based systems such as BUILD2 (Braid, 1979) and GWB (Mäntylä, 1983) provide Euler operations, which create and modify B-reps when complex shape operations, such as Boolean operations, are implemented. In many cases, then, the programmers of such systems need not be concerned with the details of solid data structure. As a result, these systems can be easier to implement.

In DESIGNBASE, Euler operations and all atomic operations for changing the data structure of solids are called **primitive operations**. **Reference functions** are used to derive geometrical information from the data structure. All shaping operations are implemented by primitive operations and reference functions, without using B-reps. Thus the implementation of operations and applications in DESIGNBASE is simple.

Chapter 3

Representation of Solids

This chapter describes methods of representing solid shapes and a process for designing solids.

3.1   INTERNAL REPRESENTATION OF A SYSTEM

Most solid modelling systems have adopted either CSG-reps or B-reps as internal representations of solids. In this section, the advantages and drawbacks of each method are discussed. We then describe why a B-rep was adopted as the internal representation in DESIGNBASE.

3.1.1   Advantages and drawbacks of CSG-reps

1.   *Advantages of a CSG-rep*

1. The data structure of a CSG-rep is simple, and its data size is small. The internal management of the data structure is therefore easy.

2. A CSG-rep always corresponds to a physically valid solid.

3. Any system using a CSG-rep as an internal representation can provide both a CSG-rep and B-rep, as it is generally possible to convert a CSG-rep to a B-rep. The system can therefore support a wide variety of applications.

4. It is easy to modify a solid shape corresponding to a CSG-rep. Figure 3.1 shows a simple example in which the radius of a cylinder hole in a block is changed. In a CSG-rep based system, the cylinder hole is created by subtracting a cylinder primitive from the original solid, so in this case, a user changes only the radius of the cylinder primitive. Because CSG-reps define not only the shape of a solid, but also the process of modelling that solid, such a modification is easy.

2.   Drawbacks of a CSG-rep

1. There are only limited operations available to create and modify a solid. Generally, it is not easy to implement operations other than Boolean operations (e.g. local operations). In an interactive design environment, users require a quick response to the shaping operation, so local operations are important modelling tools. However, most local operations simply can not be implemented. Also, to improve the 'user-friendliness' of a system, a wide variety of operations should be available.

2. The computation for generating pictures of solids (e.g. wire-frame drawings and colour-shaded pictures) requires much time. This is because boundary elements, such as faces and edges, drawn in the picture are implicitly represented in CSG-reps, and hence obtaining the elements is computationally expensive. Several algorithms, have recently been proposed for creating shaded pictures of CSG-reps and special hardwares, (Okino et al., 1984; Satoh et al., 1985; Goldfeather et al., 1986).

3.1.2   Advantages and drawbacks of B-reps

1.   Advantages of a B-rep

1. Since edges and faces are explicitly represented in a B-rep, a wire-frame picture of a B-rep is quickly drawn. It is also easy and quick to ascertain topological relationships – which vertices are connected to an edge, which edges are attached to a face, and so on.

2. In B-rep based systems there are few restrictions on the availability of operations, so a wide variety of operations can be used.

2.   Drawbacks of a B-rep

1. The data structure of a B-rep is complex, and it requires a large memory space. Procedures for manipulating the internal data are therefore complex.

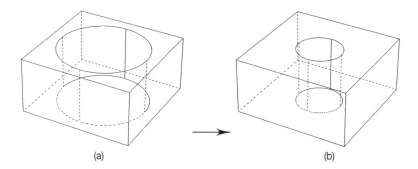

(a)   (b)

Figure 3.1   A simple shape modification.

2.   Since B-reps are only representations of solid shapes, modification is occasionally troublesome. In order to made the modification in Figure 3.1 using Boolean operations, the user must first erase the hole by adding an appropriate solid, then make a new hole by subtracting a cylinder with smaller radius. When a mistake is made in the creation or modification of a B-rep, a similar problem arises. For example, if a mistake occurs in positioning solids, and a Boolean operation is applied to two solids, important parts of the originals may be erased. Figure 3.2 shows this type of mistake in a Boolean operation. Figures 3.2(a) and (b) show two solids to be applied by a union operation. While Figure 3.2(c) shows the solid generated by the correct operation. Figure 3.2(d) shows a solid generated as the result of an error. To correct such an error, after erasing the rectangle the user must reconstruct part of the original solid.

3.   B-reps are informationally complete as representations of solids. However, they do not always correspond to valid solids. Figure 3.3 illustrates a case of an invalid solid generated by a local operation. When sweeping a face of a solid as shown in Figure 3.3(a), a user specifies the distance the face is to be translated. The shape of the solid is then changed, as shown in Figure 3.3(b). If a user makes mistakes in specifying the distance, self-intersecting objects will sometimes be generated, as shown in Figure 3.3(c). In most cases, the user can regenerate the original solid by using other local operations. However, occasionally this is very difficult. For example, when the distance specified is very large, it is not always possible to see the whole of the solid in the graphic display. When the distance is very small, it is difficult to specify elements such as edges, faces and vertices, using an input device (e.g. a mouse). Because of these problems in modifying B-reps, designers need to take care in specifying operations.

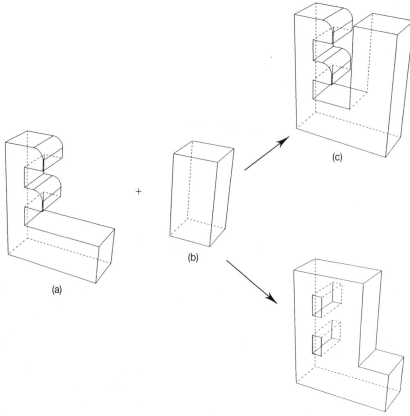

Figure 3.2   Mistakes in Boolean operations.

To solve the problems generated by users' mistakes, a solid data recovery facility is required in B-rep based systems. Two methods have conventionally been implemented.

Saving data on the solid   The first method is to save all the data on the solid as a file in an external storage system, at each stage of the design process. The previously designed solid can be regenerated from the geometric information in the stored file. This method is quick because no computation is required. However, when complex solids are constructed using many commands, a vast amount of storage space is required because the data is saved repeatedly during the design process. This method is therefore economically undesirable.

Recomputing commands   The second method is to store all the commands entered by the user when generating a solid. When a previously designed solid has to be regenerated, all these operations must be re-executed. This is time-consuming if a great number of commands were

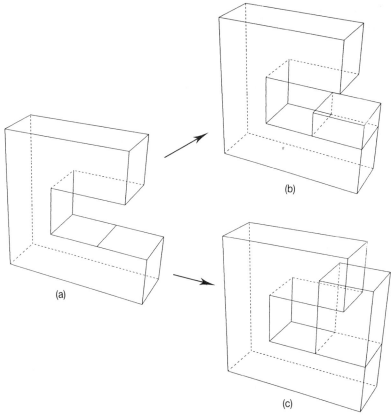

Figure 3.3   Mistakes in local operations.

input. Although very often it is the solid before the last command that is needed, this obviously is the worst case. This method is therefore not feasible for interactive design.

3.1.3   Internal representation methods in DESIGNBASE

Having considered the advantages and disadvantages of both representations, the B-rep was adopted as the internal representation of a solid shape in DESIGNBASE, as it was possible then to provide a wide variety of user operations. The primary application of DESIGNBASE is the conceptual design of aesthetic objects, so its convenience for the user is more important than having a wide range of applications which solid modelling systems can support.

However, the problem remained of reconstructing solids. To solve this problem, we implemented undo and redo operations for regenerating previously designed solids, which are supported by solid design representations using primitive operations. This set of functions includes Euler operations. Each primitive operation has a corresponding inverse operation for undoing changes. Undo and redo operations can also be implemented as a set of primative operations. In our system, Boolean operations and local operations – primitive operations – are always used to create or modify solid shapes. The primitive operations that have been invoked are then stored in tree structures. These structures represent the solid as it evolves in the design process, and support undo and redo operations.

Related to our approach, the solid modelling system GWB has been developed (Mäntylä and Solonen, 1982; Mäntylä, 1983). In GWB, the construction of solids has been implemented using Euler operations. However, the Boolean operations in the early version of GWB partially modified a solid without using Euler operations. In DESIGNBASE, however, high-level operations without exception use primitive operations to modify solids, and all the primitive operations used are stored as tree structures. Thus our system can quickly regenerate any previously designed solid, and users need not worry that an error might destroy their work.

3.2   BOUNDARY REPRESENTATION

This section describes a B-rep of a solid modelling system. The B-rep method used in DESIGNBASE is then described as a practical example.

3.2.1   Winged-edge representation

In the early stages of computer graphics, surface models were widely used to represent 3-D shapes. A surface model is represented by tables of faces, edges and vertices. The face table stores information on all the edges attached to each face. The given order of edges defining a face is counterclockwise, viewing the face from outside the solid. The edge table records the two vertices attached to each edge. In the vertex table, the co-ordinates (X, Y, Z) of each vertex are stored. For example, the rectangular pyramid shown in Figure 3.4 is represented by Table 3.1. Any hidden lines or surface-removal algorithms to display 3-D shapes need to be similarly represented. However, the following problems arise if such surface models are used to represent solids in a solid modelling system.

1.   Management of the face table

Although a face is defined by the edges attached to it, the number of the edges is not constant. For example in Table 3.1 although face F_1 has four edges, face F_2 has three edges. Thus the size of a table representing a face

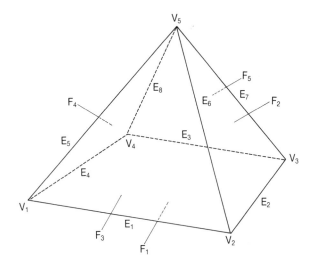

Figure 3.4 A solid composed of faces, edges and vertices.

must be variable. In the process of constructing a solid, faces are frequently added or deleted. Therefore, it is not easy to implement a program to manage the record of a face.

2. *Topological information*

All edges and vertices attached to a specified face are easily obtained from the information stored in the tables. However, it is not easy to ascertain from the tables which faces meet a specific edge. Also, although a vertex is connected to some edges, it is not easy to check which edges are attached to a specific vertex. Thus we can see that the topological information about the surface model is incomplete. Although many solid

Table 3.1   Tables of a surface model.

face	*Face table* *edges*	*edge*	*Edge table* *vertices*	*vertex*	*Vertex table* *coordinate*
F_1	E_4, E_3, E_2, E_1	E_1	V_1, V_2	V_1	x_1, y_1, z_1
F_2	E_2, E_7, E_6	E_2	V_3, V_2	V_2	x_2, y_2, z_2
F_3	E_1, E_6, E_5	E_3	V_3, V_4	V_3	x_3, y_3, z_3
F_4	E_4, E_5, E_8	E_4	V_1, V_4	V_4	x_4, y_4, z_4
F_5	E_3, E_7, E_8	E_5	V_1, V_5	V_5	x_5, y_5, z_5
		E_6	V_2, V_5		
		E_7	V_3, V_5		
		E_8	V_4, V_5		

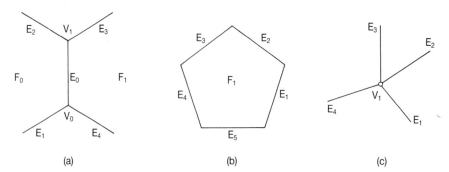

Figure 3.5   The winged-edge structure representation of a solid.

modelling procedures require the topological relationships between faces, edges and vertices, the surface model can not satisfy this requirement.

The **winged-edge structure representation** method proposed by Baumgart (1974) produced solutions to these problems. The representation consists of structures of three elements: an edge, a face and a vertex. Figure 3.5 shows the information stored in the structure of each element. Figure 3.5(a) shows edge E_1, E_2, E_3 and E_4. These four edges are called **winged-edges**. In this book, E_1, E_2, E_3 and E_4 respectively refer to an **SL-edge** (starting and left edge), **EL-edge** (end and left edge), **ER-edge** (end and right edge) and **SR-edge** (starting and right edge). Edge E_0 runs between vertices V_0 and V_1. The structure representing each edge stores the four winged-edges, the two faces and the two vertices shown in Figure 3.5. Although face F_1 is attached to some edges E_i ($i = 1, \ldots, 5$), as shown in Figure 3.5(b), the structure of each face stores any one of the edges attached to it. Figure 3.5(c) shows that vertex V_1 is connected to edges E_i ($i = 1, \ldots, 4$). The structure of each vertex stores that any one of the edges attached to the vertex and the coordinate of that vertex. Such information makes it possible easily to check the topological relationships between faces, edges and vertices. Thus, the second problem is solved. The first problem is also solved because in this representation method the size of each face, edge and vertex structure is constant. The management of the structure is therefore simple.

3.2.2   Winged-edge representation with loops

Since the usefulness of winged-edge representations have been widely recognized, many solid modelling systems have adopted winged-edge representations as B-reps. However, Baumgart's method did not treat holes in solids. There are many holes in mechanical parts, and they play a functionally important role. Subsequently Braid (1979) extended a

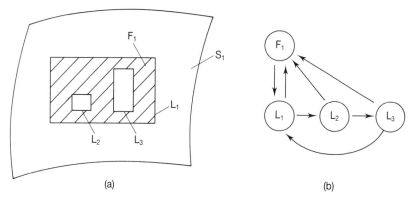

Figure 3.6   A face defined by loops.

winged-edge method to represent solids with holes. This representation method has been adopted in the solid modelling system BUILD2.

In Braids's method, a face is represented using several **loops**. Figure 3.6 illustrates a face defined in this way. In Figure 3.6(a), face F_1 is a finite area on surface S_1, given by a single equation. The boundaries of face F_1 are defined by loops: loop L_1 is an outside boundary, loops L_2 and L_3 are boundaries representing holes in a face, and each loop belongs to the same face. The relationships between a face and loops are stored as face and loop structures, as shown in Figure 3.6(b). In the structure of a face, any one of several loops is stored for defining the face. The structures of loops which belong to the same face are chained in a one-way chain, and they all store the face. One of the edges attached to the loop is also stored. In the structure of an edge, instead of faces, two loops which meet the edge are stored, as shown in Figure 3.7.

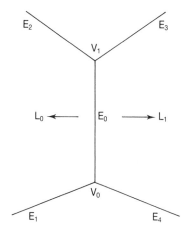

Figure 3.7   Winged-edges.

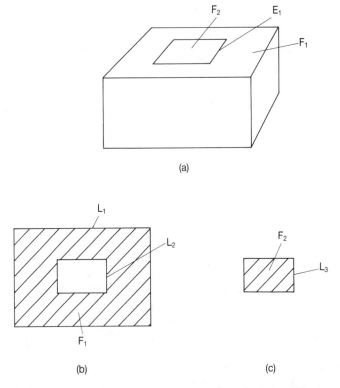

Figure 3.8   The winged-edge representation method with loops.

Figure 3.8 shows an example to illustrate the winged-edge representation method with loops. Figure 3.8(a) shows two faces F_1 and F_2 in a solid and edge E_1 meeting F_1 and F_2. Face F_1 has two loops L_1 and L_2, as shown in Figure 3.8(b). Face F_2 also has a loop L_3, as shown in Figure 3.8(c). Although loops L_2 and L_3 seem to be the same, these loops must be different according to the rule that a loop belongs to a single face. Loops L_2 and L_3 are stored in the structure of edge E_1.

3.2.3   B-reps in DESIGNBASE

The B-rep of a solid in DESIGNBASE is similar to the winged-edge representation using loops proposed by Braid. Although the topological elements in his method are the solid, face, loop, edge and vertex, face tables are not used in DESIGNBASE. Instead of a face, there are two types of loops: the **P-loop** (parent-loop) and the **C-loop** (child-loop), as shown in Figure 3.9. A P-loop is an outside boundary of a face and corresponds to a face. For every face there is a single P-loop, so the

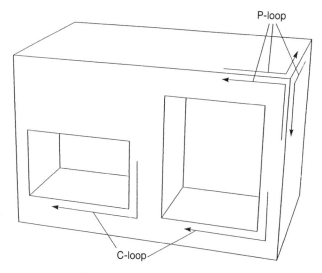

Figure 3.9   P-loops and C-loops.

number of faces in a solid is the same as the number of P-loops. A C-loop is a boundary indicating a hole in a face. A face may have several C-loops. Since there are fewer topological elements, the internal management of a solid's data structure becomes easier. Each topological element is described in detail below.

A solid has both an external name and an internal name. The external name is a string given by a user. The internal name is an integer from 1 to *n* which the system assigns. Similarly the faces, edges and vertices of each solid have internal names from 1 to *n*. The internal names of each face, edge and vertex are localized in each solid. The data structure of the solid table is described using the struct of language C, as follows:

```
struct SolidTable{
        char * Name;
        int NumberEdege;
        int NumberLoop;
        int NumberVertex;
        struct EdgeTable * EdgeTable;
        struct LoopTable * LoopTable;
        struct VertexTable * VertexTable;
};.
```

The table of a solid stores the numbers of edges, loops and vertices representing that solid. It also stores pointers to the edge table, face table and vertex table.

The data structure of the edge table is

```
struct EdgeTable{
        int LeftLoop;
        int RightLoop;
        int StartVertex;
        int EndVertex;
        int LeftEdge;
        int RightEdge;
};.
```

In the table of edge E_0, shown in Figure 3.7, LeftLoop, RightLoop, StartVertex, EndVertex, LeftEdge and RightEdge stores L_0, L_1, V_0, V_1, E_2 and E_4, respectively. Although the winged-edge representation stores four winged-edges in the edge table, in our method only two edges, an EL-edge and an SR-edge are stored. This reduces the primitive operations required to create and modify the data structure of a solid. For example, if edge E_0 in Figure 3.7 is deleted in the primitive operation, the tables of four edges E_1, E_2, E_3 and E_4 must be updated in the method with four winged-edges. On the other hand, since in our method, the tables of edge E_2 and E_4 do not store E_0, only the two edge tables for E_1 and E_3 need to be updated.

The loop table is

```
struct LoopTable{
        int Edge;
        int CLoop;
        int PLoop;
};.
```

Edge in a loop table stores one of several edges attached to the loop. However, it is not the case that any edge is stored in the table and occasionally it is necessary to select which edge should be stored. Figure 3.10 illustrates the selection process. In Figures 3.10(a) and (b), loops of both sides of edges E_1 and E_2 are the same, respectively. In such a case, one of the other edges is stored in the loop table so that edges in a given loop can be easily found in the counterclockwise order. The program is shown in Figure 3.11. Figure 3.10(c) shows a case in which the loops of both sides of all edges are the same. Since a loop has no surface area, we cannot define the counterclockwise order. It is therefore allowed to save any edge in the table.

The relationship between a P-loop and a C-loop is represented in the table by PLoop and CLoop. If the loop is a P-loop, CLoop stores one of the C-loops which belong to the P-loop, and PLoop = 0. If the loop is a C-loop, Ploop stores a P-loop to which the C-loop belongs, and CLoop stores one of the other C-loops which belong to the same P-loop. As a

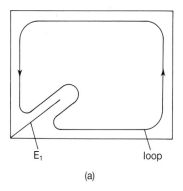

(a)

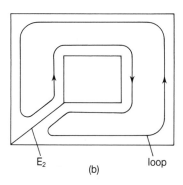

(b)

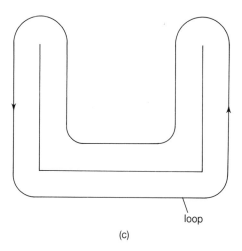

(c)

Figure 3.10   Saving an edge in the loop table.

Figure 3.11 A function EVLoop determines the edges and vertices which are attached to a loop. If the loop is a P-loop, the order of edges and vertices given by the function is counterclockwise. If the loop is a C-loop, the order of edges and vertices is clockwise.

```
struct SolidTable SolidTable[SSIZE];
struct EdgeTable EdgeTable[ESIZE];
struct LoopTable LoopTable[LSIZE];

/* edges and vertices attached to a loop */
EVLoop(solid, loop, nedge, max, edge, vertex)
int solid;
int loop;
int max;        /* size of edge and vertex */
int *nedge;     /* number of edges */
int edge[ ];
int vertex[ ];
{
    struct EdgeTable *EdgeTable;
    struct LoopTable *LoopTable;
    int i;
    int nextedge;

    EdgeTable = SolidTable[solid].EdgeTable;
    LoopTable = SolidTable[solid].LoopTable;

    /* first edge and vertex */
    edge[0] = LoopTable[loop].Edge;
```

result, in a loop table, PLoop indicates whether a loop is a P-loop or a C-loop. If PLoop = 0, a loop is a P-loop. Otherwise, a loop is a C-loop. For example, if loop L_1 is a P-loop and a face of a loop L_1 has no C-loop, then

LoopTable[L_1].CLoop = 0   and
LoopTable[L_1].PLoop = 0

If loop L_1 is a P-loop and a face of loop L_1 has C-loops L_2 and L_3,

LoopTable[L_1].CLoop = L_2
LoopTable[L_1].PLoop = 0

LoopTable[L_2].CLoop = L_3
LoopTable[L_2].PLoop = L_1

LoopTable[L_3].CLoop = 0   and
LoopTable[L_3].PLoop = L_1

Figure 3.11   (cont.)

```
if(EdgeTable[edge[0]].LeftLoop == loop) {
    vertex[0]   = EdgeTable[edge[0]].EndVertex;
    nextedge  = EdgeTable[edge[0]].LeftEdge;
}

if(EdgeTable[edge[0]].RightLoop == loop) {
    vertex[0]   = EdgeTable[edge[0]].StartVertex;
    nextedge  = EdgeTable[edge[0]].RightEdge;
}

for(i = 1;  i < max;  i++) {
    edge[i] = nextedge;

    if(EdgeTable[edge[i]].StartVertex == vertex[i − 1]) {
        vertex[i] = EdgeTable[edge[i]].EndVertex;
        nextedge = EdgeTable[edge[i]].LeftEdge;
    }

    if(EdgeTable[edge[i]].EndVertex == vertex[i − 1]) {
        vertex[i] = EdgeTable[edge[i]].StartVertex;
        nextedge = EdgeTable[edge[i]].RightEdge;
    }
    if(edge[i] == edge[0] && vertex[i] == vertex[0]) break;

}
*nedge = i;
}
```

The table of a vertex is

```
struct VertexTable{
    int Edge;
    double X;
    double Y;
    double Z;
};.
```

Edge in the table of vertex V stores any one of the edges attached to vertex V. The coordinates of vertex V are stored in X, Y and Z. From the tables shown above, it is easy to check which edges and loops are attached to a vertex. The program is shown in Figure 3.12.

Since two out of four winged-edges are not stored in the edge table, the procedure of manipulating a solid's data stucture becomes easy. However, this method has one restriction concerning the topology of a

Figure 3.12   A function ELVertex determines the edges and loops which are attached to a vertex. The order of edges and vertices is clockwise.

```
struct SolidTable SolidTable[SSIZE];
struct EdgeTable EdgeTable[ESIZE];
struct VertexTable VertexTable[LSIZE];

/* edges and loops attached to a vertex */
EL Vertex(solid, vertex, nedge, max, edge, loop)
int solid;
int vertex;
int max;        /* size of edge and vertex */
int *nedge;     /* number of edges */
int edge[ ];
int loop[ ];
}
    struct EdgeTable * EdgeTable;
    struct VertexTable * VertexTable;
    int i;
    int nextedge;

    EdgeTable = SolidTable[solid].EdgeTable;
    LoopTable = SolidTable[solid].LoopTable;
    VertexTable = SolidTable[solid].VertexTable;
```

particular solid represented in DESIGNBASE. Figure 3.13 shows a cylinder and its topology. Edge E_1 is attached to the same vertex V_1 twice. Namely, the start vertex of edge E_1 is the same as its end vertex. The topology of such a solid can not be represented like this in DESIGNBASE. To be able to represent such a solid, a vertex V_2 must be made on edge E_1, and E_1 be separated into two edges E_1 and E_2, as shown in Figure 3.13(b). We consider that the ease with which data structures can be manipulated is more important than the representation of the particular topology shown in Figure 3.13(a). However, if a designer of a solid modelling system wishes to represent this particular topology in the system, either four winged-edges can be stored in the edge table, or some other representation method (Weiler, 1985) can be used.

3.3   PRIMITIVE OPERATIONS

In DESIGNBASE, the data structure of a solid is always created and modified by primitive operations. This section introduces how each primitive operation modifies a solid, and then explains how each one is

```
    nextedge = VertexTable[vertex].Edge;

    for(i = 0;  i < max;  i ++){
        edge[i] = nextedge;

        if(EdgeTable[edge[i]].StartVertex == vertex) {
            loop[i] = EdgeTable[edge[i]].RightLoop;
            nextedge = EdgeTable[edge[i]].RightEdge;
        }

        if(EdgeTable[edge[i]].EndVertex == vertex) {
            loop[i] = EdgeTable[edge[i]].LeftLoop;
            nextedge = EdgeTable[edge[i]].LeftEdge;
        }
        if(edge[i] == edge[0]) break;

    }
    *nedge = i;
}
```

implemented. Every primitive operation has its inverse in a set of primitive operations. There are three kinds of primitive operations: topological, geometric and global.

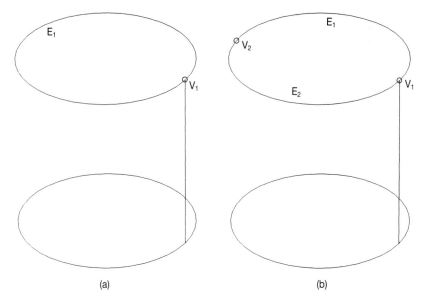

(a)   (b)

Figure 3.13   A cylinder and its topology.

3.3.1 Geometric computations

Before introducing the primitive operations, we will first describe the algorithms of geometric computations which are required in the procedures of primitive operations.

1. *Edge in a corner*

Figure 3.14 shows corners defined by three points P_0, P_1, P_2. Although the angle θ of a corner shown in Figure 3.14(a) is smaller than 180°, the angle θ shown in Figure 3.14(b) is larger than 180°. To make a new edge E between points Q and P_0, we must decide whether or not edge E is included in the corner. This algorithm consists of two phases and is described below.

Phase 1: Angle of a corner   First, we decide if the angle θ of a corner is smaller or larger than 180°. To do so we calculate a normal vector **n** of a face including the corner and the cross product of two vectors, $\overrightarrow{P_1P_0}\ \times$

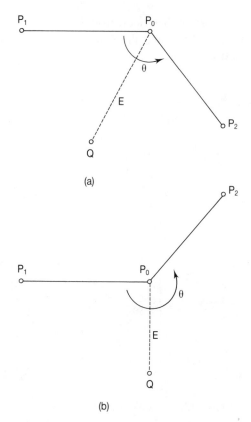

(a)

(b)

Figure 3.14 Making an edge on a corner.

$\overrightarrow{P_0P_2}$. Although the face normal **n** can have two directions, we select one from inside the solid to outside. Then the dot product of the two vectors

$$\mathbf{n} \cdot (\overrightarrow{P_1P_0} \times \overrightarrow{P_0P_2})$$

is calculated. If the value of the dot product is larger than 0, θ is smaller than 180°. If the value is smaller than 0, θ is larger than 180°.

Phase 2: Side of an edge   If the angle θ is smaller than 180° and a new edge E is in the corner, edge E must lie on the left side of $\overrightarrow{P_0P_1}$ and on the right side of $\overrightarrow{P_0P_2}$. Also, if θ is larger than 180° and E is in the corner, edge E must lie on the left side of $\overrightarrow{P_0P_1}$ or on the right side of $\overrightarrow{P_0P_2}$. To detect this,

$$a = (\overrightarrow{P_1P_0} \times \overrightarrow{P_0Q}) \cdot \mathbf{n}$$
$$b = (\overrightarrow{P_2P_0} \times \overrightarrow{P_0Q}) \cdot \mathbf{n}$$

are calculated. As a result, if $\theta < 180°$, and $a > 0$ and $b < 0$, the new edge E lies in the corner. Also, if $\theta > 180°$, and $a > 0$ or $b < 0$, E lies in the corner. Otherwise, E is not included in the corner.

2.   *Normal vector of a loop*

Figure 3.15 shows loop L which is defined by edges E_i $(i = 1, \ldots , n)$ and vertices V_i $(i = 1, \ldots , n)$. Here, the coordinate of vertex V_i is (x_i, y_i, z_i). The unit normal vector **n** (a, b, c) of loop L is calculated as follows (Sutherland *et al.*, 1974):

$$j = (\text{if } i = n \text{ then } 1 \text{ else } i + 1)$$

$$a1 = \sum_{i=1}^{n} (y_i - y_j)(z_i + z_j)$$

$$b1 = \sum_{i=1}^{n} (z_i - z_j)(x_i + x_j)$$

$$c1 = \sum_{i=1}^{n} (x_i - x_j)(y_i + y_j)$$

$$d = \sqrt{a1^2 + b1^2 + c1^2}$$

$$a = \frac{a1}{d}$$

$$b = \frac{b1}{d}$$

$$c = \frac{c1}{d}$$

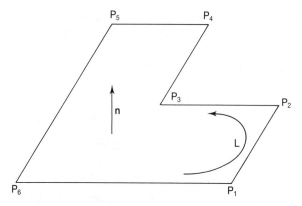

Figure 3.15   The normal vector of a loop.

If a loop is not planar, this method will produce a plane equation closely related to the loop, but not the best-fit plane equation.

3.   Surrounding loop

Figure 3.16 shows loop L and four points A, B, C and D. To detect whether or not a loop surrounds a point, we define any line from the point to infinity, and count the number of times the line crosses the boundary of the loop (Sutherland *et al.*, 1974). If the crossing number is even, the point is outside the loop, like point B. If the number is odd, the

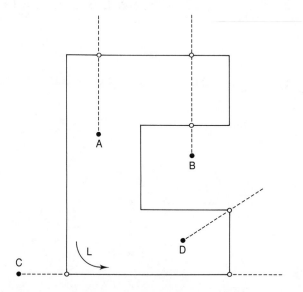

Figure 3.16   Points included in a loop. ● point; ○ intersection.

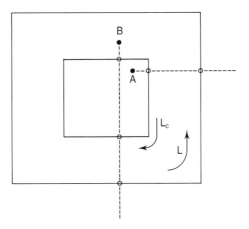

Figure 3.17 Points included in a loop with a C-loop.

point is inside, like point A. When the edge lies on the line, like point C, or the vertex lies on the line, like point D, the procedure described above can not be used for the check. One simple way of avoiding such cases is to select the other semi-infinite line from the point.

Figure 3.17 shows loop L with C-loop L_c. In this case, we similarly count the number of intersections between the semi-infinite line and all the edges of loops L and L_c. If the crossing number is even, the point is outside the loop, like point A. Otherwise, the point is inside, like point B. Figure 3.18 also shows loop L which has edges E_1 and E_2. The loops of both sides of E_1 and E_2 are the same. In this case, we count the number of intersections between edges other than E_1 and E_2 and the semi-infinite line.

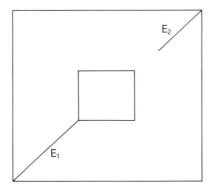

Figure 3.18 Points included in a loop.

3.3.2 Topological operations

We will now describe the topological operations which generate and modify the topology of a solid. Because such operations add or delete faces, edges and vertices according to the **Euler formula** for solid objects, they are called **Euler operations** (Baumgart, 1975). The Euler formula for a solid with no holes is

$$F + V - E = 2$$

where E, F and V are the number of edges, faces and vertices, respectively. In the cube shown in Figure 3.19(a), $E = 12$, $F = 6$ and $V = 8$. The formula for an arbitrary solid is

$$F + V - E - R = 2(S - H)$$

where, H is the number of **holes** which pass through the solid, and R is the number of **rings** which are cavities in the faces. Figure 3.19(b) shows a ring R_1 in a face F_1 and a ring R_2 in a face F_2. S is the number of **shells**, or disconnected surfaces. In the solid shown in Figure 3.19(b), $E = 24$, $F = 10$, $V = 16$, $S = 1$, $H = 1$ and $R = 2$. The terms on the left of the formula can be found directly from the data structure described in Section 3.2. F and R correspond to the number of P-loops and C-loops, respectively. The term on the right is implicitly represented in the data structure.

We now discuss topological operations in detail. In the expression of operation variables, $\uparrow$ and $\downarrow$ mean output and input respectively.

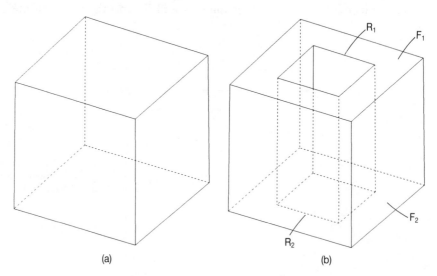

(a)   (b)

Figure 3.19   The Euler formula.

1. MEL (Make an Edge and a Loop)

$$\text{MEL} \, (\overset{\downarrow}{A}, \overset{\uparrow}{E_1}, \overset{\uparrow}{L_2}, \overset{\downarrow}{L_1}, \overset{\downarrow}{V_1}, \overset{\downarrow}{V_2})$$

Edge E_1 is generated between vertices V_1 and V_2 in loop L_1 of solid A, as shown in Figure 3.20(a). At the same time, loop L_1 is separated into two loops L_1 and L_2. Although loop L_1 may be either a P-loop or a C-loop, as shown in Figure 3.20(b), the new loop made in MEL, loop L_2, is always a P-loop. The MEL procedure consists of three phases.

Phase 1: Finding winged-edges   Figure 3.21 shows that edge E_1 is in loop L_1. To make a table of the new edge E_1, the winged-edges of edge E_1 must be found. In the case shown in Figure 3.21(a), four winged-edges E_2, E_3, E_4 and E_5 are easily found from the topological information of the solid. However, in the case shown in Figure 3.21(b), we must check whether edge E_1 should be made at a corner between edges E_3 and E_6 or between

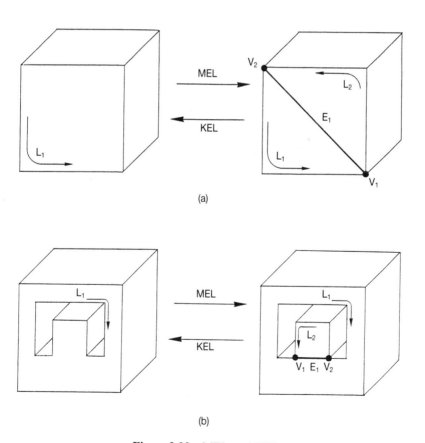

(a)

(b)

Figure 3.20   MEL and KEL.

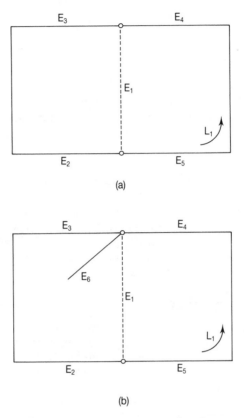

Figure 3.21   Making an edge in a loop.

edges E_6 and E_4. To do this, the geometric calculation described in Section 3.3.1, part 1 is required. After the winged-edges are found, an EL-edge and an SR-edge are stored in a new edge table, and elements in the table of an ER-edge and an SL-edge are modified. If edges E_3, E_4 and E_6 do not exist on the same plane, it is difficult to find the corner for creating a new edge. In a case like this we are hindered in making an edge.

Phase 2: Procedure for a new loop   Figure 3.22(a) shows P-loop L_3 with C-Loop L_2. If MEL creates a new edge E_1 attached to C-loop L_2 in phase 1, loop L_2 is separated into L_1 and L_2, as shown in Figure 3.22(b). As a result, either loop L_1 or L_2 is a C-loop which belongs to P-loop L_3, and the other is a P-loop. However, from the topological information it is difficult to decide which loop is a P-loop. To do so, the normal vectors of loops L_1, L_2 and L_3 are calculated using the algorithm in Section 3.3.1, part 2. Here, we consider two loops which are closed and belong to the same plane face. If the direction of the normal vector of one loop is opposite to that of the other loop, one is a P-loop and the other is a C-loop.

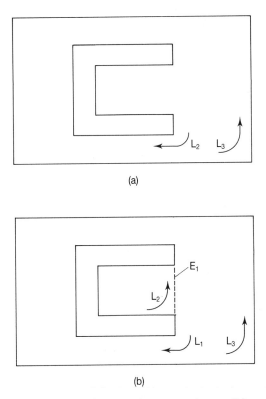

(a)

(b)

Figure 3.22 Making an edge to attach to a C-loop.

Therefore, if the direction of the vector of loop L_3 is the same as that of loop L_2, the tables of loops L_1, L_2 and L_3 are modified so that C-loop L_1 belongs to P-loop L_3, and loop L_2 is a P-loop. Otherwise, no action is taken since L_2 is already a C-loop.

Phase 3: Procedure for C-loops Figure 3.23(a) shows loop L_2 with C-loop L_3. If a new edge E_1 in loop L_2 is created in phase 1 of MEL, loop L_2 is separated into two loops L_1 and L_2. In such a case, we must check to which P-loop (L_1 or L_2) C-loop L_3 belongs. To do so, it is necessary to check whether or not any point attached to a C-loop is included in a P-loop by using the algorithm in Section 3.3.1, part 3. As a result, if C-loop L_3 is included in the new P-loop L_1, the table of loops L_3 and L_1 are modified so that L_1 can be a P-loop with C-loop L_3. On the other hand, if L_3 is included in L_2, no action is taken since L_3 already belongs to L_2.

When loops L_3 and L_2 are both flat, and L_2 and L_3 lie on the same plane, a check can easily be done to determine the relationship between a

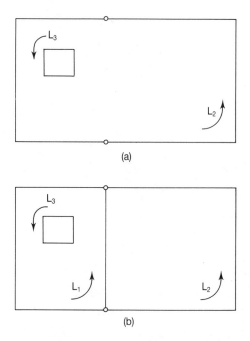

Figure 3.23   Making an edge in a P-loop with C-loops.

point and a loop. However, when the loop is curved, or L_2 and L_3 do not lie on the same plane, the check is harder. It is therefore difficult to perform MEL in such a case. If a user wishes to make an edge in loop L_2, loop L_3 must be changed to a P-loop before the MEL procedure.

2.   KEL (Kill an Edge and a Loop)

$$\begin{array}{cccccc} \downarrow & \downarrow & \uparrow & \uparrow & \uparrow & \uparrow \end{array}$$
$$\text{KEL } (A, E_1, L_2, L_1, V_1, V_2)$$

Edge E_1 of solid A is deleted, as shown in Figure 3.20. At the same time, two loops L_1 and L_2 are combined, and a new loop L_2 is created. KEL is the inverse operation of MEL. For the procedure, the tables of edge E_1 and loop L_1 are removed. The tables of an SL-edge and an ER-edge of E_1 are updated. Figure 3.24 shows edge E_1 and P-loops L_1 and L_2 on both sides of E_1. L_1 and L_2 have C-loops L_3 and L_4, respectively. If edge E_1 and loop L_1 are killed using a KEL operation, the P-loop belonging to C-loop L_3 becomes P-loop L_2.

In DESIGNBASE, each primitive operation must always be invertible in order to undo the shaping operation. However, if KEL is

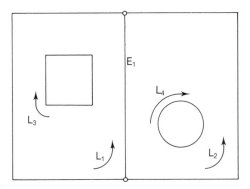

Figure 3.24   Making an edge in a P-loop with C-loops.

performed when the shape of either L_1 or L_2 in Figure 3.24 is curved, KEL may not be invertible, the reason being that it is difficult to check to which P-loop (L_1 or L_2) the C-loops L_3 and L_4 belong. It is therefore not possible to perform KEL in such a case.

3.   MVE (Make a Vertex and an Edge)

$$\overset{\downarrow}{} \overset{\uparrow}{} \overset{\uparrow}{} \overset{\downarrow}{} \overset{\downarrow}{} \overset{\downarrow}{} \overset{\downarrow}{}$$
$$\text{MVE } (A, V_1, E_1, E_2, x, y, z)$$

Vertex V_1 of solid A is generated at a point (x, y, z) on edge E_2, as shown in Figure 3.25. As a result, edge E_2 is separated into two edges E_1 and E_2.

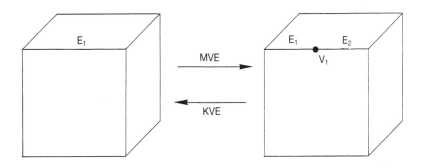

Figure 3.25   MVE and KVE.

4. KVE (Kill a Vertex and an Edge)

$$\overset{\downarrow\;\;\downarrow\;\;\uparrow\;\;\uparrow\;\;\uparrow\;\uparrow}{\text{KVE (A, } V_1, E_1, E_2, x, y, z)}$$

Vertex V_1 is deleted, as shown in Figure 3.25. As a result, two edges E_1 and E_2 are combined, and a new edge E_2 is generated. KVE is the inverse operation of MVE.

5. KCLMPL (Kill a C-Loop and Make a P-Loop)

$$\overset{\downarrow\;\;\uparrow\;\;\downarrow}{\text{KCLMPL (A, } L_1, L_2)}$$

This procedure changes the C-loop L_2 to P-loop L_2, as shown in Figure 3.26. Before the operation, C-loop L_2 belongs to a face which has P-loop L_1.

6. KPLMCL (Kill a P-Loop and Make a C-Loop)

$$\overset{\downarrow\;\;\downarrow\;\;\downarrow}{\text{KPLMCL (A, } L_1, L_2)}$$

This operation changes the P-loop L_2 to C-loop L_2 which belongs to P-loop L_1, as shown in Figure 3.26. This is the inverse operation of KCLMPL.

7. MEV (Make an Edge and a Vertex)

$$\overset{\downarrow\;\;\uparrow\;\;\uparrow\;\;\downarrow\;\;\downarrow\;\;\downarrow\;\downarrow}{\text{MVE (A, } E_1, V_1, V_2, L_1, x, y, z)}$$

Edge E_1 is generated between vertex V_2 in loop L_1 and a point (x, y, z), as shown in Figure 3.27. At the same time, vertex V_1 is generated at the same point (x, y, z). Loop L_1 may be either a P-loop or a C-loop. For this procedure, the winged-edges of a new edge are found, as in phase 1 of MEL. The new edge table is then constructed, and the tables of the winged-edges are updated.

8. KEV (Kill an Edge and a Vertex)

$$\overset{\downarrow\;\;\downarrow\;\;\downarrow\;\;\uparrow\;\;\uparrow\;\;\uparrow\;\uparrow}{\text{KEV (A, } E_1, V_1, V_2, L_1, x, y, z)}$$

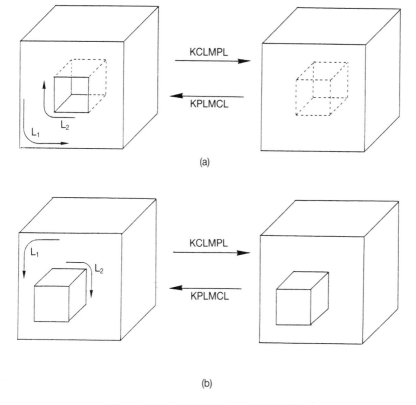

Figure 3.26   KCLMPL and KPLMCL.

Edge E_1 and vertex V_1 are deleted, as shown in Figure 3.27. KEV is the inverse operation of MEV.

9.   MEKL (Make an Edge and Kill a Loop)

$$
\begin{array}{ccccccc}
\downarrow & \uparrow & \downarrow & \downarrow & \downarrow & \downarrow \\
\end{array}
$$
MEKL $(A, E_1, L_1, L_2, V_1, V_2)$

As shown in Figures 3.28(a) and (b), edge E_1 is generated between vertex V_1 in Loop L_1 and vertex V_2 in loop L_2. As a result, two loops L_1 and L_2 are combined, and loop L_2 is generated. The two loops L_1 and L_2 must be the same type. In particular, when the loops are both C-loops, they must belong to the same face, as shown in Figure 3.28(b). If loops L_1 and L_2 are different types, a C-loop is changed to a P-loop using KCLMPL before MEKL, as shown in Figure 3.28(c).

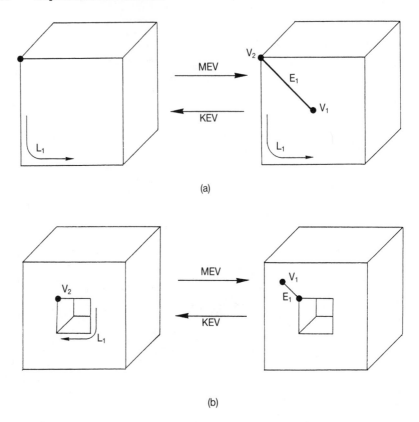

(a)

(b)

Figure 3.27   MEV and KEV.

10. KEML (Kill an Edge and Make a Loop)

$$\text{KEML (A, E}_1\text{, L}_1\text{, L}_2\text{, V}_1\text{, V}_2)$$

As shown in Figure 3.28, edge E_1 is deleted, and loop L_2 is separated into two loops L_1 and L_2. The generated loop L_1 is the same type as loop L_2. KEML is the inverse operation of MEKL.

11. MEVVL (Make an Edge, a Vertex, a Vertex and a Loop)

$$\text{MEVVL (A, E}_1\text{, V}_1\text{, V}_2\text{, L}_1\text{, } x_1\text{, } y_1\text{, } z_1\text{, } x_2\text{, } y_2\text{, } z_2)$$

Edge E_1 is generated between a point (x_1, y_1, z_1) and a point (x_2, y_2, z_2), as shown in Figure 3.29. At the same time, vertices V_1, V_2 and loop L_1 are generated.

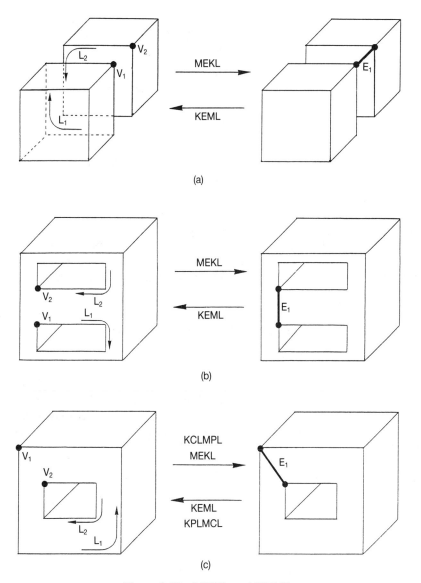

Figure 3.28   MEKL and KEML.

12.   KEVVL (Kill an Edge, a Vertex, a Vertex and a Loop)

$$\text{KEVVL } (A, E_1, V_1, V_2, L_1, x_1, y_1, z_1, x_2, y_2, z_2)$$

Edge E_1 is deleted, as shown in Figure 3.29, and vertices V_1, V_2 and loop L_1 are also deleted. KEVVL is the inverse operation of MEVVL.

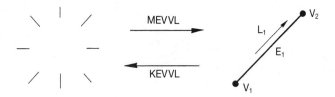

Figure 3.29 MEVVL and KEVVL.

13. *MZEV (Make a Zero-length Edge and a Vertex)*

$$\text{MZEV } (A, E_1, V_1, V_2, E_2, E_3)$$

Figure 3.30(a) shows vertex V_2 which is attached to edges E_2, E_3, E_4 and E_5 and faces F_1, F_2, F_3 and F_4. The MZEV operation replaces a vertex V_2 with a zero-length edge E_1 and two vertices V_1 and V_2, as shown in Figure 3.30(b). To apply MZEV to a vertex, the vertex must be attached to two or more edges.

14. *KZEV (Kill a Zero-length Edge and a Vertex)*

$$\text{KZEV } (A, E_1, V_1, V_2, E_2, E_3)$$

A zero-length edge E_1 is deleted, as shown in Figure 3.30. At the same time vertex V_1 is deleted. To apply KZEV to a zero-length edge, both vertices attched to the edge must be connected to two or more edges, respectively. KZEV is the inverse of MZEV.

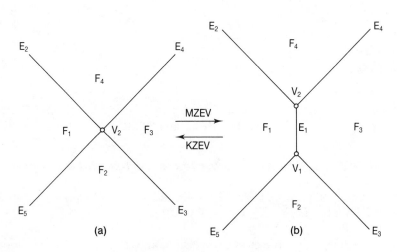

Figure 3.30 MZEV and KZEV.

3.3.3 Geometric operations

1. TV (Translate a Vertex)

$$\text{TV}\ (A,\ V_1,\ x,\ y,\ z)$$

The vertex V_1 of solid A is translated, as shown in Figure 3.31. The translation vector is (x, y, z). The internal representation of a solid in DESIGNBASE does not store the surface equation of a face, so a solid can have a twisted face, as shown in Figure 3.31(b).

2. CLB (Change a Line to a Bézier curve)

$$\text{CLB}\ (A,\ E_1,\ x_1,\ y_1,\ z_1,\ x_2,\ y_2,\ z_2)$$

In DESIGNBASE, the shape of an edge is represented by either a line or a cubic Bézier curve (see Section 5.2). This procedure changes a straight line edge E_1 into a cubic Bézier curve, as shown in Figure 3.32. Although a cubic Bézier curve is defined by four control points $P_i (i = 0, \ldots, 3)$, P_0 and P_3 are two vertices attached to edge E_1. The coordinates of control points P_1 and P_2 are (x_1, y_1, z_1) and (x_2, y_2, z_2), respectively. In this book, we refer to the control point of a Bézier curve as a **Bézier point**.

3. CBL (Change a Bézier curve to a line)

$$\text{CBL}\ (A,\ E_1,\ x_1,\ y_1,\ z_1,\ x_2,\ y_2,\ z_2)$$

This changes a Bézier curve edge E_1 into a straight line, as shown in Figure 3.32. CBL is the inverse operation of CLB.

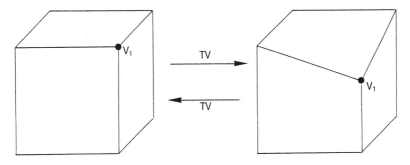

Figure 3.31 TV.

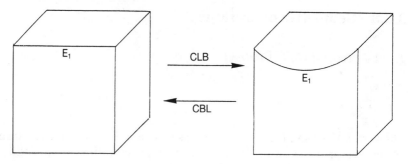

Figure 3.32 CLB and CBL.

4. TB (Translate a Bézier point)

$$\overset{\downarrow\quad\downarrow\quad\downarrow\;\downarrow\;\downarrow\;\downarrow}{\mathrm{TB}\,(\mathrm{A},\,\mathrm{E}_1,\,i,\,x,\,y,\,z)}$$

This translates the ith (1 or 2) control point of a Bézier curve edge E_1, as shown in Figure 3.33. The translation vector is (x, y, z).

In DESIGNBASE, if a curve other than a Bézier curve (e.g. an arc, a parabola or an ellipse) is used as a new type of edge shape, a primitive operation for changing a line edge to the new type, plus its inverse operation, must be added.

3.3.4 Global operations

1. TS (Translate a Solid)

$$\overset{\downarrow\;\downarrow\;\downarrow\;\downarrow}{\mathrm{TB}\,(\mathrm{A},\,x,\,y,\,z)}$$

Solid A is translated in space. The translation vector is (x, y, z).

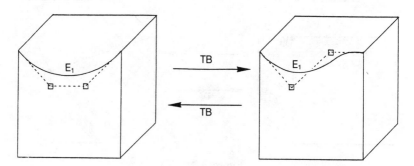

Figure 3.33 TB.

2. RS (Rotate a Solid)

$$\overset{\downarrow \ \ \downarrow \ \downarrow}{RS\,(A,\,i,\,\theta)}$$

Solid A is rotated about an *i*-axis (*i* indicates *x*, *y*, *z*). θ is the angle of rotation. The rotation of a solid about an arbitrary line in space is performed by a combination of TS and RS.

3. NS (Negate a Solid)

$$\overset{\downarrow}{NS\,(A)}$$

All the faces of solid A are turned over so that their normal vectors are reversed. For this procedure, all the edge tables are modified. Figure 3.34 shows edge E_0 on which two loops L_1 and L_2 meet, and the winged-edges of E_0 and E_1, E_2, E_3 and E_4. First, a left loop L_1 and right loop L_2 in the table are swapped. EL-edge E_2 and SR-edge E_4 are replaced by E_3 and E_1, respectively. In doing this the order of edges and vertices defining each loop become reversed, as do the order of edges and loops around each vertex. This operation is used in Boolean operations and in generating a mirror image solid (see Section 4.4).

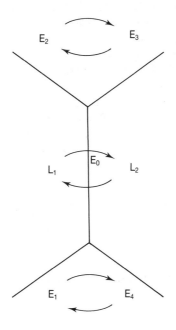

Figure 3.34   NS.

4.   CS *(Combine two Solids)*

    ↓ ↓ ↓
CS (A, B, C)

Solids A and B are combined, and solid C is generated. The geometry and the topology of solids A and B are not changed; this combination means simply that the two solids are considered as one in the data structure. This primitive operation is used in combinational operations of two solids, such as a Boolean operation and a glue operation (see Section 4.5).

5.   SS *(Separate a Solid)*

    ↓ ↓ ↓
SS (A, B, C)

By separating the data structure of solid C, two solids A and B are generated. This operation is the inverse of CS, and is used to undo both a Boolean operation and a glue operation.

3.4   REPRESENTING THE SOLID DESIGN PROCESS

In DESIGNBASE, all high-level operations for creating or modifying a solid are implemented by primitive operations. All the primitive operations used in a design are stored in a tree which represents the history of the design process. We will call such a tree a **solid design process tree** (SDP tree). By invoking the sequences of primitive operations stored in an SDP-tree, the system quickly regenerates any previously designed solid. Such a solid is referred to as an **ancestor solid**. This method of representing a design process as a hierarchical tree structure naturally supports undo and redo operations. The user simply specifies a path moving up the tree to undo a sequence of operations, or moving down the tree to redo a previously specified sequence. The following section presents detailed descriptions of the undo and redo operations.

3.4.1   Procedures for constructing a single solid

Operations for creating or modifying solids can be grouped into two. Those in the first create or modify individual solids and are called **single-solid operations**. Edge-rounding and face-sweeping operations are classified within this group. The others are called **compound-solid operations**, in which a new solid is generated from two existing solids. This group includes Boolean operations and glue operations. The procedure for constructing a solid using single-solid operations is presented below. The representation for compound-solid operations is given in Section 3.4.2.

A user constructs a solid by specifying commands that invoke primitive operations. The first command generates the initial solid and subsequent commands modify it. At the same time, a data tree is constructed to represent the design process itself. Each node of the tree represents the solid at a specific stage of design. The node also represents the specific single-solid commands and the primitive operations used to execute these commands. The system assigns an identifier (ID) to each node so that a user can easily specify each stage of the solid design. This arrangement supports undo and redo operations, by allowing users to recover from errors and to recall any stage of the design process.

Figure 3.35 shows the procedure for constructing a solid A and a tree structure representing its design process.

1. The root node A_0 of the design representation tree is generated first. This node represents a null solid. Another node is then generated to represent the initial solid. This node's ID is $A_{1,1}$, which thus indicates the first solid in the first design stage of solid A. Node $A_{1,1}$ stores the sequence of primitive operations used to create solid $A_{1,1}$.

2. An edge is created in face F_1 of solid A, thereby dividing F_1 into two faces F_1 and F_2. The resulting solid has the node ID $A_{1,2}$. Then, by sweeping face F_1, a node $A_{1,3}$ is generated. Finally, edge E_1 is rounded and this is node $A_{1,4}$.

3. An undo operation is specified twice to regenerate the solid identified by node $A_{1,2}$. For this procedure, the sequence of primitive operations stored in nodes $A_{1,4}$ and $A_{1,3}$ are retrieved. The inverse of each primitive operation is then applied to solid $A_{1,4}$, in reverse order.

4. Face F_2 of solid $A_{1,2}$ is swept. When a solid is modified after an undo operation, the stage number is incremented. Therefore, the node ID of the solid is labelled $A_{2,1}$. Edge E_2 is then rounded and the node is $A_{2,2}$.

5. By specifying two undo operations and one redo operation, the solid identified by node $A_{1,3}$ is generated. Face F_3 is then swept. This new solid's node is labelled $A_{3,1}$.

By specifying any sequence of undo and redo operations in this way, the user can regenerate ancestor solids. When an undo operation is specified, a solid higher up the tree hierarchy is regenerated from the current solid by applying the inverse operations of the primitive operations. When a redo operation is specified, a solid lower down in the tree hierarchy is generated. If there are two or more lower solids, the system selects the solid with the largest stage number. Alternatively, the user can select the solid. Furthermore, any ancestor solid can be

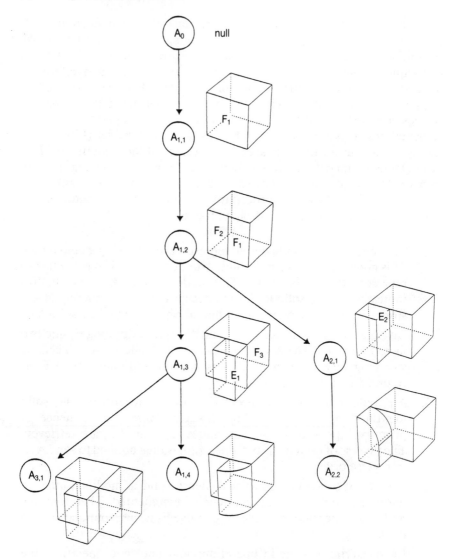

Figure 3.35   Construction of single-solid tree.

regenerated simply by specifying the state (i.e. the node ID) of that solid. The computation time of these undo and redo operations is far less than that of their corresponding commands. This is because the execution of the command involves many procedures other than primitive operations, e.g. intersection detection and input data checks.

Many solid modelling systems assign global internal definitions to edges and vertices. For example, if edge names are assigned from 1 to n, all solids have the same set of names in common. To implement inverse operations in such a system, a solid must not be defined using the names of edges or vertices removed from other solids or ancestor solids. Keeping track of such conditions uses a lot of memory. In DESIGN-BASE, internal definitions of edges, loops and vertices are locally assigned, e.g. each element of a body is given an ID from 1 to n. The current solid can therefore use the memory space which the ancestor solid occupied, and memory use is economical.

3.4.2   Representating compound-solid operations

Once a solid has been constructed using single-solid operations, compound-solid operations such as Boolean and glue operations can be applied to it. This section describes the representation of the design process using compound-solid operations. Figure 3.36 explains the design process using a compound-solid operation and its representation. In this figure, solids A and B are first produced using single-solid operations. The internal node IDs of the solids are $A_{2,1}$ and $B_{1,2}$. Solid C is then generated from solids A and B using a difference Boolean operation. For the procedure, new nodes $A_{2,2}$, $B_{1,3}$, C_0 and $C_{1,1}$ are created. The primitive operations applied to solids A, B and C are stored in nodes $A_{2,2}$, $B_{1,3}$ and $C_{1,1}$, respectively. The $\oplus$ node corresponding to a compound-solid operation is created. The emergent arc of this node is connected to node C_0; the two incident arcs are connected to nodes $A_{2,2}$ and $B_{1,3}$. The $\oplus$ node indicates that the two solids are now treated as a single solid. The values of function variables of a CS primitive operation are stored in the $\oplus$ node. After the Boolean operation, several edges of solid C are changed to fillet surfaces using a rounding operation. The node ID of solid C becomes $C_{1,2}$. If two undo operations are applied to solid C, the B-reps of two solids A and B are regenerated from solid C, and the B-rep of solid C is deleted.

3.4.3   Tree displays

Two kinds of trees representing the solid design process are displayed on a screen to enable the user to understand the process. One kind is a tree representing the design process of a single solid, and is called a **single-solid tree**. The other is a tree representing the relationships of solids which are combined using Boolean or glue operations, and is called a **compound-solid tree**. In Figure 3.37, the two kinds of trees are displayed in one of the windows of the user-interface. Our screen uses three windows, i.e. a menu-window, text-window and graphics-window. It is implemented by SunWindows (SUN, 1985) on the SUN workstation. In this figure, the compound-solid tree appears in the upper area of the text-window. This tree shows that a solid E was made from two solids C and D, and that solid D was made from solids A and B. In this tree, solid E

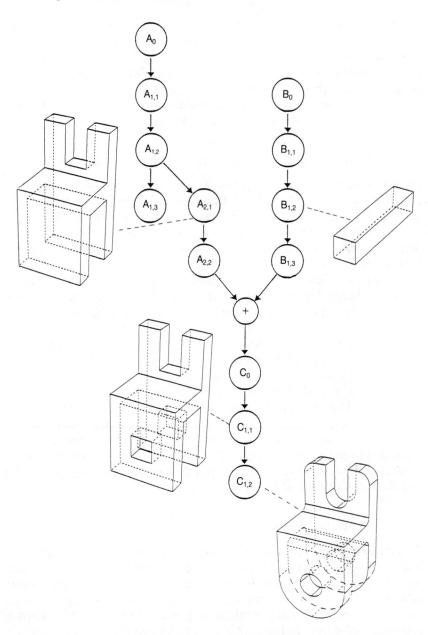

Figure 3.36   A compound-solid tree.

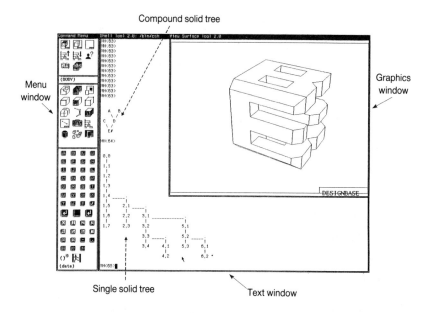

Compound solid tree

Menu
window

Graphics
window

Single solid tree   Text window

Figure 3.37   The DESIGNBASE–user interface.

marked by # is a current solid. The single-solid tree of a solid appears
drawn in the lower area of the text-window. The node ID marked by *
indicates the current state of a solid. Using such tree pictures, a designer
can enter undo or redo commands to regenerate a previous solid. It is also
possible to regenerate a solid by specifying the internal ID of its
corresponding ancestor solid.

3.5   THE MODULAR STRUCTURE OF DESIGNBASE

Figure 3.38 outlines the DESIGNBASE software structure. The circles
indicate data which represent solids, and the box indicates a program
module. To generate or modify a solid, the user gives commands to the
geometric modelling module, which applies primitive operations to the B-
rep of that solid. Local operations and Boolean operations are included in
this module. At the same time, the **tree processor** stores the primitive
operations in SDP trees, and the **display program module** draws the
resulting solid on the screen. The display program module does not get
the information for drawing the solid directly from the B-rep, but from
the **reference function module**. The reference function formats the data
on the solid to facilitate the implementation of the geometric modelling

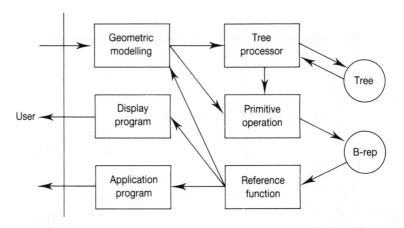

Figure 3.38   The software structure of DESIGNBASE.

and display program. The reference functions in DESIGNBASE are illustrated in Appendix A. The **application program module** also receives information about a solid through the reference functions. The programs for generating a cutter path to make a 3-D model and for computing the volume of a solid are both included in the application program module.

Our system uses a winged-edge structure as a B-rep of a solid. However, most programmers need not be aware of this, because the geometric modelling module, display program and application program are independent of the characteristics of the B-rep structure. However, it is necessary for programmers of the geometric modelling module to understand how to use the primitive operations and the reference function. It is also necessary for programmers of the display program and the application program to understand how to use the the reference function. Therefore, these modules are more easily implemented corresponding functions in conventional systems.

Chapter 4

Implementing High-level Operations

This chapter describes how various high-level operations for creating or modifying solid shapes are implemented in DESIGNBASE. Solid shapes are always created and modified by primitive operations.

4.1   GENERATING AN INITIAL SOLID

The initial solid in DESIGNBASE is either a **two-and-a-half dimensional solid** or a **rotational object**, sometimes called a **translational sweeping object** and a **rotation sweeping object**, respectively. This section describes how primitive operations are used to create these solids.

1.   *Two-and-a-half dimensional object*

To construct a two-and-a-half dimensional object, a user allocates n points P_i $(i = 1, \ldots, n)$ on an XY-plane to define a polygon and the height of the object. The object is created in the following way.

1.   An object composed of one edge E_1, two vertices V_1 and V_2, and one loop L_1 is created using an MEVVL operation (Figure 4.1(a)).

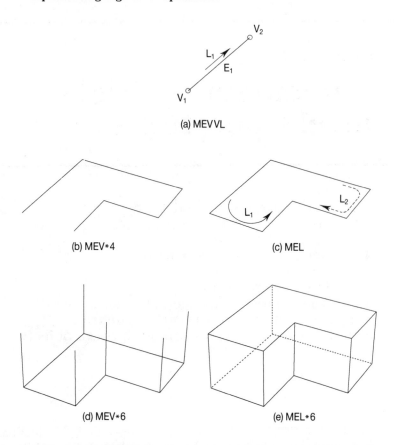

(a) MEVVL

(b) MEV∗4   (c) MEL

(d) MEV∗6   (e) MEL∗6

Figure 4.1   Generating a two-and-a-half dimensional object.

2. An MEV operation is applied to the object $n - 2$ times, and $n - 2$ edges are generated (Figure 4.1(b)).

3. An MEL operation is applied to the object, and loop L_1 is separated into two loops L_1 and L_2 (Figure 4.1(c)). L_1 is a loop with normal $(0, 0, 1)$, and L_2 is a loop with normal $(0, 0, -1)$. The object becomes a **lamina**.

4. An MEV operation is applied to the object n times, which generates n edges attached to all vertices in loop L_1 (Figure 4.1(d)).

5. Lastly, an MEL operation is applied n times and the object becomes a true solid.

2. *Rotational object*

For a rotational object, a user defines a line on an XZ-plane which passes through points P_i $(i = 1, \ldots, n)$. The solid is created as follows.

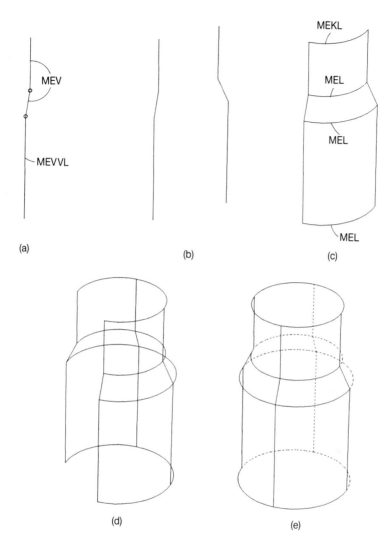

Figure 4.2 Generating a rotational object.

1. A line is created using MEVVL and MEV (Figure 4.2(a)).
2. The same line is created and then rotated about a Z-axis (Figure 4.2(b)). In this case, the angle of rotation is 90°.
3. Between the corresponding end points of the two lines, two edges are generated using MEKL and MEL. The resulting object has two loops: an inside loop and an outside loop. Next, MEL is used to create edges between the interior points in the outside loop (Figure 4.2(c)). These edges are changed to curved ones approximating arcs.

4. A procedure similar to (2) and (3) is applied to the object, which generates the solid shown in Figure 4.2(d). Finally, MEL is used to create edges between the corresponding points, and the rotational solid is completed (Figure 4.2(e)).

4.2 PRODUCING AND DELETING EDGES

There are three types of user commands for producing an edge in a solid, as described below.

1. Edge between two vertices on the same face

To generate an edge between two vertices in the same face, a user specifies two vertices which are attached to the same face. To do this, an input device such as a mouse is used to pick two vertices of a solid shown on the display screen. Examples of such operations are shown in Figure 4.3. In Figure 4.3(a), a user specifies two vertices in the same loop. For

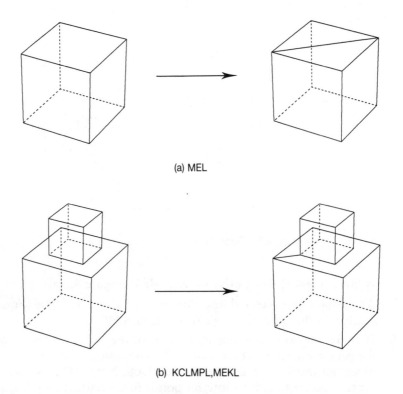

(a) MEL

(b) KCLMPL,MEKL

Figure 4.3 Producing an edge between two vertices on the same face.

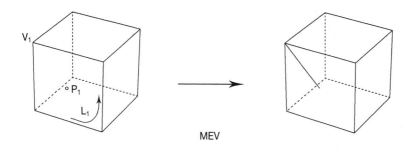

Figure 4.4   Producing an edge between a vertex and a point.

this procedure, an MEL operation is applied to the solid. In Figure 4.3(b), a user specifies two vertices which are attached respectively to the different loops. The two loops belong to the same face. For this procedure, KCLMPL and MEKL operations are applied. In the process of these commands, it is necessary to check whether or not two vertices are attached to the same face. Furthermore, if the same face exists, the system will detect which loop primitive operations are applied, otherwise the procedure can not continue.

2.   Edge between a vertex and a point

To produce an edge between a vertex and a point, a user chooses vertex V_1, loop L_1 attached to V_1 and the coordinate of point P_1, as shown in Figure 4.4. The system then makes an edge between V_1 and P_1 using MEV. Although in DESIGNBASE a user picks three vertices to specify a loop, the first vertex becomes a vertex attached to a new edge.

3.   Edge between different loops

To generate an edge between different loops, two vertices must be chosen which are attached to different loops. Although the types of the two loops may be the same, the loops must not belong to the same face. Figure 4.5 shows shape modifications using this command. In Figure 4.5(a), the operation is used to combine two different solids. MEKL is first used to make an edge between the different P-loops, and then MEL is used three times. In Figure 4.5(b), an edge is made between the different C-loops and a penetrating hole is then created in the solid.

As we have just discussed, there are three kinds of commands for making edges. However, there is only one user command for deleting an edge. Although there are four kinds of primitive operations for deleting an edge (i.e. KEL, KEV, KEML and KEVVL), the system can automatically check which operation should be used. The algorithm is shown in Figure 4.6.

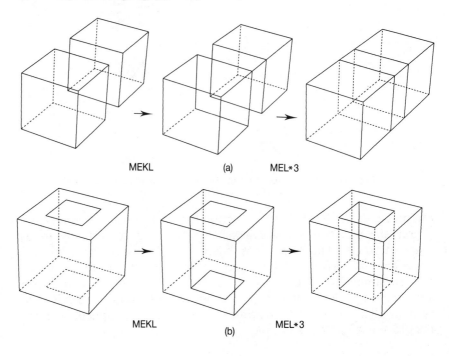

Figure 4.5 Producing an edge between different loops.

4.3 THE LIFT OPERATION

The topological elements of solids, such as faces, edges and vertices are swept using the lift operation. The user specifies the element and how far that element should be moved. Figure 4.7 shows how the lift operation is applied to a face using primitive operations. First, MEV operations are applied to the solid, and edges are created attached to all vertices in the face. Then edges are created between new vertices using an MEL operation. In the specification of the lift operation, if a minus value is given to the distance, a hole is created in the solid, as shown in Figure 4.8. Figure 4.9 also shows the lift operation applied to a face which is composed of P-loop L_1 and C-loop L_2. First, L_2 is changed to a P-loop using a KCLMPL operation, as shown in Figure 4.9(b). Then edges are generated using MEV and MEL operations, as shown in Figure 4.9(c). Lastly, P-loop L_3, which lies on a plane including a new P-loop L_4, is found and L_3 is changed to a C-loop belonging to L_4 by a KPLMCL operation, as shown in Figure 4.9(d). Figures 4.10 and 4.11 show the lift operation applied to an edge and a vertex, respectively.

Figure 4.6   An algorithm for deleting an edge.

```
DeleteEdge(body, edge)
int body;
int edge;
{
    int vertex1, vertex2;
    int loop1, loop2;
    int n1,n2;

    /* two end vertices are given */
    rbE Vertex(body, edge, &vertex1, &vertex2);

    /* the number of edges attached to each vertex */
    rbVEdNm(body, vertex1, &n1);
    rbVEdNm(body, vertex2, &n2);

    /* kill an edge */
    if(n1 == 1 && n2 == 1) {
        KEVVL(body, edge);
        return;
    }
    if(n1 == 1 || n2 == 1) {
        KEV(body, edge);
        return;
    }
    /* both side loops of the edge are given */
    rbELoop(body, edge, &loop1, &loop2);

    /* if both side loops are the same, then KEML */
    if(loop1 == loop2) KEML(body, edge);
    else KEL(body, edge);
}
```

4.4   GENERATING A MIRROR IMAGE

Many objects that an engineer might wish to design are symmetrical, so a modelling system needs to be able to generate the mirror image of a solid (see Figure 4.12). For the operation, a mirror, which is either a plane in space or a plane face of the original solid, must be specified. For the procedure, an identical solid is first generated by a copy operation. The positions of all vertices in a mirror image of the original solid are then computed. In addition, the positions of all Bézier control points of any curved edges are computed. Next, the vertices and the control points of

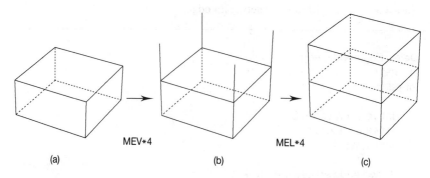

MEV*4   MEL*4

(a)   (b)   (c)

Figure 4.7 Lifting a face.

the original solid are translated to those of the mirror image solid using the primitive operations TV and TB, respectively. Finally, the solid is negated using the primitive operation NS, resulting in a mirror image of the original solid. If a face in the original solid is specified as a mirror, the two solids are combined using a glue operation.

4.5 THE GLUE OPERATION

The glue operation combines two contiguous solids into a single solid, provided there is no interference between the two. Although the same procedure can be accomplished using Boolean operations, the computation time is longer, since many of the processes required for Boolean operations are simply not necessary in glue operations. Because the glue operation includes the restriction that there is no interference between the two solids, the algorithm is simplified, thereby reducing the response

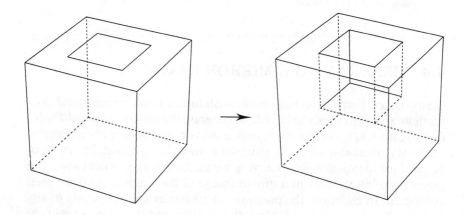

Figure 4.8 Lifting a face composed of a P-loop and a C-loop.

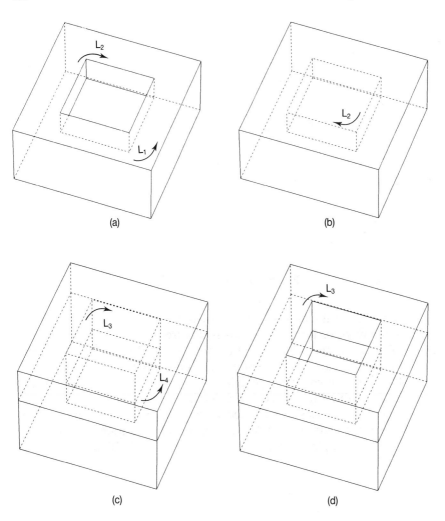

Figure 4.9 Lifting a face with a hole.

time. The program is also more reliable. The glue operation is therefore important in a system which uses B-reps as internal models of solids.

Two kinds of glue operations have been implemented in DESIGN-BASE, as explained below.

1. The first type of glue operation is applied when two faces of the same shape are to be joined. Figure 4.13 shows how a glue operation is implemented using primitive operations. Figure 4.13(a) shows the two solids that are to be glued together. Although the solids do not appear to be contiguous, they were only drawn this way for

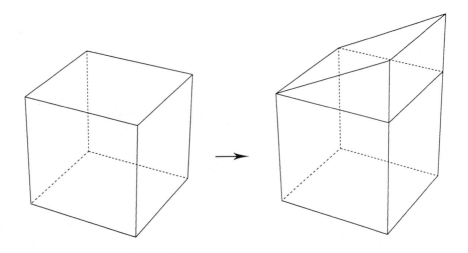

Figure 4.10   Lifting an edge.

purposes of illustration, i.e. the distance between the two cubes is actually zero. First, as shown in Figure 4.13(b), four zero-length edges are generated between the two solids using MEKL and MEL operations, and the two solids are combined into a single solid. Next, unwanted edges are deleted, as shown in Figure 4.13(c). The edges of the original solids are deleted using a KEL operation, and zero-length edges are deleted using a KZEV operation. Finally, unwanted vertices are deleted using a KVE operation, and the glued solid is complete, as shown in Figure 4.13(d). If the faces to be

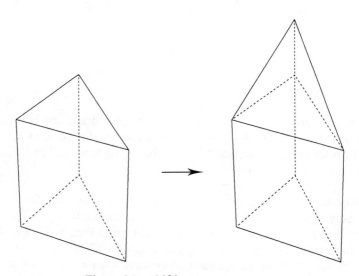

Figure 4.11   Lifting a vertex.

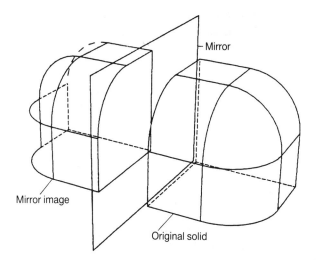

Figure 4.12   Generating a mirror image.

joined include C-loops, all the C-loops are first changed to P-loops by KCLMPL before the edges are generated. The same procedure is then applied to the solids.

2. The second type of glue operation is applied when two faces lie in the same plane, and one face includes the other. An example is shown in Figure 4.14, where loop L_2 in one solid includes loop L_1 in the other solid. For this procedure, the P-loop L_1 is changed to a C-loop by KPLMCL, and the P-loop of C-loop L_1 becomes L_2. Figure 4.15 shows how two loops which have C-loops are joined. In such a case, the two C-loops are first changed to P-loops, and the original P-loops are then joined.

If a user makes a mistake in the positioning of two solids, thereby combining interfering solids in a glue operation, a self-intersecting solid is sometimes generated. It is difficult to recover the original solids from a self-intersecting solid using conventional operations. However, in DE-SIGNBASE an undo operation can always be used to regenerate the original solids, so users need not worry greatly about making mistakes.

4.6   THE CUT OPERATION

In the cut operation, intersection lines between a solid and a plane are computed, and these lines are added to the solid as edges, as shown in Figure 4.16. A plane is defined by three points in space. The points are specified either using coordinates in the case of a space or by vertices in the case of a solid. First, all the intersection points between the plane and the edges of a solid are computed. Vertices are then created at these

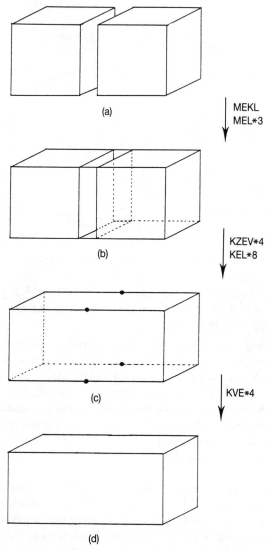

MEKL
MEL*3

KZEV*4
KEL*8

KVE*4

(a)

(b)

(c)

(d)

Figure 4.13 The glue operation applied to faces with the same shapes.

points using an MVE operation. Lastly, edges are created between new vertices. If two vertices between which a new edge is created belong to the same loop, MEL is performed. If two vertices belonging to the same loop also belong to different loops, the types of the two loops are checked. If the loops are same type, MEKL is applied. Otherwise, KCLMPL is used to change the C-loop to a P-loop and MEKL is then applied. The cut operation can optionally separate a solid into two. It can also remove part of a solid.

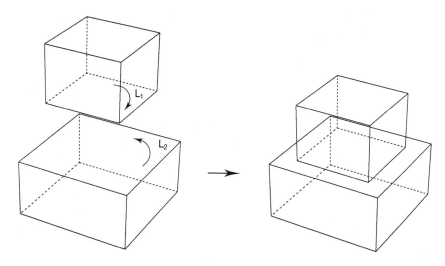

Figure 4.14 The glue operation.

4.7 OPERATIONS FOR A FACE-SET

4.7.1 Specification of a face-set

In DESIGNBASE, part of a solid can be either translated, lifted or deleted. For these procedures, a particular part of a solid is defined as a **face-set**, and a user assigns it a name. To define a face-set, a user must specify an **edge-sequence**. There are two types of specification methods, as explained below.

1. Closed edge-sequence

In Figure 4.17(a), the shaded part is a face-set composed of three faces F_1, F_2 and F_3. This face-set is defined by the closed edge-sequence (E_1, E_2, E_3), which is the closed boundary of the face-set. The order of edges must be counterclockwise when the face-set is viewed from outside the solid. If the order of edges in the edge-sequence is reversed, this defines a face-set composed of all faces except F_1, F_2 and F_3. This face-set is the shaded portion in Figure 4.17(b).

2. Open edge-sequence

Figure 4.18(a) shows an open edge-sequence (E_1, E_2). If such an edge-sequence is given, all the edges which can be traversed from the edge-sequence are collected. Then all the faces which have these edges as boundaries are specified as a face-set. In Figure 4.18(b), the shaded part shows a face-set composed of five faces.

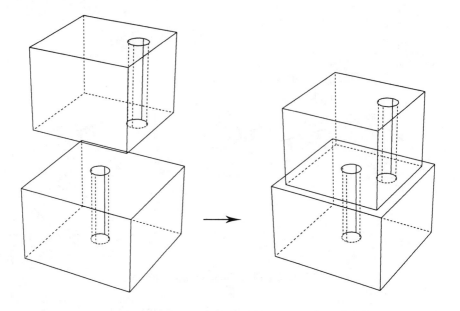

Figure 4.15   The glue operation.

4.7.2   A lift operation applied to a face-set

Figure 4.19 shows a lift operation applied to a face-set defined by a closed edge-sequence. For this procedure, an MZEV operation is applied to all the vertices in a close edge-sequence, and each vertex is replaced by two vertices and a zero-length edge. Figure 4.19(c) shows how a vertex V_1 in the original solid is changed. In the figure, E_1 is a new edge and V_2 a new vertex. New edges are then created between new vertices using MEL. Finally, all vertices and Bézier points in the face-set are translated. This operation can not be applied to a face-set defined by an open edge-sequence.

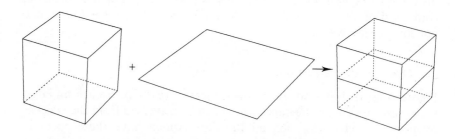

Figure 4.16   The cut operation.

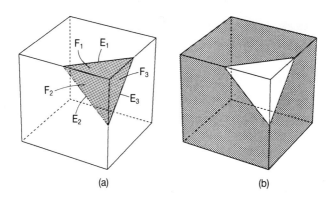

Figure 4.17   Defining a face-set by a closed edge-sequence.

4.7.3   Translating a face-set

Figure 4.20 shows the translation of a face-set defined by an open edge-sequence.

4.7.4   Deleting a face-set

When deleting a face-set, all the edges of the face-set are deleted using the primitive operations KEL, KEML, KEV and KEVVL. Although KEML, KEV and KEVVL can always be used, the use of KEL is restricted (see Section 3.3.1), since, in order to support an undo operation, an edge in a curved loop with C-loops should not be killed. Thus all C-loops in a face-set are first changed to P-loops using the KCLMPL primitive. All the

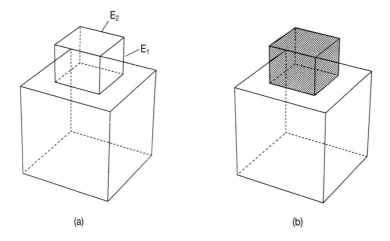

Figure 4.18   Defining a face-set by an open edge-sequence.

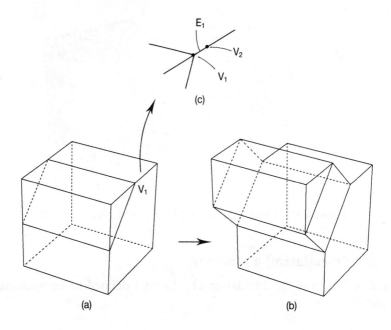

Figure 4.19   The lifting operation applied to a face-set.

curved edges are then changed to straight edges using the geometric primitive CBL. Lastly all edges are deleted, in arbitrary order. Figures 4.21 and 4.22 are both examples of face-sets being deleted.

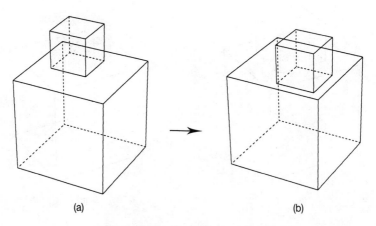

Figure 4.20   Translating a face-set.

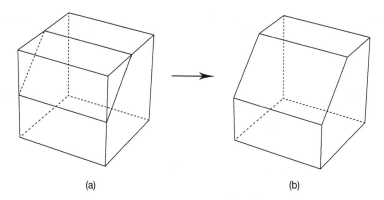

(a)   (b)

Figure 4.21   Deleting a face-set.

4.8   BOOLEAN OPERATIONS ON POLYHEDRA

4.8.1   Overview of Boolean operations

There are three kinds of Boolean operations: union, difference and intersection. Both the difference and intersection operations of two solids A and B are accomplished by a combination of the union operation and the NS primitive operation. These are defined as

difference (A, B) = NS (union (NS(A), B)

intersection (A, B) = NS (union (NS(A), NS(B)))

Here we will describe the union operation, which can be applied only to polyhedra.

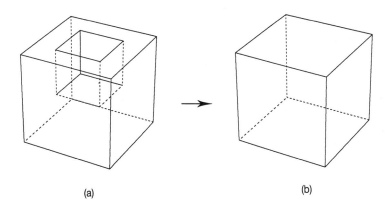

(a)   (b)

Figure 4.22   Deleting a face-set.

Figure 4.23(a) shows two intersecting solids A and B. When a union operation is applied it consists of the following four steps.

1. Calculating J-points and J-lines

The intersection lines between two solids are calculated. These lines are called **J-lines** (junction lines). The end points of the J-lines are called **J-points** (junction points).

2. Generating J-edges and J-vertices

The system generates **J-vertices** on J-points, and **J-edges** on J-lines using primitive operations. Figure 4.23(b) shows J-vertices V_i $(i = 1, \ldots, 8)$ and J-edges E_i $(i = 1, \ldots, 8)$. Each J-vertex of solid A corresponds to that of solid B. Similarly, each J-edge of solid A corresponds to that of solid B.

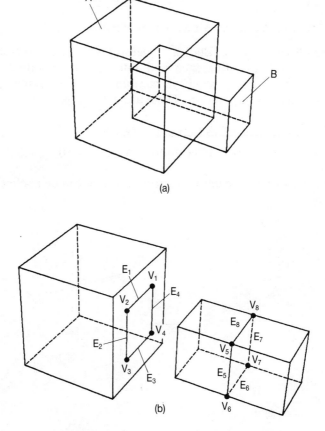

(a)

(b)

Figure 4.23 The union Boolean operation.

3. Removing the included part

The portion of solid B that is included in solid A is now removed, as is the portion of solid A in solid B. All the edges in these parts are usually removed using primitive operations, as shown in Figure 4.23(c).

4. Joining the two solids

To join the two solids, zero-length edges are generated between their corresponding J-vertices. Figure 4.23(d) shows zero-length edges E_i $(i = 9, \ldots, 12)$. The Boolean operation is complete when all unnecessary edges and vertices have been eliminated. Figure 4.23(e) shows the resulting solid.

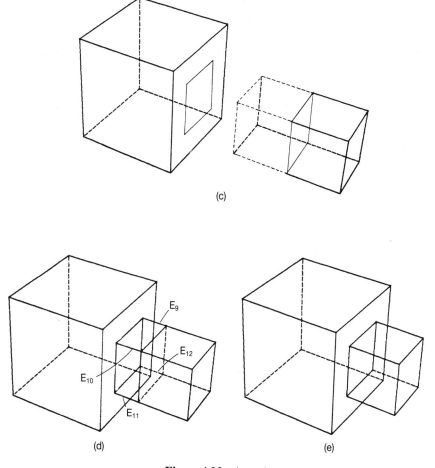

(c)

(d)   (e)

Figure 4.23 (cont.)

4.8.2   Calculating J-points and J-lines

This section describes the method of determining J-points and J-lines, which consists of the following three steps.

1.   Rough intersection check

To find pairs of intersecting faces, the smallest 3-D box that can contain a face is generated for every face of both solids. The intersections between the faces can be roughly checked using these boxes, and the candidate pairs of intersecting faces are then stored.

2.   Computation of J-points and J-lines

J-points and J-lines are computed from each pair of intersecting faces. Figure 4.24 shows intersecting faces F_a and F_b which belong to solids A and B, respectively. First we calculate the intersection points between all the edges of face F_a and a plane which includes face F_b. In the figure, the intersection points are P_1, P_3, P_4 and P_5. Next the system checks whether or not each point is included in face F_b (the algorithm is described in Section 3.3.1). If the point is included, it is a J-point; points P_3, P_4 and P_5 are J-points. The same procedure is then applied to all the edges of face F_b and a plane which includes F_a, and the J-points P_2, P_3, P_4 and P_5 are found.

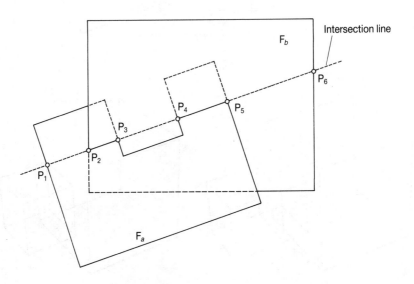

Figure 4.24   Two intersecting faces.

J-points on the intersection line are sorted, and the line segments between J-points are then given. The system checks whether or not each line segment lies on both faces. To do so, the mid-point of each line segment is calculated, and the system checks if the point lies on both faces. If it does, it is a J-line. In Figure 4.24, lines $\overline{P_2P_3}$ and $\overline{P_4P_5}$ are J-lines.

3. Making tables of J-points and J-lines

The system tabulates the information on the J-points and J-lines. The J-point table is as follows:

```
struct Jpoint{
        double x;
        double y;
        double z;
        int relationship;
        int vertex;
}
```

x, y, and z store the position of each J-point and relationship represents the relationship between the J-point and its parent solid. The possible relationships are as follows:

1. A J-point is on a vertex of a solid.
2. A J-point is on an edge.
3. A J-point is enclosed in a loop.

The initial value of vertex is zero. In the next procedure, when the J-point becomes a J-vertex, vertex stores its vertex ID. The J-line table is as follows:

```
struct Jline{
        int Jpoint1;
        int Jpoint2;
        int edge;
}
```

Jpoint1 and Jpoint2 store two J-points attached to each J-line. When the J-line becomes a J-edge, edge stores its edge ID.

4.8.3   Generating J-edges and J-vertices

The system now generates J-vertices and J-edges using information from the J-point and J-line tables. J-vertices are first created at some J-points, and J-edges are then created between the J-vertices.

1. Generating J-vertices

If a J-point corresponds to an existing vertex of one of the solids to be joined, the system regards that vertex as a J-vertex, and does not generate a new one. In the J-point table, vertex stores the ID of the original vertex. If a J-point lies on an edge of the solid, the primitive operation MVE is used to generate a J-vertex on a J-point. vertex stores the ID of the new vertex. All the remaining J-points are on a loop. No action is taken because the corresponding J-vertices are created when an edge is produced, starting from this point. Creating J-vertices in this way makes it easier to determine which primitive operation should be applied to produce a J-edge.

2. Generating J-edges

Using information from the J-line and J-point tables, the system generates J-edges on J-lines by primitive operations. A J-line falls into one of three categories depending on its stage of development:

1. Neither of its J-vertices (end points) has yet been generated. In this case, MEVVL is used to generate a J-edge, both J-vertices and a loop (Figure 4.25(a)).

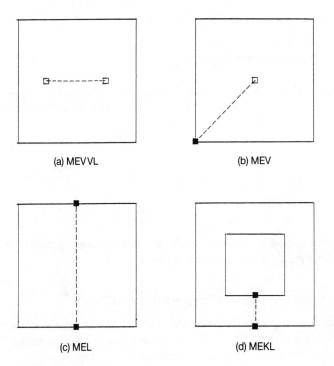

(a) MEVVL   (b) MEV

(c) MEL   (d) MEKL

Figure 4.25 Making a J-edge. □ J-point; ■ J-vertex; ---- J-line.

2. Only one of its J-vertices has been generated. In this case, MEV is used to generate a J-edge and a J-vertex (Figure 4.25(b)).
3. Both its J-vertices have been generated. In this case, if both J-vertices lie on the same loop (as in Figure 4.25(c)), MEL is used to generate a J-edge and a loop; if the J-vertices lie on the same face, but in different loops (as in Figure 4.25(d)), MEKL is used.

Unnecessary calculation can be avoided by applying primitive operations in the logical sequence. For example, Figure 4.26(a) shows the creation of two edges E_1 and E_2 in loop L_1. If E_2 is created by MEL before E_1 is created, loop L_1 is divided into two loops L_1 and L_2, as shown in Figure 4.26(b). When edge E_1 is created, the system must determine the loop to which this edge will belong. This calculation is not required if E_1 is produced first, using the MEV operation, before E_2 is created.

Figure 4.27 provides another example of the importance of the sequence in which primitive operations are applied. Here, the quadrilateral PQRS forms a loop. Creating edges PQ and RS by MEVVL results in two loops, L_1 and L_2. If either edge QR or PS is produced by MEKL, loop L_1 or loop L_2 must be killed. The superfluous loop can be avoided by creating edges PQ, QR, RS and SP in that order. The algorithm used to create J-edges is shown in Figure 4.28.

4.8.4   Removing included parts

In our union operation, any part of a solid that penetrates the boundary of another solid is called an **included part**. This section describes the third phase of a Boolean operation, the removal of included parts. The procedure itself consists of the following three steps.

1.   *Assigning three types of marks to faces*

Figure 4.29 shows a J-edge generated on an intersection of two faces, and its adjacent faces F_1, F_2, F_3 and F_4. Faces F_1 and F_2 belong to solid A, and

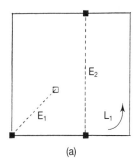   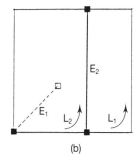

(a)   (b)

Figure 4.26   Making a J-edge.

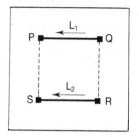

Figure 4.27   Making a J-edge.

Figure 4.28   An algorithm for making J-edges.

```
MakeJedges(Jpoint, Jline, njl)
struct Jpoint Jpoint[ ];          /* J-point table */
struct Jline Jline[ ];            /* J-line table */
int njl;                          /* the number of J-lines */
{
     int i;
     int ne;         /* the number of edges */
     int vertex1;
     int vertex2;
     int jpoint1;
     int jpoint2;
     int edge;
     int loop;

     for (;;) {
         ne = 0;
         for(i = 1;  i <= njl;  i ++) {

             if(Jline[i].edge != 0) continue;
             jpoint1 = Jline[i].Jpoint1;
             jpoint2 = Jline[i].Jpoint2;

             /* making an edge using MEVVL */
             if(Jpoint[jpoint1].vertex == 0 & &
               Jpoint[jpoint2].vertex == 0) {
                 MEVVL(&edge, &vertex1, &vertex2);
                 Jline[i].edge = edge;
                 Jpoint[jpoint1].vertex = vertex1;
                 Jpoint[jpoint2].vertex = vertex2;
                 ne++;
             }

             /* making an edge using MEV */
             if(Jpoint[jpoint1].vertex != 0 &&
               Jpoint[jpoint2].vertex == 0) {
                 MEV(&edge, &vertex1);
```

F_3 and F_4 belong to solid B. In the figure, the shaded side of each face shows the inside of a solid. Faces attached to J-edges can be divided into three types:

1. A face of one solid which is not included in the other solid.
2. A face of one solid which is included in the other solid.
3. A face of one solid which lies on the boundary of the other solid.

The system internally marks faces of the above groups with $+$, $-$ and 0, respectively. While $+$ indicates that the face is to be kept in the

Figure 4.28   (cont.)

```
                    Jline[i].edge = edge;
                    Jpoint[jpoint1].vertex = vertex1;
                    ne++;
            }

            /* making an edge using MEV */
            if(Jpoint[jpoint1].vertex == 0 &&
                Jpoint[jpoint2].vertex != 0) {
                    MEV(&edge, &vertex2);
                    Jline[i].edge = edge;
                    Jpoint[jpoint2].vertex = vertex2;
                    ne++;
            }
        }

        /* if there is no edge which can be made by MEVVL or MEV */
        if(ne == 0) break;
    }

    for(i = 1;  i <= njl;  i++) {

        /* get two vertices to be connected to a new J-edge */
        if(Jline[i].edge != 0) continue;
        jpoint1 = Jline[i].Jpoint1;
        jpoint2 = Jline[i].Jpoint2;
        vertex1 = Jpoint[jpoint1].vertex;
        vertex2 = Jpoint[jpoint2].vertex;

        /* get the common loop including vertex1 and vertex2 */
        GetCommonLoop(vertex1, vertex2, &loop);
        if(loop != 0) MEL;
        else MEKL;
    }
}
```

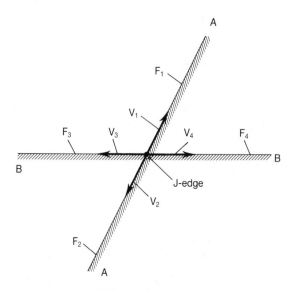

Figure 4.29   The intersection of two faces.

procedure of the Boolean operation, $-$ indicates that the face is to be removed. 0 will be replaced by either $+$ or $-$ in the next step. In Figure 4.29, faces F_1 and F_3 are marked $+$, and faces F_2 and F_4 are marked $-$. The mark given to each face is checked by computing a vector V_i $(i = 1, \ldots, 4)$ which lies on each face and is perpendicular to the intersecting line. The system then checks whether or not the vector on a face of one solid is included in the corner between two vectors indicating the inside of the other solid. If the vector on the face is included in the corner, the face is marked $+$. If the vector of one solid is the same as either of the two vectors of the other solid, the face is marked 0. Otherwise the face is marked $-$. This is geometric computation on a plane (the algorithm is similar to that described in Section 3.3.1).

2.   Detecting faces in the included part

J-edges can be divided into three groups:

1.   J-edges generated at an intersection of two faces. This case was shown in Figure 4.29.
2.   J-edges generated at an intersection between a face of one solid and an edge of another. All possible cases are shown in Figure 4.30.
3.   J-edges generated at an intersection between two edges. All possible cases are shown in Figure 4.31.

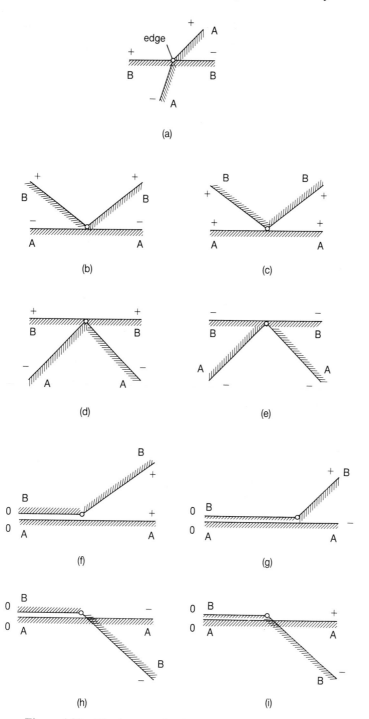

Figure 4.30   The intersection between a face and an edge.

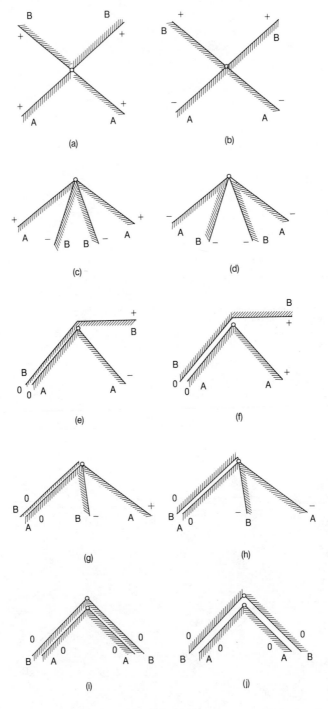

Figure 4.31   The intersection of two edges.

Although there are many kinds of intersection, there are eight combinations of marks, as shown in Figure 4.32. Cases 5, 6, 7 and 8 in the figure include mark 0. In these cases, 0 will be changed to either + or −. The process of change for each case is described below.

Case 5 Case 5 includes two different cases, as shown in Figures 4.31(i) and (j). In Figure 4.31(i), pairs of faces which lie on the same plane have the same normal vectors. In this case, two faces of one solid have to be deleted. Since the check on which faces are to be deleted is performed by detecting an included part, all 0's are replaced by +'s. In Figure 4.31(j), the normal vector of one face is opposite to that of the corresponding face. All four faces are therefore to be deleted since they are included in the resultant solid. So the 0 mark on these faces is replaced by −.

Case 6 Figures 4.30(f) and 4.31(f) show examples of case 6. The normal of one face marked 0 is opposite to that of the other face marked 0, and the two faces are included in the resulting solid. Both 0 marks are therefore replaced by −.

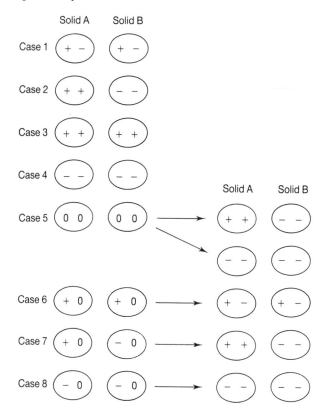

Figure 4.32 Combining +, − and 0.

Case 7   Figures 4.30(g) and (i) and 4.31(e) and (g) show examples of case 7. One face is to be removed, and the other is to be kept. The 0 mark in one solid is therefore changed to +, and the 0 in the other solid is changed to −.

Case 8   Figures 4.30(h) and 4.31(h) show examples of case 8. The four faces are to be deleted since they are included in the resulting solid. Thus on all these faces 0 is replaced by −.

The combinations give four cases, as described below.

Case 1   A J-edge becomes one of the boundary edges of an included part. Thus, **R-flags** (remove-flags) are given to the two faces marked −.

Case 2   R-flags are given to the two faces marked −. In this case, a J-edge does not become one of the boundary edges of an included part and the information on J-edges is removed.

Case 3   This is the case in which an intersection between two solids is a line, as shown in Figure 4.33. The information on J-edges is removed because such parts are not combined.

Case 4   R-flags are given to the four faces marked −. The information on J-edges is removed.

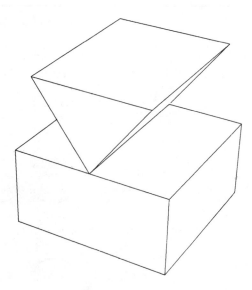

Figure 4.33   The intersection of two solids.

After the above procedure is completed, the sequence of J-edges becomes a loop. This J-edge loop is the boundary of an included part.

3. Removal of edges in the included part

All edges and faces of the included part from the J-edge loop and the faces with R-flags are traversed using the topological information. This procedure does not require geometric computation. All the edges and faces of the included part are then removed by primitive operations. In order to regenerate solids efficiently using undo operations, all C-loops in the included part are first changed into P-loops using KCLMPL. All the edges are then removed using either KEV, KEVVL, KEL or KEML. The procedure is the same as that used in deleting a face-set.

4.8.5   Joining two solids

This section describes the fourth phase of a Boolean operation, the procedure of joining two solids, which consists of the following two steps:

1. Joining J-loops

As a result of removing the included part, the two solids now meet at J-edges. These J-edges form pairs of loops which are referred to as **J-loops**. To join the two solids, the system generates zero-length edges between corresponding J-vertices on two J-loops using MEKL and MEL operations. Once the solids are joined, all zero-length edges and the J-vertices of one solid are removed using KZEV operations. The procedure is the same as that used in a glue operation.

Our method of joining two solids requires all the J-vertices connected in the J-loop of one solid to correspond to the J-vertices in the J-loop of the other. However, this requirement is not always satisfied. Figure 4.34 illustrates one such example. Figure 4.34(a) shows two solids A and B to which a Boolean operation is applied. Figure 4.34(b) and (c), respectively, show the two solids after the removal of an included part. While solid A has two J-loops L_1 and L_2, solid B has only one, L_3. In the vertex sequence of loop L_3, vertex V_1 appears twice. J-loop L_3 is called a **constricted loop**, and vertex V_1 is called a **C-vertex**. Since the shapes of such J-loops do not correspond directly to those of the intersecting solid, the above procedure can not be used to join the solids.

In the case just described, the loop shapes are modified using Euler operations so that corresponding loops have the same shape. Figure 4.35 illustrates how the constricted loop L_3 is separated at the C-vertex V_1. This separation is accomplished in two steps. First, the C-vertex V_1 is replaced by two C-vertices V_1 and V_2 and a zero-length edge E_1 using

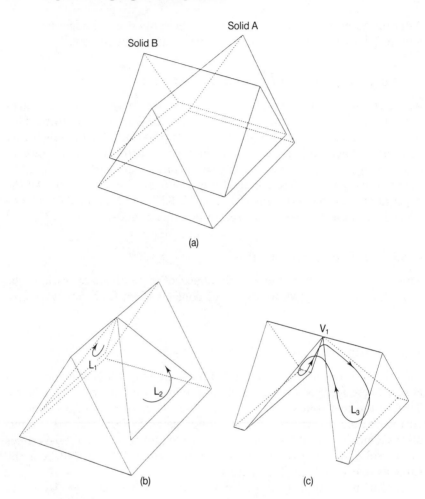

Figure 4.34   A constricted loop.

MZEV (Figure 4.35(b)). The zero-length edge between two the C-vertices is then removed using KEML (Figure 4.35(c)). The constricted loop is thereby separated into two non-constricted loops L_3 and L_4. In other cases where there are no corresponding J-loops, a similar procedure using Euler operations is applied.

2.   Removing J-edges

The two solids are now joined at duplicate J-loops. In this step, some J-edges are removed. All the J-edges of one solid are first removed using KEL operations, learning only the J-edges of the other solid. If the normal vectors of both faces attached to such a J-edge lie in the same direction,

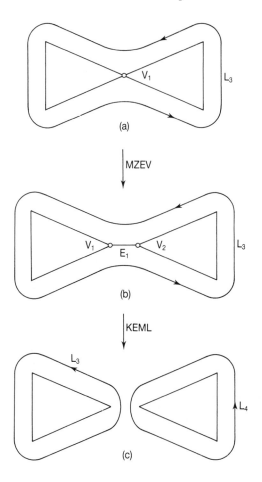

Figure 4.35   Separating a constricted loop.

the edge is not needed in the representation of the solid. It is therefore removed using KEL or KVE.

The union operation is now complete. An example of solid generation using Boolean operations is shown below. Figures 4.36(a), (b) and (c) show three solids which were generated by sweeping the 2-D shapes of letters G, E and B, respectively. First, the intersection operation is applied to solids G and E, and the solid shown in Figure 4.36(d) is generated. Next, the intersection operation is applied to the new solid and solid B, and the solid shown in Figure 4.36(e) is generated. Finally, all edges of the resulting solid are changed to fillet surfaces using a rounding operation (see Section 6.4), as shown in Plate 1. This image was generated using a scan-line shading algorithm (see Section 9.2.2).

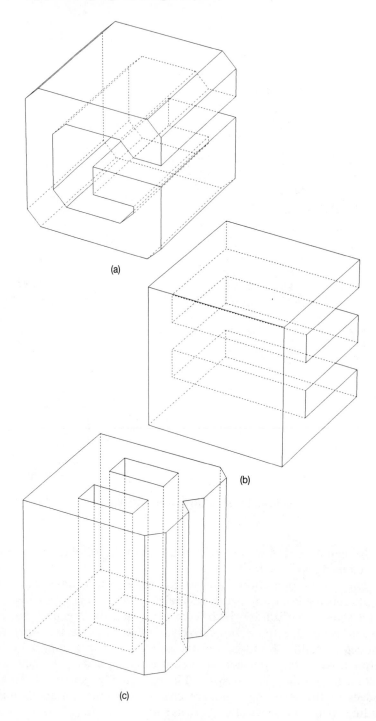

(a)

(b)

(c)

Figure 4.36   Examples of Boolean operations.

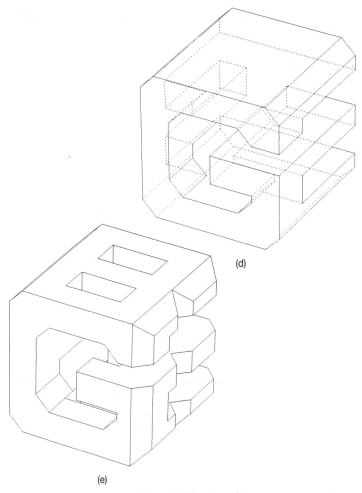

Figure 4.36 (cont.)

4.8.6 Numerical errors in Boolean operations

The coordinates of the vertices of a solid generated by a Boolean
operation are given as the intersections between planes and lines. The
coordinates of vertices therefore include numerical errors, and the plane
faces attached to these vertices become slightly curved. As a Boolean
operation is repeatedly applied to the solid, the numerical error becomes
larger. Finally, a further Boolean operation can not be performed on the
solid because the program assumes that all faces are planar. When a solid
is rotated, the coordinates similarly include the numerical error since
they are multiplied by the values of sin and cos. The problem of
numerical error is very serious in solid modelling, and there has been
some research in this area (Segal and Séquin, 1985).

4.9   BOOLEAN OPERATIONS ON SCULPTURED OBJECTS

Although in DESIGNBASE the development of Boolean operations applied to sculptured objects has not yet been completed, we introduce several techniques to implement Boolean operations.

4.9.1   Intersection of free-form surfaces

To implement this Boolean operation, the intersecting curves between the different free-form surfaces need to be computed. However, if bicubic parametric patches, which are popular in industry, are used as surface expressions in the solid modelling system, the degree of the intersecting curve between the patches becomes 324. And the degree of the curve between the patch and a plane is 18. The computation of polynomials of such high degrees is very expensive. It is also difficult to deal with high degree polynomials in the system. So, in existing systems supporting Boolean operations, points on the intersection curves are computed, and then spline curves are used to interpolate these points.

To compute the intersection points, two kinds of methods have been applied: branch following and subdivision (Thomas, 1987). The branch following method (Barnhill *et al.*, 1987) first finds at least one point on the intersection curve. The differential equation is then used to follow the curve in both directions from this point. The subdivision method (Carlson, 1982; Thomas, 1984; Houghton *et al.*, 1985) uses surface subdivision to approximate each surface by collecting plane segments. The intersection curve is then approximated as the intersection of the surface approximation.

4.9.2   Trimmed surface patches

As a result of the Boolean operation, the solid shape is represented by part of a surface patch. The face represented by a patch has a boundary which is the intersection line between the free-form surfaces. We call such a patch a **trimmed surface patch**. The trimmed surface patch is not rectangular and may have an arbitrary topology with disconnected pieces and holes. Figure 4.37 shows an example of a trimmed surface patch. The shaded portion indicates the region which is removed by the Boolean operation.

Two approaches have been taken to represent trimmed surfaces. The repatching approach (Sarraga and Waters, 1984) attempts to replace the retained regions with several new surface patches. The advantage is that a whole region of a patch is used to represent the shape and it is therefore easy to deal with the data structure of the solid. This approach requires the region to be subdivided into several rectangular areas since

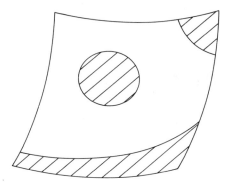

Figure 4.37   A trimmed surface patch.

the topology of the region is highly non-rectangular. However, it is not clear how effectively to do this automatically. The other approach (Casale, 1987) is to support a trimmed surface patch in the data structure of the system. The region is bounded by a number of loops, each of which is composed of one or more intersection curves or parts of the boundary of the original patch. If a trimmed surface patch is used to represent the shape, the system procedure becomes relatively complex.

Chapter 5

Free-form Curves

In this chapter we will describe methods for generating and modifying free-form curves. Since curves generated in DESIGNBASE are expressed using cubic Bézier curves, the emphasis will be on methods involving Bézier curves.

5.1   PARAMETRIC CURVES

Although a space or plane curve can be represented by either an implicit or a parametric form, it is the parametric form which has been widely used in both CAD and computer graphics. The parametric curve has the advantage that its shape is independent of any axes and it is therefore easy to represent a closed curve. In addition, the points on the curve which are required in order to draw it can be computed simply by varying the value of the parameter. The parametric curve $\mathbf{P}(t)$ in a space is generally expressed as

$$\mathbf{P}(t) = \begin{bmatrix} P_x(t) \\ P_y(t) \\ P_z(t) \end{bmatrix}$$

where

$$t_0 \leq t \leq t_1$$

For computational simplicity, the curve represented by a polynomial is popular. Its equation is

$$\mathbf{P}(t) = \mathbf{C}_n t^n + \mathbf{C}_{n-1} t^{n-1} + \ldots + \mathbf{C}_0$$

where $\mathbf{C}_i$ $(i = 0, \ldots, n)$ are coefficient vectors composed of x, y and z values. To define the parametric curve of degree n, a user has to specify $n + 1$ coefficients. However, since the relationship between the coefficients and the curve shape is not clear, it is difficult for a designer to specify coefficients which define a particular curve. Thus methods of defining a curve using **control points** have been widely used. Of these, Bézier curves (Bézier, 1972; Forrest, 1972a) and B-spline curves (Riesenfeld, 1973) are the most popular. These curves are described in Sections 5.2 and 5.3.

5.2   BÉZIER CURVES

A Bézier curve $\mathbf{R}(t)$ of degree n, defined by control points $\mathbf{P}_i$ $(i = 0, \ldots, n)$, is expressed as

$$\mathbf{R}(t) = \sum_{i=0}^{n} \binom{n}{i} t^i (1-t)^{n-i} \mathbf{P}_i \qquad (0 \leq t \leq 1)$$

where

$$\binom{n}{i} = \frac{n!}{i!(n-i)!}$$

Figure 5.1 shows Bézier curves of degrees 3, 4 and 5 and their control points. Figure 5.2 gives FORTRAN programs which compute a point on a Bézier curve. A Bézier curve can be elegantly expressed as follows:

$$\mathbf{R}(t) = (1 - t + tE)^n \mathbf{P}_0, \qquad E\mathbf{P}_i = \mathbf{P}_{i+1}$$

where E is a shift operator (Hosaka and Kimura, 1980). The properties of a Bézier curve are described below.

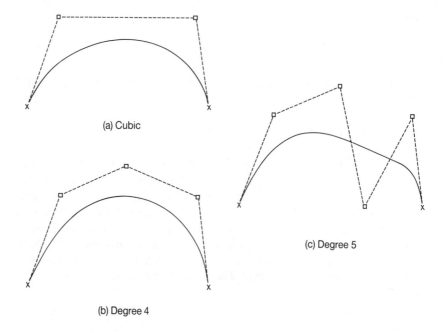

(a) Cubic

(c) Degree 5

(b) Degree 4

Figure 5.1 Bézier curves.

1. Convex hull property

In the formulation of a Bézier curve, since the weights given to control points are binomial coefficients, the total sum of the weights is always 1:

$$\sum_{i=0}^{n} \binom{n}{i} t^{i}(1-t)^{n-i} = 1$$

Thus any point on a Bézier curve is always included in a convex hull defined by control points. Figure 5.3 shows two cubic Bézier curves and their corresponding convex hulls. The shaded areas are the convex hulls. This property is useful in checking the interference between the different curves. In many CAD and computer graphics procedures, the interference check is performed often. If an intersection point of two curves has to be computed to check whether or not two curves intersect then the procedure is expensive. On the other hand, by comparing the convex hulls of two curves, we can quickly determine whether or not those two curves intersect.

2. Relationship between a curve and a control polygon

A designer can readily understand the relationship between the shape of a Bézier curve and a polygon of control points. The first and last control

Figure 5.2   FORTRAN programs for computing a point on a Bézier curve.

```
C---------------------------------------------------------------
C
C      >> POSITION ON BEZIER CURVE <<
C
       SUBROUTINE CPOSZ (IS, ID, ZP, T, SDR)
       DIMENSION ZP(IS, 1), SDR(IS)
C
C      /I/ IS.. =2:PLANE CURVE =3:SPACE CURVE
C      /I/ ID.. DEGREE OF CURVE
C      /I/ ZP.. BEZIER POINTS
C      /I/ T .. PARAMETER VALUE
C      /O/ SDR.. POSITION
C
C      - CLEAR SDR -
C

       DO 110 K=1,IS
         SDR(K)=0.0
110    CONTINUE
C
C      - POSITION -
C
       IAEN=ID+1
       DO 200 IA=1,IAEN
         I=IA-1
         W1=1.0
       IF(I.NE.0) W1=T**I
         W2=1.0
       IF(I.NE.ID) W2=( 1.0-T)**(ID-I)
       W=CBNC(ID,I)*W1*W2
       DO 230 K=1,IS
         SDR(K)=SDR(K)+ZP(K,I+1)*W
230      CONTINUE
200    CONTINUE
C
       RETURN
       END
C
C---------------------------------------------------------------
C      >> BINOMIAL COEFFICIENT <<
C
       FUNCTION CBNC(N,I)
C
       CBNC=1.0
       IF(N.LE.0) RETURN
       IF(I.LE.0) RETURN
       IF(I.GE.N) RETURN
```

Figure 5.2 (cont.)

```
C
      IA=I
      NA=N
      IF(I.GT.N/2) IA=N-I
C
      DO 100 K=1,IA
         CBNC=CBNC*FLOAT(NA)/FLOAT(K)
         NA=NA-1
100   CONTINUE
      RETURN
      END
C--------------------------------------------------------------------
```

points are the end points of a curve. The characteristics of the polygon are similar to those of the curve, and the curve is smoother than the polygon. In other words, if there is no wave in the polygon, the curve does not include a wave. This property enables a designer easily to define the shape of a curve by manipulating the control points.

3. Derivative vectors

The first derivative of a Bézier curve $\mathbf{R}(t)$ of degree n with respect to t is represented using a Bézier expression of degree $n-1$, as follows:

$$\frac{d\mathbf{R}(t)}{dt} = \dot{\mathbf{R}}(t) = n\sum_{i=0}^{n-1}\binom{n-1}{i}t^{i}(1-t)^{n-1-i}\mathbf{a}_i$$

where $\mathbf{a}_i$ $(i = 0,\ldots,n-1)$ are the vectors between control points expressed as

$$\mathbf{a}_i = \mathbf{P}_{i+1} - \mathbf{P}_i$$

Proof The first derivative of $\mathbf{R}(t)$ with respect to t is expressed as

$$\frac{d\mathbf{R}(t)}{dt} = \dot{\mathbf{R}}(t) = \sum_{i=0}^{n}i\binom{n}{i}t^{i-1}(1-t)^{n-i}\mathbf{P}_i$$

$$-\sum_{i=0}^{n}(n-i)\binom{n}{i}t^{i}(1-t)^{n-i-1}\mathbf{P}_i$$

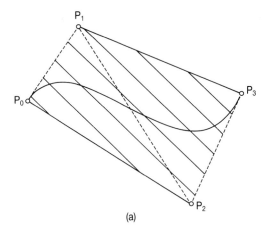

(a)

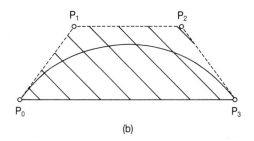

(b)

Figure 5.3 Bézier curves and their convex hulls.

Then

$$\dot{\mathbf{R}}(t) = \sum_{i=1}^{n} i \binom{n}{i} t^{i-1}(1-t)^{n-i}\mathbf{P}_i$$

$$- \sum_{i=0}^{n-1}(n-i)\binom{n}{i} t^{i}(1-t)^{n-i-1}\mathbf{P}_i$$

$$\dot{\mathbf{R}}(t) = \sum_{i=0}^{n-1}(i+1)\binom{n}{i+1} t^{i}(1-t)^{n-1-i}\mathbf{P}_i$$

$$- \sum_{i=0}^{n-1}(n-i)\binom{n}{i} t^{i}(1-t)^{n-1-i}\mathbf{P}_i$$

In the equation,

$$(i+1)\binom{n}{i+1} = n\binom{n-1}{i}, \qquad (n-i)\binom{n}{i} = n\binom{n-1}{i}$$

We then obtain

$$\dot{\mathbf{R}}(t) = n \sum_{i=0}^{n-1} \binom{n-1}{i} t^i (1-t)^{n-1-i} \mathbf{a}_i$$

where

$$\mathbf{a}_i = P_{i+1} - P_i \qquad (i = 0, \ldots, n-1) \qquad \blacksquare$$

From the above equation, the first derivatives on the end points of a Bézier curve are given by

$$\dot{\mathbf{R}}(0) = n \times (\mathbf{P}_1 - \mathbf{P}_0)$$
$$\dot{\mathbf{R}}(1) = n \times (\mathbf{P}_n - \mathbf{P}_{n-1})$$

Figure 5.4 shows a polygon of a cubic Bézier curve and the first derivative on a starting point of the curve. The second derivative with respect to t is

$$\frac{d^2 \mathbf{R}(t)}{dt^2} = \ddot{\mathbf{R}}(t) = n(n-1) \sum_{i=0}^{n-2} \binom{n-2}{i} t^i (1-t)^{n-2-i} \mathbf{b}_i$$

where

$$\mathbf{b}_i = \mathbf{a}_{i+1} - \mathbf{a}_i \, (i = 0, \ldots, n-2)$$

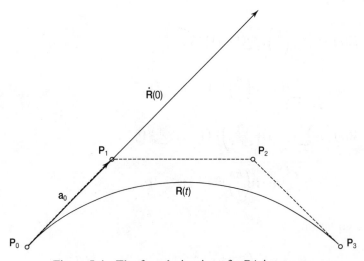

Figure 5.4   The first derivative of a Bézier curve.

This property enables us visually to understand the derivatives of the Bézier curve. Figure 5.5 gives a program to compute the derivatives.

4. Elevation of a degree

A Bézier curve of degree n can be represented by a Bézier curve of degree $n + 1$. The elevation of the degree of a Bézier curve is expressed as

$$\mathbf{R}(t) = (1-t)\mathbf{R}(t) + t\mathbf{R}(t)$$

Here, a Bézier curve $\mathbf{R}(t)$ defined by control points $\mathbf{P}_i (i = 0, \ldots, n)$ is rewritten as

$$\mathbf{R}(t) = \sum_{i=0}^{n} \binom{n}{i} t^i (1-t)^{n-i} \mathbf{P}_i = \{\mathbf{P}_0, \mathbf{P}_1, \ldots, \mathbf{P}_n\} \qquad (5.1)$$

We then obtain

$$t\mathbf{R}(t) = t\{\mathbf{P}_0, \mathbf{P}_1, \ldots, \mathbf{P}_n\}$$
$$= \left\{ 0, \frac{\mathbf{P}_0}{n+1}, \frac{2\mathbf{P}_1}{n+1}, \ldots, \frac{n\mathbf{P}_{n-1}}{n+1}, \mathbf{P}_n \right\} \qquad (5.2)$$
$$(1-t)\mathbf{R}(t) = (1-t)\{\mathbf{P}_0, \mathbf{P}_1, \ldots, \mathbf{P}_n\}$$
$$= \left\{ \mathbf{P}_0, \frac{n\mathbf{P}_1}{n+1}, \frac{(n-1)\mathbf{P}_2}{n+1}, \ldots, \frac{\mathbf{P}_n}{n+1}, 0 \right\} \qquad (5.3)$$

Proof

$$t\mathbf{R}(t) = \sum_{i=0}^{n} \binom{n}{i} t^{i+1} (1-t)^{n-i} \mathbf{P}_i$$

Here, $k = i + 1$ and $m = n + 1$.

$$t\mathbf{R}(t) = \sum_{k=1}^{m} \binom{m-1}{k-1} t^k (1-t)^{m-k} \mathbf{P}_{k-1}$$

In the equation,

$$\binom{m-1}{k-1} = \frac{k}{m} \binom{m}{k}$$

Figure 5.5 Program for computing the first derivative of a Bézier curve.

```
C-------------------------------------------------------------
C     >> ORDER-N DERIVATINE ON BEZIER CURVE<<
C
      SUBROUTINE CNDEZ(IS, ID, ZP, T, IN, SDR, ZPA)
      DIMENSION ZP(IS, 1), SDR(IS, 1), ZPA(IS, 1)
C
C     /I/ IS.. = 2:PLANE CURVE  =3:SPACE CURVE
C     /I/ ID.. DEGREE OF CURVE
C     /I/ ZP.. BEZIER POLYGON
C     /I/ IN.. ORDER OF DERIVATIVE
C     /I/ T .. PARAMETER VALUE
C     /O/ SDR
C     // ( ,1).. POSITION
C     // ( ,2).. FIRST DERIVATIVE
C     // ( ,3).. SECOND DERIVATIVE
C
C     - ZP TO ZPA -
C
```

Consequently, we obtain

$$t\mathbf{R}(t) = \sum_{k=0}^{m}\binom{m}{k}t^k(1-t)^{m-k}\frac{k}{m}\mathbf{P}_{k-1}$$

The following equation is similarly obtained.

$$(1-t)\mathbf{R}(t) = \sum_{k=0}^{m}\binom{m}{k}t^k(1-t)^{m-k}\frac{m-k}{m}\mathbf{P}_k \qquad \blacksquare$$

Therefore, the control points of a Bézier curve of degree $n+1$ are given by

$$\mathbf{R}(t) = \left\{\mathbf{P}_0, \frac{\mathbf{P}_0+n\mathbf{P}_1}{n+1}, \frac{2\mathbf{P}_1+(n-1)\mathbf{P}_2}{n+1}, \ldots, \frac{n\mathbf{P}_{n-1}+\mathbf{P}_n}{n+1}, \mathbf{P}_n\right\}$$

As described above, it is simple to elevate the degree of a Bézier curve. Figure 5.6 shows an example in which $\mathbf{P}_i$ ($i = 0, \ldots, 3$) are the control points of a cubic Bézier curve, and $\mathbf{Q}_i$ ($i = 0, \ldots, 4$) are the control points of a fourth-degree curve defining the same curve.

Figure 5.5   (cont.)

```
        ID1=ID+1
        DO 100 I=1, ID1
          DO 110 K=1, IS
            ZPA(K, I)=ZP(K, I)
110       CONTINUE
100     CONTINUE
C
        IDA=ID
        IPEN=IN+1
        DO 210 IP=1, IPEN
          CALL CPOSZ(IS, IDA, ZPA, T, SDR(1, IP))
          DO 300 I=1, IDA
            DO 310 K=1, IS
              ZPA(K, I)=(ZPA(K, I+1)-ZPA(K, I))*FLOAT(IDA)
310         CONTINUE
300       CONTINUE
C
          IDA=IDA-1
210     CONTINUE
C
        RETURN
        END
C-----------------------------------------------------------
```

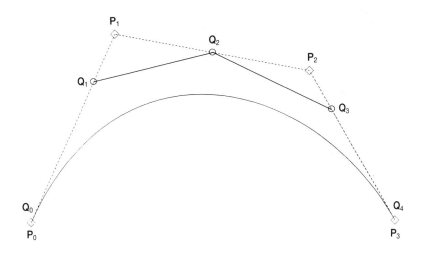

Figure 5.6   Degree elevation of a Bézier curve.

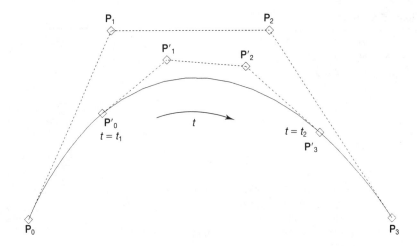

Figure 5.7   Subdivision of a Bézier curve.

5. *Subdivision of a Bézier curve*

Part of a Bézier curve can be represented as a Bézier curve. As an example, we will describe how to subdivide a cubic Bézier curve. Figure 5.7 shows a cubic Bézier curve $\mathbf{R}(t)$ defined by four control points $\mathbf{P}_i$ $(i = 0, \ldots, 3)$. A curve between parameters t_1 and t_2 $(0 \le t_1 \le t_2 \le 1)$ on curve $\mathbf{R}(t)$ is represented as a cubic Bézier curve $\mathbf{R}'(t')$ $(0 \le t' \le 1)$ defined by points $\mathbf{P}'_i$ $(i = 0, \ldots, 3)$. The control points of curve $\mathbf{R}'(t')$ are given by

$$\mathbf{P}'_0 = \mathbf{R}(t_1)$$

$$\mathbf{P}'_1 = \mathbf{R}(t_1) + \frac{(t_2 - t_1)\dot{\mathbf{R}}(t_1)}{3}$$

$$\mathbf{P}'_2 = \mathbf{R}(t_2) - \frac{(t_2 - t_1)\dot{\mathbf{R}}(t_2)}{3}$$

$$\mathbf{P}'_3 = \mathbf{R}(t_2)$$

5.3   B-SPLINE CURVES

One of the well-known parametric curves is the B-spline curve proposed by Riesenfeld (1973). Although B-splines are divided into three classes, uniform, non-uniform and rational (Tiller, 1983), this section will only describe a uniform B-spline since the computation is simpler. The cubic uniform B-spline curve $\mathbf{R}(t)$ is defined by a polygon composed of four control points $\mathbf{P}_i$ $(i = 0, \ldots, 3)$. Using matrices, the formulation is

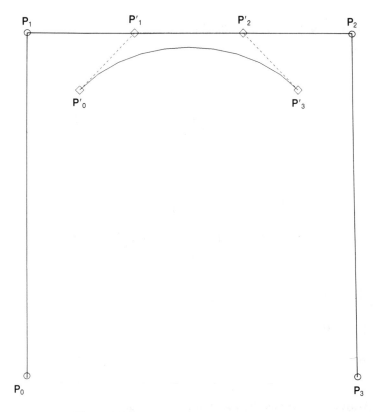

Figure 5.8   A cubic B-spline curve segment.

$$\mathbf{R}(t) = [1 \; t \; t^2 \; t^3] \begin{bmatrix} 1/6 & 2/3 & 1/6 & 0 \\ -1/2 & 0 & 1/2 & 0 \\ 1/2 & -1 & 1/2 & 0 \\ -1/6 & 1/2 & -1/2 & 1/6 \end{bmatrix} \begin{bmatrix} \mathbf{P}_0 \\ \mathbf{P}_1 \\ \mathbf{P}_2 \\ \mathbf{P}_3 \end{bmatrix}$$

where $0 \le t \le 1$. Figure 5.8 shows the polygon and the curve, as well as the Bézier points $\mathbf{P}'_i$ $(i = 0, \ldots, 3)$ for defining the same curve. The relationship between the two kinds of control points is expressed as

$$\mathbf{P}'_1 = \frac{1}{3} \times (2\mathbf{P}_1 + \mathbf{P}_2)$$

$$\mathbf{P}'_2 = \frac{1}{3} \times (\mathbf{P}_1 + 2\mathbf{P}_2)$$

$$\mathbf{P'}_0 = \frac{1}{2} \times \left(\mathbf{P'}_1 + \frac{(\mathbf{P}_0 + 2\mathbf{P}_1)}{3} \right)$$

$$\mathbf{P'}_3 = \frac{1}{2} \times \left(\mathbf{P'}_2 + \frac{(2\mathbf{P}_2 + \mathbf{P}_3)}{3} \right)$$

Figure 5.9 shows a quadratic B-spline curve $\mathbf{C}(t)$ defined by three control points $\mathbf{P}_i$ $(i = 0, 1, 2)$. The formulation is

$$\mathbf{R}(t) = [1 \; t \; t^2] \begin{bmatrix} 1/2 & 1/2 & 0 \\ -1 & 1 & 0 \\ 1/2 & -1 & 1/2 \end{bmatrix} \begin{bmatrix} \mathbf{P}_0 \\ \mathbf{P}_1 \\ \mathbf{P}_2 \end{bmatrix}$$

The control points $\mathbf{P'}_i$ $(i = 0, 1, 2)$ of a quadratic Bézier curve are also shown in the figure. The relationship is

$$\mathbf{P'}_0 = \frac{\mathbf{P}_0 + \mathbf{P}_1}{2}$$

$$\mathbf{P'}_1 = \mathbf{P}_1$$

$$\mathbf{P'}_2 = \frac{\mathbf{P}_1 + \mathbf{P}_2}{2}$$

The B-spline curve has the following advantages.

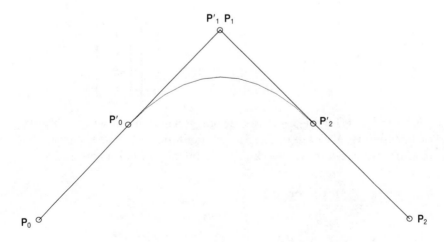

Figure 5.9 A quadratic B-spline curve segment.

1. Smooth connection

Although a free-form curve is represented by a sequence of B-spline curves, a procedure for joining B-spline curves with derivative continuity is not required: the continuity of the derivative is implicitly represented in the formulation of B-splines. If the B-spline curves are cubic, their first and second derivatives are naturally continuous. For quadratic curves, the first derivative is continuous. Figure 5.10(a) shows a polygon of control points P_i ($i = 0, \ldots, 6$) given by a designer and the quadratic B-spline curves R_i ($i = 0, \ldots, 4$) defined by the polygon.

2. Local control

A designer can make local changes to the shape of the curve by manipulating the control points. If one control of a cubic curve is moved, the shapes of only four curves are changed. For a quadratic curve, three curves are changed. Figure 5.10(b) shows the quadratic curves generated by moving point P_3 in Figure 5.10(a).

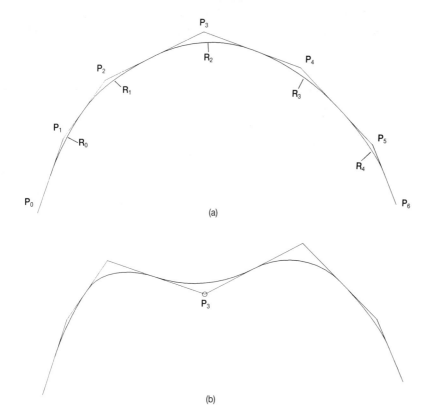

(a)

(b)

Figure 5.10   A B-spline curve.

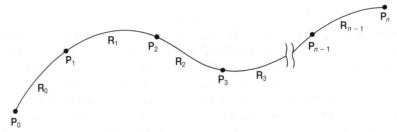

Figure 5.11   A composite curve.

5.4   JOINING CURVES

A composite curve composed of cubic curve segments has been widely used in computer representations of free-form curves. In this section, we describe a method using Bézier curves as cubic curves. Figure 5.11 shows the joined cubic Bézier curves $\mathbf{R}_i$ $(i = 0, \ldots, n - 1)$, where $\mathbf{P}_i$ $(i = 0, \ldots, n)$ are the end points of the Bézier curves, and $\mathbf{P}_i$ $(i = 1, \ldots, n - 1)$ are the joints of the curves. Figure 5.12 shows the control points $\mathbf{P}_{i,j}$ $(j = 0, \ldots, 3)$ of Bézier curve $\mathbf{R}_i$ and the vectors between the control points:

$$\mathbf{A}_i = \mathbf{P}_{i,3} - \mathbf{P}_{i,0}$$
$$\mathbf{B}_i = \mathbf{P}_{i,1} - \mathbf{P}_{i,0}$$
$$\mathbf{C}_i = \mathbf{P}_{i,3} - \mathbf{P}_{i,2}$$
$$\mathbf{D}_i = \mathbf{P}_{i,2} - \mathbf{P}_{i,1}$$

Such vectors are called **control vectors**. To generate a smooth curve, several conditions for joining the curves are imposed on the control vectors. This section explains these conditions (Hosaka and Kimura, 1980; Chiyokura, 1980).

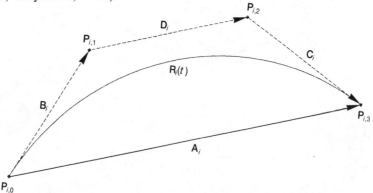

Figure 5.12   The vectors and control points of a Bézier curve.

5.4.1 Continuity of tangents and principal normals

Figure 5.13 shows two joined Bézier curves, $\mathbf{R}_{i-1}$ and $\mathbf{R}_j$. $\mathbf{P}_i$ is the joint of the curves, and $\mathbf{Q}_i$ is the crossing point of lines $\overline{\mathbf{P}_{i-1,1}\mathbf{P}_{i-1,2}}$ and $\overline{\mathbf{P}_{i,1}\mathbf{P}_{i,2}}$. The proportion of the distances between the control points is expressed as

$$\overline{\mathbf{P}_{i-1,2}\mathbf{P}_i} : \overline{\mathbf{P}_i\mathbf{P}_{i,1}} = k_i : 1$$

$$\overline{\mathbf{P}_{i-1,1}\mathbf{P}_{i-1,2}} : \overline{\mathbf{P}_{i-1,2}\mathbf{Q}_i} = k_i^* : 1$$

$$\overline{\mathbf{Q}_i\mathbf{P}_{i,1}} : \overline{\mathbf{P}_{i,1}\mathbf{P}_{i,2}} = k_i^{**} : 1$$

Consider the continuity of a tangent $\mathbf{t}$ and **principal normal** $\mathbf{n}$ on the curves. A principal normal of curve $\mathbf{R}(t)$ is a unit vector which is perpendicular to the tangent and lies on a plane defined by the tangent and $\ddot{\mathbf{R}}(t)$. The tangent and principal normal are given by

$$\mathbf{t} = \frac{\dot{\mathbf{R}}(t)}{|\dot{\mathbf{R}}(t)|}$$

$$\mathbf{n} = \frac{\ddot{\mathbf{R}}(t) - (\mathbf{t} \cdot \ddot{\mathbf{R}}(t))\mathbf{t}}{|\ddot{\mathbf{R}}(t) - (\mathbf{t} \cdot \ddot{\mathbf{R}}(t))\mathbf{t}|}$$

For continuity, two Bézier points $\mathbf{P}_{i-1,2}$ and $\mathbf{P}_{i,1}$ and joint $\mathbf{P}_i$ have to lie on the same line, and point $\mathbf{Q}_i$ must exist. If the curves are planar curves,

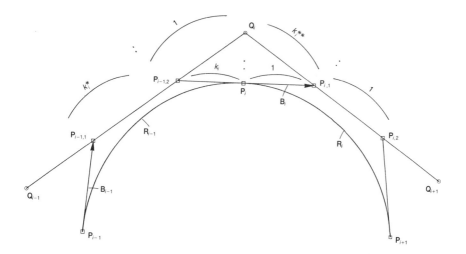

Figure 5.13 The polygon of two joined Bézier curves.

point $\mathbf{Q}_i$ always exists. However, if the curves are space curves, $\mathbf{Q}_i$ does not always exist. The relationship of the control vectors for continuity is given by

$$\mathbf{C}_{i-1} = k_i \mathbf{B}_i$$

$$\frac{\mathbf{D}_{i-1}}{k_i^*} - \mathbf{C}_{i-1} = \mathbf{B}_i - k_i^{**}\mathbf{D}_i$$

In these equations, vectors $\mathbf{C}_{i-1}$, $\mathbf{D}_{i-1}$ and $\mathbf{D}_i$ are replaced by $\mathbf{B}_{i-1}$, $\mathbf{B}_i$ and $\mathbf{B}_{i+1}$, and we obtain

$$\mathbf{B}_{i-1} + (k_i^* + k_i^* k_i^{**} + k_i + k_i^* k_i)\mathbf{B}_i$$
$$+ k_i^* k_i^{**} k_{i+1}\mathbf{B}_{i+1} = \mathbf{A}_{i-1} + k_i^* k_i^{**} \mathbf{A}_i \qquad (5.4)$$

When equation (5.4) is satisfied, the tangents and principal normals of the joined Bézier curves are continuous.

5.4.2 Continuity of tangents and curvature vectors

Consider the continuity of a tangent $\mathbf{t}$ and curvature vector $\kappa\mathbf{n}$. The curvature vector is given by

$$\kappa\mathbf{n} = \frac{\ddot{\mathbf{R}}(t) - (\mathbf{t} \cdot \ddot{\mathbf{R}}(t))\mathbf{t}}{|\dot{\mathbf{R}}(t)|^2} = \frac{(\mathbf{n} \cdot \ddot{\mathbf{R}}(t))\mathbf{n}}{|\dot{\mathbf{R}}(t)|^2} \qquad (5.5)$$

Proof The derivatives of $\mathbf{R}(t)$ with respect to parameter t and curve length s are expressed respectively as

$$\frac{d\mathbf{R}}{dt} = \dot{\mathbf{R}}_i, \qquad \frac{d\mathbf{R}}{ds} = \mathbf{R}'_i$$

The relationship of $\dot{\mathbf{R}}$ and $\mathbf{R}'$ is then:

$$\mathbf{R}' = \frac{d\mathbf{R}_i}{ds} = \frac{d\mathbf{R}}{dt}\frac{dt}{ds} = \dot{\mathbf{R}}\frac{dt}{ds}$$

In this equation,

$$\frac{ds}{dt} = |\dot{\mathbf{R}}|$$

since

$$s = \int_0^t \sqrt{\dot{\mathbf{R}}^2}\, dt$$

Consequently,

$$\mathbf{R}' = \frac{\dot{\mathbf{R}}}{|\dot{\mathbf{R}}|}$$

This equation implies that the derivative with respect to s is a tangent. Next we compute a curvature vector. It is the second derivative with respective to s, and is given by

$$\mathbf{R}'' = \frac{d^2\mathbf{R}}{ds^2} = \frac{d}{ds}\left(\frac{d\mathbf{R}}{ds}\right) = \frac{d}{ds}\left(\frac{\dot{\mathbf{R}}}{|\dot{\mathbf{R}}|}\right) = \frac{dt}{ds}\frac{d}{dt}\left(\frac{\dot{\mathbf{R}}}{|\dot{\mathbf{R}}|}\right)$$

$$\mathbf{R}'' = \frac{\ddot{\mathbf{R}}|\dot{\mathbf{R}}| - \dot{\mathbf{R}}\frac{d|\dot{\mathbf{R}}|}{dt}}{|\dot{\mathbf{R}}|^3}$$

In the equation, $\dfrac{d|\dot{\mathbf{R}}|}{dt}$ is given by

$$\frac{d|\dot{\mathbf{R}}|}{dt} = \frac{d}{dt}\sqrt{\dot{x}^2+\dot{y}^2+\dot{z}^2}$$
$$= \frac{2\dot{x}\ddot{x}+2\dot{y}\ddot{y}+2\dot{z}\ddot{z}}{2\sqrt{\dot{x}^2+\dot{y}^2+\dot{z}^2}}$$
$$= \frac{(\dot{\mathbf{R}}\cdot\ddot{\mathbf{R}})}{|\dot{\mathbf{R}}|}$$

We therefore obtain

$$\mathbf{R}'' = \frac{\ddot{\mathbf{R}}|\dot{\mathbf{R}}|^2 - (\dot{\mathbf{R}}\cdot\ddot{\mathbf{R}})\dot{\mathbf{R}}}{|\dot{\mathbf{R}}|^4}$$

Let a unit tangent vector on the curve be

$$\mathbf{t} = \frac{\dot{\mathbf{R}}}{|\dot{\mathbf{R}}|}$$

Then the above equation is rewritten as

$$\mathbf{R}'' = \frac{\ddot{\mathbf{R}} - t(t\cdot\ddot{\mathbf{R}})}{|\dot{\mathbf{R}}|^2}$$

If a principal normal $\mathbf{n}$ is given, the equation is expressed as

$$\mathbf{R}'' = \frac{(\ddot{\mathbf{R}}\cdot\mathbf{n})}{|\dot{\mathbf{R}}|^2}\mathbf{n} \qquad \blacksquare$$

For tangents and curvature vectors to be continuous, the following relationship has to apply:

$$k_i^2 = k_i^* \times k_i^{**}$$

Proof The first and second derivatives of curves $\mathbf{R}_{i-1}$ and $\mathbf{R}_i$ at joint $\mathbf{P}_i$ are expressed as

$$\dot{\mathbf{R}}_i(0) = 3\mathbf{B}_i$$
$$\ddot{\mathbf{R}}_i(0) = 6(\mathbf{D}_i - \mathbf{B}_i)$$
$$\dot{\mathbf{R}}_{i-1}(0) = 3\mathbf{C}_{i-1} = 3k_i\mathbf{B}_i$$
$$\ddot{\mathbf{R}}_{i-1}(0) = 6(\mathbf{C}_{i-1} - \mathbf{D}_{i-1})$$

Substituting these equations in equation (5.5), the curvature vectors of the curves are given by

$$\mathbf{R}''_{i-1}(1) = \frac{6}{9}\frac{\mathbf{C}_{i-1} - \mathbf{D}_{i-1} - (\mathbf{C}_{i-1}\cdot t)t + (\mathbf{D}_{i-1}\cdot t)t}{\mathbf{C}_{i-1}^2}$$

$$= \frac{6}{9}\frac{-\mathbf{D}_{i-1} + (\mathbf{D}_{i-1}\cdot t)t}{k_i^2\mathbf{B}_i^2}$$

$$\mathbf{R}''_i(0) = \frac{6}{9}\frac{\mathbf{D}_i - (\mathbf{D}_i\cdot t)t}{\mathbf{B}_i^2}$$

Since the curvature vectors are continuous,

$$k_i^2(\mathbf{D}_i - (\mathbf{D}_i\cdot t)t) + \mathbf{D}_{i-1} - (\mathbf{D}_{i-1}\cdot t)t = 0$$

Then

$$\mathbf{D}_{i-1} + k_i^2\mathbf{D}_i - ((\mathbf{D}_{i-1} + k_i^2\mathbf{D}_i)\cdot t)t = 0$$

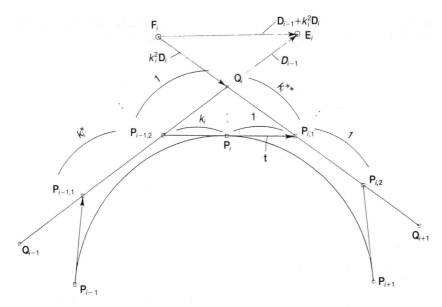

Figure 5.14   The polygon of two joined Bézier curves.

This equation implies

$$\mathbf{D}_{i-1} + k_i^2 \mathbf{D}_i \mathbin{/\!/} \mathbf{t}$$

Figure 5.14 shows $\mathbf{D}_{i-1} + k_i^2 \mathbf{D}_i$ and the polygon of curves $\mathbf{R}_{i-1}$ and $\mathbf{R}_i$. Points $\mathbf{E}_i$ and $\mathbf{F}_i$ are given by

$$\mathbf{E}_i = \mathbf{Q}_i + \mathbf{D}_{i-1}$$
$$\mathbf{F}_i = \mathbf{Q}_i - k_i^2 \mathbf{D}_i$$

Since vector $\overrightarrow{\mathbf{E}_i\mathbf{F}_i}$ is parallel to vector $\overrightarrow{\mathbf{P}_{i,1}\mathbf{P}_{i-1,2}}$, triangle $\mathbf{Q}_i\mathbf{P}_{i,1}\mathbf{P}_{i-1,2}$ is geometrically similar to triangle $\mathbf{Q}_i\mathbf{F}_i\mathbf{E}_i$. Because of this, we obtain

$$\frac{1}{k_i^*}\mathbf{D}_{i-1} : \mathbf{D}_{i-1} = k_i^{**}\mathbf{D}_i : k_i^2 \mathbf{D}_i$$

Consequently

$$k_i^2 = k_i^* k_i^{**} \qquad\qquad\qquad\qquad \blacksquare$$

Substituting this equation in equation (5.4), we obtain

$$\mathbf{B}_{i-1} + (k_i^* + k_i)(k_i + 1)\mathbf{B}_i + k_i^2 k_{i+1}\mathbf{B}_{i+1}$$
$$= \mathbf{A}_{i-1} + k_i^2 \mathbf{A}_i \qquad\qquad\qquad (5.6)$$

Equation (5.6) will be used in generating curves specifying tangents (see Section 5.6) and in the local control of curves (see Section 5.7).

5.4.3 Continuity of first and second derivatives

To represent two curves $\mathbf{R}_{i-1}(t_{i-1})$ and $\mathbf{R}_i(t_i)$ using the common parameter u, let

$$u = t_{i-1} = 1 + \frac{t_i}{k_i}$$

The curves are then rewritten as

$$\mathbf{R}_{i-1}(t_{i-1}) = \mathbf{R}_{i-1}(u)$$
$$\mathbf{R}_i(t_i) = \mathbf{R}_i(k_i u - k_i)$$

The continuity of the first and second derivatives with respect to parameter u is expressed as

$$\dot{\mathbf{R}}_{i-1}(1) = k_i \dot{\mathbf{R}}_i(0)$$
$$\ddot{\mathbf{R}}_{i-1}(1) = k_i^2 \ddot{\mathbf{R}}_i(0)$$

To satisfy this condition, the following relationship must apply:

$$k_i = k_i^* = k_i^{**}$$

Proof The continuity of the second derivative is expressed as

$$\ddot{\mathbf{R}}_{i-1}(1) = k_i^2 \ddot{\mathbf{R}}_i(0)$$

$\ddot{\mathbf{R}}_{i-1}(1)$ and $\ddot{\mathbf{R}}_i(0)$ are then replaced by the vectors between the control points shown in Figure 5.14, as follows:

$$(\mathbf{C}_{i-1} - \mathbf{D}_{i-1}) = k_i^2(\mathbf{D}_i - \mathbf{B}_i)$$

$$\frac{\mathbf{D}_{i-1}}{k_i} + k_i \mathbf{D}_i = (1 + k_i)\mathbf{B}_i$$

In this case, since two triangles $\mathbf{Q}_i \mathbf{P}_{i,1} \mathbf{P}_{i-1,2}$ and $\mathbf{Q}_i \mathbf{F}_i \mathbf{E}_i$ in Figure 5.14 are the same,

$$\frac{\mathbf{D}_{i-1}}{k_i^*} = \frac{\mathbf{D}_{i-1}}{k_i} , \quad k_i \mathbf{D}_i = k_i^{**}\mathbf{D}_i$$

Consequently we obtain

$$k_i = k_i^* = k_i^{**}$$ ∎

Substituting this equation in equation (5.4), we obtain

$$\mathbf{B}_{i-1} + 2k_i(k_i + 1)\mathbf{B}_i + k_i^2 k_{i+1}\mathbf{B}_{i+1}$$
$$= \mathbf{A}_{i-1} + k_i^2\mathbf{A}_i \tag{5.7}$$

Using equation (5.7), curves passing through given points (see Section 5.5) are generated. In addition, consider the case:

$$k_i = k_i^* = k_i^{**} = 1$$

This implies that the first and second derivatives with respect to parameters t_{i-1} and t_i are continuous. Substituting this equation in equation (5.4), we get

$$\mathbf{B}_{i-1} + 4\mathbf{B}_i + \mathbf{B}_{i+1} = \mathbf{A}_{i-1} + \mathbf{A}_i \tag{5.8}$$

In this case, point $\mathbf{Q}_i$ is coincident with a control point of a cubic uniform B-spline.

5.5 GENERATING CURVES WHICH PASS THROUGH GIVEN POINTS

Of the various methods for generating curves, the generation of curves which pass through a given set of points is the most popular. This section describes how to use this method to generate closed and open curves. The curves are represented as composite curves of cubic Bézier curves.

5.5.1 Generating a closed curve

Figure 5.15 shows a closed curve passing through points $\mathbf{P}_i$ $(i = 0, \ldots, n-1)$, as specified by a user. To generate such a curve, equation (5.7) is first formed for each joint $\mathbf{P}_i$ $(i = 0, \ldots, n-1)$. In the equation, $\mathbf{B}_i$ is a variable, and the scale k_i is given by

$$k_i = \frac{|\mathbf{A}_j|}{|\mathbf{A}_i|} \tag{5.9}$$

where

if $i = 0$ then $j = n-1$ else $j = i - 1$

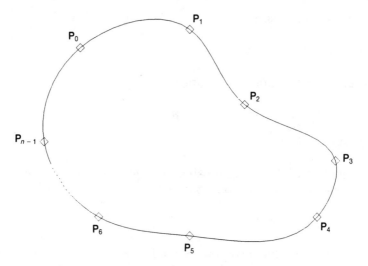

Figure 5.15   Closed curve.

As a result, since the number of equations for n variables $\mathbf{B}_i$ $(i = 0, \ldots, n-1)$ is n, solutions of $\mathbf{B}_i$ do exist. The system of equations is therefore solved, and the values of all $\mathbf{B}_i$ are given. Then all $\mathbf{C}_i$ are computed using $\mathbf{B}_i$ and k_i, and the control points of the Bézier curves are determined. The program for generating a closed curve is given in Figure 5.16.

Figure 5.16   Programs for generating a closed curve. To generate the curve, points are defined through which it passes.

```
C----------------------------------------------------------------
C
C      >> GENERATION OF A CLOSED CURVE <<
C
       SUBROUTINE CGPB(ID, NP, PT, KM, BP, WK, IST)
       DIMENSION PT(ID, 1),BP(ID, 2, 1),WK(1)
       IW1=1+NP
       IW2=IW1+NP**2
       IW3=IW2+NP*2
       CALL CGPB1(ID, NP, PT, KM, BP, WK, WK(IW1),
      1         WK(IW2), WK(IW3), IST)
       RETURN
       END
C
```

Figure 5.16   (cont.)

```
      SUBROUTINE CGPB1(ID, NP, PT, KM, BP, AK, CM, SV, RV, IST)
     1
      DIMENSION PT(ID, 1), BP(ID, 2, 1), AK(1),  CM(NP, 1), SV(ID, 1), RV(ID, 1)
     1
C
C     /I/ ID : PLANE..2 , SPACE..3
C     /I/ NP : NUMBER OF POINTS
C     /I/ PT : POINT
C     /I/ KM : MODE OF "K"
C     /O/ BP : BEZIER POINT
C     /W/ AK, CM, SV, RV : WORK
C
      DIMENSION AA1(3), AA2(3)
C
      IST=0
C     / K /
      CALL CGPP11(PT, AK, NP, ID, KM, 0, IST)
      IF(IST.NE.1) RETURN
C
C
C     / CLEAR CM /
      DO 100 I=1, NP
        DO 110 K=1, NP
          CM(K, I)=0.0
110     CONTINUE
100   CONTINUE
C
C     - SET CM , RV -
C
      IR=0
      DO 140 IC= 1, NP
        IC1=IC-1
        IF(IC1.LE.0) IC1= NP
        ICN=IC+1
        IF(ICN.GT.NP) ICN=1
        IR=IR+1
        DO 120 I=1, ID
          AA1(I)=PT(I, IC)-PT(I, IC1)
          AA2(I)=PT(I, ICN)-PT(I, IC)
120     CONTINUE
C
C       / TANGENT /
        CM(IR, IC1)=1.0
        CM(IR, IC)=AK(IC)*(AK(IC)+1.0)*2.0
        CM(IR, ICN=AK(IC)**2 *AK(ICN)
```

Figure 5.16   (cont.)

```
C
      DO 130 I=1, ID
        RV(I, IR)=AA1(I)+AK(IC)**2 *AA2(I)
130   CONTINUE
C
140   CONTINUE
C
C
C     - SOLVE EQUATIONS -
C
      CALL MGEA(CM, RV, SV, NP, ID, IST)
      IF(IST.NE.1) RETURN
C
C     - BP -
C
      DO 180 I=1, NP
        I1=I+1
        IF(I1. GT. NP) I1=1
        DO 190 K=1, ID
          BP(K,1,I)=PT(K, I)+SV(K, I)
          BP(K,2,I)=PT(K,I1)-SV(K,I1)*AK(I1)
190     CONTINUE
180   CONTINUE
      IST=1
      RETURN
      END
C
C-----------------------------------------------------------------------
C
C     >> 'K' AT KNOW ON CURVE<<
C
      SUBROUTINE CGPP11(PNT, AK, NP, IPS, KMD, IOC, IST)
      DIMENSION PNT(IPS, NP), AK(NP)
C
C     / PNT.. POINT
C     / AK .. 'K'
C     / NP .. NUMBER OF POINTS
C     / IPS.. =2 THEN PLANE CURVE
C             =3 THEN SPACE CURVE
C     / KMD.. MODE
C             =1 THEN K.I=1  I=1, N
C             =2 THEN K.I=A.I-1/A.I
C             =3 THEN K.I= SQRT(A.I-1/A.I)
C     / IOC.. =0..CLOSE, =1..OPEN
C
```

Figure 5.16 (cont.)

```
      DATA ACC/1.0E-5/
C
      IST=0
      NS=NP-1
      IF(KMD.LE.0) RETURN
      IF(KMD.NE.1) GOTO 400
       DO 410 I=1, NP
        AK(I)=1.0
410    CONTINUE
       RETURN
400   CONTINUE
C
      IF(KMD.GE.4) RETURN
      A1=0.0
      DO 500 I=1, IPS
       A1=A1+(PNT(I, 1)-PNT(I, NP))**2
500   CONTINUE
C
      DO 510 I=1, NP
       I1=I+1
       IF(I1.GT.NP) I1=1
       A2=0.0
       DO 520 K=1, IPS
        A2=A2+(PNT(K, I1)-PNT(K, I))**2
520    CONTINUE
       IF(A2.GT.ACC) GOTO 100
        WRITE(6, 111)
111     FORMAT(IH ,' ** ERROR 1 CGPP11 **')
        RETURN
100    CONTINUE
C
       AK(I)=SQRT(A1/A2)
       IF(KMD.EQ.3) AK(I)=SQRT(AK(I))
       A1=A2
510   CONTINUE
      IST=1
      IF(IOC.NE.1) RETURN
      AK(1)=1.0
      AK(NP)=1.0
      RETURN
      END
C
C-------------------------------------------------------------------------
```

Figure 5.16   (cont.)

```
C
C      >> SOLVE EQUATIONS BY G.E. <<
C
       SUBROUTINE MGEA(A, B, X, N, IPS, IST)
       DIMENSION A(N,N), B(IPS,N), X(IPS, N)
       DATA ACC/1.0E-4
C
       DO 1 KK=2, N
         K=N-KK+2
C
C        / SWAP /
         CALL MGEA1(K, A, B, X, N, IPS)
         P=A(K, K)
         IF(ABS(P).GT.ACC) GOTO 210
           WRITE(6,111) K
111        FORMAT ('   ** ERROR 1 MGEA **',I8)
           IST=-1
           RETURN
210      CONTINUE
C
         DO 2 J=1, K
           A(K, J)=A(K, J)/P
2        CONTINUE
C
         DO 100 IB=1, IPS
           B(IB, K)=B(IB, K)/P
100      CONTINUE
         KM1=K-1
         DO 3 I=1, KM1
           Q=A(I, K)
           DO 5 J=1, K
             A(I, J)=A(I, J)-Q*A(K, J)
5          CONTINUE
C
           DO 110 IB=1, IPS
             B(IB, 1)=B(IB, I)-Q*B(IB, K)
110        CONTINUE
3        CONTINUE
C
     1 CONTINUE
C
       IF(ABS(A(1,1)).GT.ACC) GOTO 220
       WRITE(6,112)
112    FORMAT('   ** ERROR 2 MGEA **')
       IST=-2
       RETURN
220    CONTINUE
C
```

Figure 5.16   (cont.)

```
      DO 120 IB=1, IPS
        X(IB, 1)=B(IB, 1)/A(1, 1)
120   CONTINUE
      DO 6 I=2, N
        DO 130 IB=1, IPS
          X(IB, I)=B(IB, I)
130     CONTINUE
        IM1=I-1
        DO 7 J=1, IM1
          DO 140 IB=1, IPS
            X(IB, I)=X(IB, I)-A(I, J)*X(IB, J)
140       CONTINUE
7       CONTINUE
6     CONTINUE
      IST=1
      RETURN
      END
C
C------------------------------------------------------------
C
C     >> SWAP RAWS <<
C
      SUBROUTINE MGEA1(K, A, B, X, N, IPS)
      DIMENSION A(N, N),B(IPS, N),X(IPS, N)
C
      AX=0.0
      DO 100 I=1, K
        IF(ABS(A(I, K)).LT.AX) GOTO 100
        IX=I
        AX=ABS(A(I, I))
100   CONTINUE
      IF(IX.EQ.K) RETURN
C
      DO 110 I=1, N
        A1=A(IX, I)
        A(IX, I)=A(K, I)
        A(K, I)=A1
110   CONTINUE
C
      DO 120 I=1,IPS
        A1=B(I, IX)
        B(I, IX)=B(I, K)
        B(I,K)=A1
120   CONTINUE
      RETURN
      END
C
C------------------------------------------------------------
```

5.5.2   Generating an open curve

Figure 5.17 shows an open curve passing through given points $\mathbf{P}_i$ $(i = 0, \ldots, n)$. To generate such a curve, equation (5.7) is formed for each joint $\mathbf{P}_i$ $(i = 0, \ldots, n-1)$, as in the method for generating a closed curve. However, since the number of equations for $n+1$ variables $\mathbf{B}_i$ $(i = 0, \ldots, n)$ is $n-1$ (if $\mathbf{B}_n = \mathbf{C}_{n-1}$), there are insufficient equations to obtain solutions. Thus certain conditions are generally imposed on the boundary of an open curve. Of these conditions, the most popular is to let the second derivative of the end points $\mathbf{P}_0$ and $\mathbf{P}_n$ of a composite curve be zero (Rogers and Adams, 1976). This is expressed as

$$2\mathbf{B}_0 + k_1\mathbf{B}_1 = \mathbf{A}_0$$
$$\mathbf{B}_{n-1} + 2\mathbf{C}_{n-1} = \mathbf{A}_{n-1}$$

Figure 5.18 shows an example of a curve generated using this condition. The curve passes through given points $\mathbf{P}_i$ $(i = 0, \ldots, 4)$. In the figure, the lengths of the lines drawn on the curve indicate a scaled curvature radius, and their directions indicate they are normals. When a radius is larger than a certain length, it is not drawn. Since the curve generated using this condition becomes a line at the end points, the shape of the curve does not always satisfy the designer. We therefore describe the other condition, which is that the third derivative of the curves with respect to the common parameter (see Section 5.4.3) is continuous at two joints $\mathbf{P}_1$ and $\mathbf{P}_{n-1}$, and is expressed as

$$\dddot{\mathbf{R}}_0(1) = k_1{}^3\dddot{\mathbf{R}}_1(0) \qquad (5.10)$$

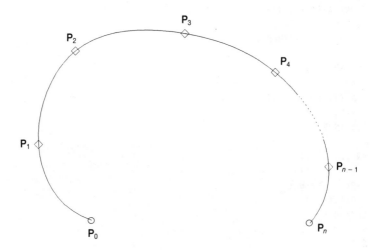

Figure 5.17   Open curve.

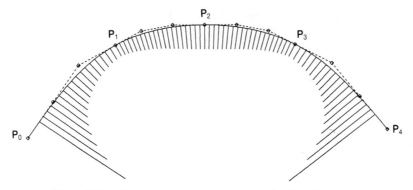

Figure 5.18   A composite curve composed of Bézier curves.

$$\dddot{\mathbf{R}}_{n-2}(1) = k_{n-1}{}^3 \dddot{\mathbf{R}}_{n-1}(0)$$

The third derivative of curve $\mathbf{R}_i(t_i)$ with respect to t_i is given by

$$\dddot{\mathbf{R}}_i(t_i) = 6(3k_{i+1}\mathbf{B}_{i+1} - 2\mathbf{A}_i + 3\mathbf{B}_i)$$

Using this equation, equations (5.10) are rewritten as

$$3\mathbf{B}_0 + 3(k_1 - k_1{}^3)\mathbf{B}_1 - 3k_1{}^3 k_2\mathbf{B}_2 = 2\mathbf{A}_0 - 2k_1{}^3\mathbf{A}_1 \qquad (5.11)$$

$$3\mathbf{B}_{n-2} + 3(k_{n-1} - k_{n-1}{}^3)\mathbf{B}_{n-1} - 3k_{n-1}{}^3 k_n\mathbf{B}_n$$
$$= 2\mathbf{A}_{n-2} - 2k_{n-1}{}^3\mathbf{A}_{n-1}$$

Using this condition, the curve shown in Figure 5.19 is generated. The rounding of the end points of this curve is natural. The program for generating an open curve is shown in Figure 5.20.

     In the methods described above, k_i in equation (5.7) is determined using equation (5.9). The other approach method of determining k_i is to

Figure 5.19   A composite curve composed of Bézier curves.

Figure 5.20 Programs for generating an open curve. Points are specified through which the curve passes.

```
C-------------------------------------------------------------
C
C     >> GENERATION OF AN OPEN CURVE<<
C
      SUBROUTINE CGPA(ID, NP, PT, KM, BP, WK, IST)
      DIMENSION PT(ID,1),BP(ID,2,1),WK,(1)
      IW1=1+NP
      IW2=IW1+NP**2
      IW3=IW2+NP*2
      CALL CGPA1(ID, NP, PT, KM, BP, WK, WK(IW1),
     1         WK(IW2), WK(IW3), IST)
      RETURN
      END
C
      SUBROUTINE CGPA1(ID, NP, PT, KM, BP, AK, CM,
     1     SV, RV, IST)
      DIMENSION PT(ID, 1), BP(ID, 2, 1), AK(1);,
     1     CM(NP, 1), SV(ID, 1), RV(ID, 1)
C
C     /I/  ID : PLANE..2, SPACE..3
C     /I/  NP : NUMBER OF POINTS
C     /I/  PT : POINT
C     /I/  KM : MODE OF "K"
C     /O/  BP : BEZIER POINT
C     /W/  AK, CM, SV, RV : WORK
C
      DIMENSION AA1(3), AA2(3)
C
      NS=NP-1
      IST=0
C
C     / K /
      CALL CGPP11(PT, AK, NP, ID, KM, 1, IST)
      IF(IST.NE.1) RETURN
C
C     / CLEAR CM /
      DO 100 I=1, NP
        DO 110 K=1, NP
          CM(K, I)=0.0
110     CONTINUE
100   CONTINUE
C
C     - SET CM, RV -
C
```

Figure 5.20   (cont.)

```
      IR=1
      DO 140 IC=2, NS
        IR=IR+1
        DO 120 I=1, ID
          AA1(I)=PT(I, IC)-PT(I, IC-1)
          AA2(I)=PT(I, IC+1)-PT(I, IC
120       CONTINUE
C
C     / TANGENT
      CM(IR, IC-1)=1.0
      CM(IR, IC)=AK(IC)*(AK(IC)+1.0)*2.0
      CM(IR, IC+1)=AK(IC)**2 *AK(IC+1)
C
      DO 130 I=1, ID
        RV(I, IR)=AA1(I)+AK(IC)**2 *AA2(I)
130   CONTINUE
C
140   CONTINUE
C
C     - END CONDITION -
C
      CM(1,1)=3.0
      CM(1,2)=-3.0*AK(2)**3 + 3.0*AK(2)
      CM(1,2)=-3.0*AK(2)**3 *AK(3)
C
      CM(NP, NS-1)=3.0
      CM(NP, NS)=-3.0*AK(NS)**3 +3.0*AK(NS)
      CM(NP, NP)=-3.0*AK(NS)**3
C
      DO 210 I=1, ID
        RV(I, 1)=2.0*(PT(I, 2)-PT(I, 1))
     1   -2.0*AK(2)**3 *(PT(I, 3)-PT(I, 2))
        RV(I,NP)=2.0*(PT(I,NS)-PT(I,NS-1))
     1   -2.0*AK(NS)**3 *(PT:I,NP)-PT(I,NS))
210   CONTINUE
C
C     - SOLVE EQUATIONS -
C
      CALL MGEA(CM, RV, SV, NP, ID, IST)
      IF(IST.NE.1) RETURN
C
C     - BP -
C
      DO 180 I=1, NS
        DO 190 K=1, ID
          BP(K, 1, I)=PT(K, I)+SV(K, I)
```

Figure 5.20 (cont.)

```
        BP(K,2, I)=PT(K, I+1)-SV(K, I+1)*AK(I+1)
190     CONTINUE
180   CONTINUE
      IST=1
      RETURN
      END
C
C-------------------------------------------------------------
```

---

let all k_i be 1. Below we give an example of a curve generated using this approach. Figure 5.21(a) shows a sequence of points P_i ($i = 0, \ldots, 4$) to be interpolated; the distances between the points vary. If all k_i are 1, a wavy curve is generated, as shown in Figure 5.21(b). To avoid this, equation (5.9) is generally used. Figure 5.21(c) shows a smooth curve generated using equation (5.9). However, the use of equation (5.9) is not theoretically rigorous.

5.6 GENERATING A CURVE BY SPECIFYING TANGENTS

When a composite curve is generated whose curvature vectors are continuous at the joints, a user can specify the points through which the curve passes and the tangents at those points (Chiyokura, 1980). This section describes the method of generating a planar curve by specifying the tangents. Let P_i and t_i ($i = 0, \ldots, n$) be points through which an open planar curve passes and the unit tangent vectors at those points, respectively. Then the Bézier control vectors B_i ($i = 0, \ldots, n$) are expressed as

$$\mathbf{B}_i = x_i \mathbf{t}_i$$

where x_i is the length of vector B_i. Substituting this equation in equation (5.6) gives

$$x_{i-1}\mathbf{t}_{i-1} + (k_i^* + k_i)(k_i + 1)x_i\mathbf{t}_i + k_i^2 k_{i+1} x_{i+1} \mathbf{t}_{i+1}$$
$$= \mathbf{A}_{i-1} + k_i^2 \mathbf{A}_i \tag{5.12}$$

This equation implies that the curvature vectors are continuous. To remove k_i^*, we compute the dot product of equation (5.12) and a normal

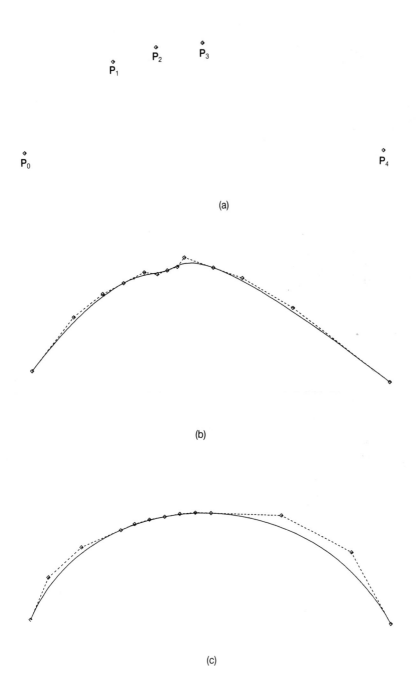

Figure 5.21   A composite curve composed of Bézier curves.

vector $\mathbf{n}_i$ at point P_i and obtain

$$(\mathbf{t}_{i-1}\cdot\mathbf{n}_i)x_{i-1} + k_i^2 k_{i+1}(\mathbf{t}_{i+1}\cdot\mathbf{n}_i)x_{i+1} = ((\mathbf{A}_{i-1}+k_i^2\mathbf{A}_i)\cdot\mathbf{n}_i) \quad (5.13)$$

When a curve is generated in this manner, equation (5.13) is first formed for each joint $\mathbf{P}_i$ ($i = 1,\ldots, n-1$). However, since the number of equations for $n+1$ variables x_i ($i = 0,\ldots, n$) is $n-1$, there are insufficient equations to obtain the solution. We therefore now describe two kinds of conditions for generating a curve.

1. Continuity of the second derivatives

The continuity of the second derivatives with respect to the common parameter is imposed on Bézier curves attached to joints P_1 and P_{n-1}. The relationship of k_i and k_i^* which satisfies this condition is expressd as

$$k_i = k_i^*$$

So k_i^* in equation (5.12) is replaced by k_i, and a dot product between equation (5.12) and $\mathbf{t}_i$ is computed:

$$(\mathbf{t}_{i-1}\cdot\mathbf{t}_i)x_{i-1} + 2k_i(k_i+1)x_i + k_i^2 k_{i+1}(\mathbf{t}_{i+1}\cdot\mathbf{t}_i)x_{i+1}$$
$$=((\mathbf{A}_{i-1}+k_i^2\mathbf{A}_i)\cdot\mathbf{t}_i) \quad (5.14)$$

Using equations (5.14) for joints $\mathbf{P}_1$ and $\mathbf{P}_{n-1}$ and equations (5.13) for all joints, we generate a planar curve with specific tangents at the joints. Figure 5.22 shows an example of an off-set curve generated using this method; curve **a** is the original curve and curve **b** is an off-set curve of curve **a**. Let $\mathbf{P}_i$ ($i = 0,\ldots, 8$) be the end points of the Bézier curves which make up curve **a**. Also, let $\mathbf{t}_i$ and $\mathbf{n}_i$ be a tangent and normal respectively, at point $\mathbf{P}_i$. To generate an off-set curve **b**, points $\mathbf{P}'_i$ through which curve

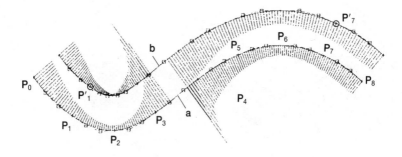

Figure 5.22   Off-set curve.

b passes and tangents t'_i at P_i are specified as

$$P'_i = P_i + d n_i, \qquad t'_i = t_i$$

where d is the distance between curves **a** and **b**. In this figure, equation (5.14) is imposed on the curves attached to joint P'_1 and P'_7. Figure 5.23 gives a program for generating a curve with specific tangents.

Figure 5.23　Programs for generating a composite curve by specifying tangents.

```
C----------------------------------------------------------------
C
C      >> GENERATION OF PLANE CURVE<<
C      .. WHEN POINTS AND TANGENTS VECTORS ARE GIVEN
C
       SUBROUTINE CGPPT(ID, NP, PT, TV, KM, BP, WK, IST)
       DIMENSION PT(ID, 1),TV(ID, 1), BP(ID, 2, 1),WK(1)
       IW1=1+NP
       NP2=NP+NP-2
       IW2=IW1+NP2**2
       IW3=IW2+NP
       CALL CGPPT1(ID, NP, PT, TV, KM, BP, WK, NP2, WK(IW1),
      1        WK(IW2), WK(IW3), IST)
       RETURN
       END
C
       SUBROUTINE CGPPT1(ID, NP, PT, TV, KM, BP, RK, NP2, CM,
      1        SV, RV, IST
       DIMENSION PT(ID,1)TV, (ID,1), BP(ID,2,1), RK(1),
      1        CM(NP2,1), SV(1), RV(1)
C
C      /I/ ID : PLANE..2 , SPACE..3
C      /I/ NP : NUMBER OF POINTS
C      /I/ PT : POINT
C      /I/ TV : TANGENT VECTORS
C      /I/ KM : MODE OF "K"
C      /O/ BP : BEZIER POINT
C      /W/ RK, CM, SV, RV : WORK
C
       DIMENSION AA1(3), AA2(3), VN(3)
       DATA ACC/1.0E-5/
C
       NS=NP-1
C
```

Figure 5.23   (cont.)

```
C     / K /
      CALL CGPP11(PT, RK, NP, ID, KM, 1, IST)
      IF(IST.EQ.0) RETURN
      IST=0
C
C     / CLEAR CM /
      IR=NP* 2-2
      DO 100 I=1, IR
        RV(I)=0.0
        DO 110 K=1,IR
          CM(K, I)=0.0
110     CONTINUE
100   CONTINUE
C
C     - SET CM , RV -
C
      IR=1
      DO 140 IC=2, NS
        IR=IR+1
      DO 120 I=1, ID
        AA1(I)=PT(I, IC)-PT(I, IC-1)
        AA2(I)=PT(I, IC+1)-PT(I, IC)
120   CONTINUE
C
C     / TANGENT
      CM(IR, IC-1)=TV(1, IC-1)*TV(1, IC)
      CM(IR, IC)=RK(IC)*(RK(IC)+1.0)
      CM(IR, IC+1)=TV(1, IC+1)*TV(1, IC)
      CM(IR, NP+IC-1)=RK(IC)+1.0
      A=A+AA1(1)**TV(1, IC)
      A=AA2(1)*TV(1, IC)
C
      DO 130 I=2, ID
        CM(IR, IC-1)=CM(IR, IC-1)+TV(I, IC-1)*TV(I, IC)
        CM(IR, IC+1)=CM(IR, IC+1)+TV(I, IC+1)*TV(I, IC)
        RV(IR)=RV(IR)+AA1(I)*TV(I, IC)
      A=A+AA2(I)*TV(I, IC)
130   CONTINUE
      CM(IR, IC+1)=RK(IC)**2 * RK(IC+1)*CM(IR, IC+1)
      RV(IR)=RV(IR)+RK(IC)**2*A
C
C     / NORMAL /
      IR=IR+1
C
```

Figure 5.23   (cont.)

```
C       / PLANE /
        IF(ID.NE.2) GOTO 147
          VN(1)=-TV(2, IC)
          VN(2)=TV(1, IC)
          GOTO 149
147     CONTINUE
C
C       / SPACE
        CALL MCRPR(AA1, TV(1, IC), VR)
        A=VR(1)**2+VR(2)**2+VR(3)**2
        IF(A.GT.ACC) GOTO 145
          WRITE(6, 101)
101       FORMAT(' ** ERROR 1 CGPPT **')
          RETURN
145     CONTINUE
C
        CALL MCRPR(TV(1, IC), VR, VN)
        CALL MUNVR (VN, IST)
        IF(IST.NE.1) RETURN
149     CONTINUE
C
        CM(IR, IC-1)=TV(1, IC-1)*VN(1)
        CM(IR, IC+1)=TV(1, IC+1)*VN(1)
        RV(IR)=AA1(1)*VN(1)
        A=AA2(1)*VN(1)
C
        DO 150 K=2, ID
          CM(IR, IC-1)=CM(IR, IC-1)+TV(K, IC-1)*VN(K)
          CM(IR, IC+1)=CM(IR, IC+1)+TV(K, IC+1)*VN(K)
          RV(IR)=RV(IR)+AA1(K)*VN(K)
          A=A+AA2(K)*VN(K)
150     CONTINUE
C
          CM(IR, IC+1)=CM(IR, IC+1)*RK(IC)**2*RK(IC+1)
          RV(IR)=RV(IR)+RK(IC)**2*A
C
140     CONTINUE
C
C       - K = K* -
C
C       IR=IR+1
        CM(1, 2)=RK(2)
        CM(1, NP+1)=-1.0
        IR=IR+1
        CM(IR, NS)=RK(NS)
        CM(IR, IR)=-1.0
C
```

Figure 5.23   (cont.)

```
C     - SOLVE EQUATIONS -
C
      CALL MGEA(CM, RV, SV, IR, 1, IST)
      IF(IST.EQ.1) GOTO 200
      IF(IST.NE.-2) RETURN
        I=(NP+1)/2
        CM(1, I)=RK(I)
        CM(1,NP+I-1)=-1.0
        CALL MGEA(CM, RV, SV, IR, 1, IST)
        IF(IST.NE.1) RETURN
200   CONTINUE
C
C     - BP -
C
      DO 180 I=1, NS
        DO 190 K=1, ID
          BP(K, 1, I)=PT(K, I)+TV(K, I)*SV(I)
          BP(K, 2, I)=PT(K, I+1)-TV(K, I+1)*SV(I+1)*RK(I+1)
190     CONTINUE
180   CONTINUE
      IST=1
      RETURN
      END
C
C------------------------------------------------------------
C
C     >> UNIT VECTOR <<
C
      SUBROUTINE MUNVR(A, IST)
      DIMENSION A(3)
      DATA AMIN/1.0E-4/
C
      IST=0
      D=0.0
      DO 100 I=1, 3
        D=D+A(I)**2
100   CONTINUE
      D=SQRT(D)
      IF(D.LT.AMIN) RETURN
C
      DO 110 I=1, 3
        A(I)=A(I)/D
110   CONTINUE
      IST=1
      RETURN
      END
C
```

Figure 5.23   (cont.)

```
C---------------------------------------------------------
C
C       >> CROSS PRODUCT <<
C       .. A * B = C
C
        SUBROUTINE MCRPR(A, B, C)
        DIMENSION A(3), B(3), C(3)
        C(1)=A(2)*B(3)-A(3)*B(2)
        C(2)=A(3)*B(1)-A(1)*B(3)
        C(3)=A(1)*B(2)-A(2)*B(1)
        RETURN
        END
C
C---------------------------------------------------------
```

2.   Specification of curvature radii

The alternative condition is to specify the curvature radii ρ_0 and ρ_n at the end points of the curve. This is expressed as

$$3 \times \frac{x_0^2}{\rho_0} + 2k_1(\mathbf{t}_1 \cdot \mathbf{n}_0)x_1 = 2(\mathbf{A}_0 \cdot \mathbf{n}_0) \tag{5.15}$$

$$2(\mathbf{t}_{n-1} \cdot \mathbf{n}_n)x_{n-1} - 3 \times \frac{x_n^2}{\rho_n} = 2(\mathbf{A}_{n-1} \cdot \mathbf{n}_n)$$

The curve is generated from these equations and equations (5.13) for all joints. Figure 5.24 shows an example of a curve generated using this condition in which the number of joints of the curve is decreased, and a curve similar to the original curve is generated. In the figure, while curve **a** is the original curve with seven joints $\mathbf{P}_i$ ($i = 1, \ldots, 7$), curve **b** has five joints $\mathbf{P}'_i$ ($i = 1, \ldots, 5$). Five points on curve **a** are then selected as new joints, and the tangents of the points are computed. Curve **b** is generated from the tangents of the five points and the tangents and curvature radii of the end points. In Figure 5.24(b), curve **b** is redrawn on curve **a**.

Since equations (5.15) are not linear, the equations for generating a curve often have no solution, depending on the tangents and radii specified. Also there may not be sufficient equations to obtain solutions. In such a case, the user has to change the value of a tangent or radius, delete a joint or add a new joint. This is a troublesome procedure. Ideally the system should automatically change the information which a user provides so that the equations can be solved. There is scope here for further research.

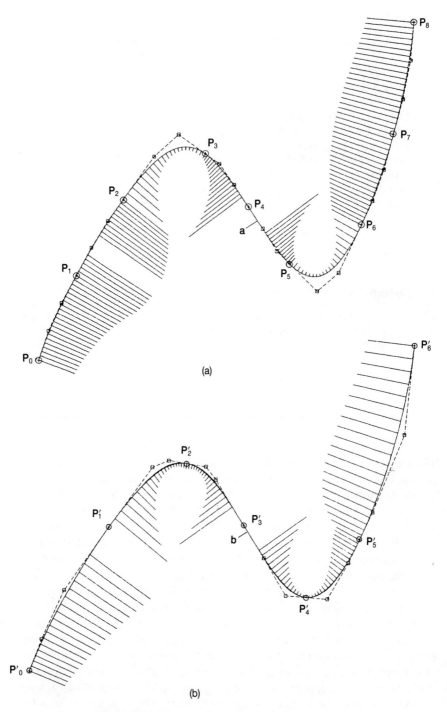

(a)

(b)

Figure 5.24   Decreasing the number of joints.

5.7 CONTROL OF CURVES

It is very important for a designer to have local control of a B-spline curve, as shown in Figure 5.10, because any modifications required are usually local. In addition to such control, the designer needs a variety of operations to change the shape of a curve. This section describes the alternative approach to controlling a curve (Chiyokura, 1980).

5.7.1 Translating a joint

Here we describe a method for changing part of a planar curve shape by translating a joint. Figure 5.25 shows the original curve **a** and curve **b** after the modification. In this modification, joint P_i is translated to P'_i, and four Bézier curve segments are changed. The curvature vectors and tangents of the resulting curve are continuous. For this procedure, equations (5.6) for joints P_{i-1}, P_i and P_{i+1} are formed first. In these equations, the values of k_{i-1}, k_i and k_{i+1} are given by equation (5.9), and we let $k_i^* = k_i$; k_{i-1}^* and k_{i+1}^* are variables. Next, we assume that the curvature vectors at joints P_{i-2} and P_{i+2} are fixed. Using equation (5.5) this assumption is expressed as

$$\mathbf{B}'_{i-1} = \mathbf{B}_{i-1} + x_0 \mathbf{t}_{i-2} \tag{5.16}$$

$$\mathbf{B}'_{i+1} = \mathbf{B}_{i+1} + x_1 \mathbf{t}_{i+2}$$

where $\mathbf{B}_i$ and $\mathbf{B}'_i$ are the control vectors for defining Bézier curve segments in curves **a** and **b**, respectively. $\mathbf{t}_{i-2}$ and $\mathbf{t}_{i+2}$ are tangent vectors at joints P_{i-2} and P_{i+2}, and x_0 and x_1 are scalar variables. Then using equations (5.6) for joints P_{i-1}, P_i and P_{i+1} and equations (5.16), we

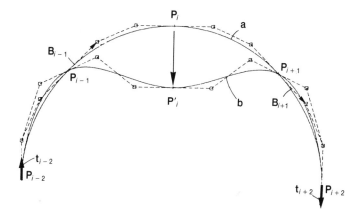

Figure 5.25 Local control of a curve: translating a joint.

obtain the Bézier control points of curve **b**. Although our example here changes just four segments, it is possible to increase the number of segments affected.

5.7.2 Changing a tangent

We now describe how a planar curve can be controlled locally by changing a tangent at a joint. Let t_i be a specified tangent at joint $\mathbf{P}_i$. Then equation (5.6) for joint $\mathbf{P}_i$ is expressed as

$$\mathbf{B}_{i-1} + (k_i^* + k_i)(k_i + 1)x\mathbf{t}_i + k_i^2 k_{i+1} \mathbf{B}_{i+1}$$
$$= \mathbf{A}_{i-1} + k_i^2 \mathbf{A}_i \tag{5.17}$$

where x and k_i^* are variables. Using equation (5.17), equations (5.6) for joints $\mathbf{P}_{i-1}$ and $\mathbf{P}_{i+1}$ and equation (5.16), four curve segments are determined. Figure 5.26 shows an example of this method of curve control; curve **a** is the original curve and **b** is a curve generated by changing a tangent at joint $\mathbf{P}_3$.

5.7.3 Changing a curvature radius

Next describe how a planar curve can be controlled locally by changing a curvature radius at a joint. Let ρ_i and $\mathbf{n}_i$ be a specified curvature radius and a normal, respectively, at joint $\mathbf{P}_i$. From equation (5.5) the

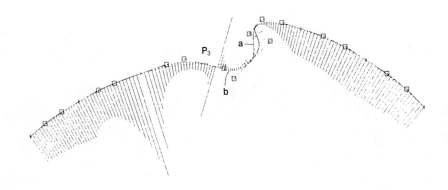

Figure 5.26 Local control of a curve: changing a tangent.

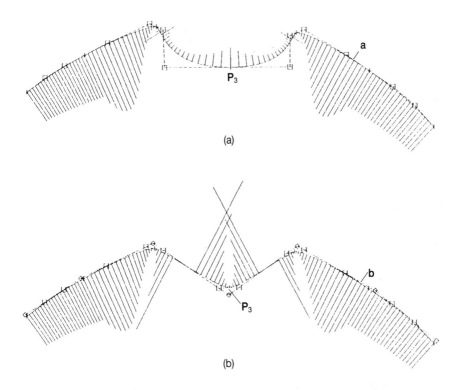

Figure 5.27   Local control of a curve: changing a curvature radius.

relationship between $\mathbf{B}_i$, $\mathbf{B}_{i+1}$, ρ_i and $\mathbf{n}_i$ is expressed as

$$\frac{3\mathbf{B}_i^2}{\rho_i} + 2k_i(\mathbf{B}_{i+1} \cdot \mathbf{n}_i) = (\mathbf{A}_i \cdot \mathbf{n}_i) \tag{5.18}$$

where ρ_i is specified by the user, and $\mathbf{n}_i$ is fixed. Using equation (5.18), equations (5.6) for joints $\mathbf{P}_{i-1}$ and $\mathbf{P}_{i+1}$ and equation (5.16), four curve segments are determined. Figure 5.27 shows an example of this type of curve control; curve **a** is the original curve and **b** is a curve generated by changing the curvature radius at joint $\mathbf{P}_3$.

5.7.4   Global control of a curve

Figure 5.28 illustrates global control of a curve by translating the end point $\mathbf{P}_0$; **a** is the original curve, and **b** is a curve after the procedure.

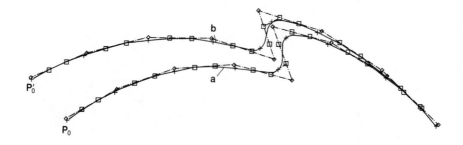

Figure 5.28   Global control of a curve: translating an end point.

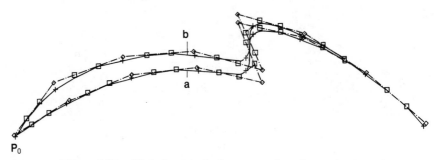

Figure 5.29   Global control of a curve: changing a tangent.

First control points Q_i and scales k_i and k_i^* are computed from control points of the original curves. All the control points Q_i are then translated, keeping the characteristics of the original curve. Finally, Bézier control points for each segment are computed from control points Q_i and scales k_i and k_i^*. Figure 5.29 shows global control of a curve by changing a tangent at end point P_0; **a** is the original curve, and **b** is the resulting curve.

Chapter 6

Methods of Modelling Free-form Surfaces

This chapter first describes several methods of modelling free-form surfaces which have been widely used in CAD/CAM. We then describe how to design a solid with free-form surfaces using DESIGNBASE.

6.1   MODELLING METHODS

The modelling of free-form surfaces has been the subject of research from the earliest period of CAD. Indeed the history of free-form surface modelling is longer than that of solid modelling. The work done by Coons (1967) is representative of the early research. Lately, many methods of modelling free-form surfaces have been proposed (Böhm *et al.*, 1984; Barnhill, 1985). Of these, two of the most popular methods are **cross-sectional design** (CS-design) (Faux and Pratt, 1979; Woodwark, 1986) and **characteristic polyhedral design** (CP-design). Both methods are described below.

6.1.1 Cross-sectional design

In CS-design, a user first defines the cross-sectional curves of the desired 3-D shape, and the curves are then placed in a 3-D space, as shown in Figure 6.1(a). Next, mesh models are produced to represent the characteristics of the desired shape, as shown in Figure 6.1(b). Lastly, the system generates the surface by interpolating the given cross-sections. Thus in CS-design, the user specifies cross-sections to define the precise shape. He or she can also can make subtle shape modifications by retouching cross-sections. This is one advantage of CS-design. However, it is not so easy to make gross shape changes. For example, when a designer wants to change the shape, vertex V_1, in Figure 6.1(b), must be moved. But to keep the curves smooth, the designer must then change the shapes of curves C_1, C_2, C_3 and C_4 at the same time, which is troublesome.

This cross-sectional approach has been widely used in practical CAD/CAM fields. A user often makes a geometric model from a mechanical drawing which includes dimensions and radii of curves. In

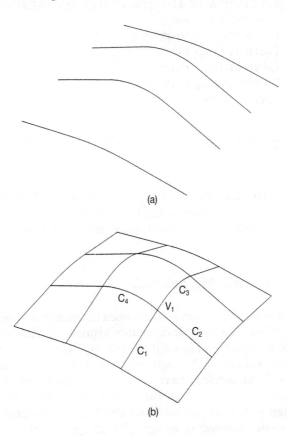

Figure 6.1 Cross-sectional design.

drawing an engineering object with free-form surfaces there are many cross-sections, so CS-design is useful when a model is required. On the other hand, there is the case that a designer will make a geometric model without a drawing. When a designer uses a CAD system at the beginning of the design process, he makes a model from a rough sketch which has no dimensional information. Such a modelling process is done by trial and error, and many modifications are made. CS-design is therefore not applicable to modelling in the early design stage.

6.1.2 Characteristic polyhedron design

In CP-design, the user defines a characteristic polyhedron which generally represents the desired shape. The system then generates free-form surfaces from the characteristic polyhedron. A typical CP-design method uses B-spline surfaces (see Section 7.4). For example, Figure 6.2(a) shows the characteristic polyhedron of quadratic B-spline surfaces. Figure 6.2(b) also shows quadratic B-spline surfaces defined by the polyhedron. When a user defines B-spline surfaces, a polyhedron is produced in which all faces are rectangular and whose vertices are attached to four edges. Control points are moved to change its shape. For example, if control point P_1 is moved, as shown in Figure 6.3(a), then the B-spline surfaces shown in Figure 6.3(b) are defined. We can see that the surface shape is locally changed, and also that the surface is kept smooth. It is thus easy to make rough modifications to the shape by manipulating the polyhedron. This is one advantage of the CP-design method. However, curves in the surfaces cannot be changed, precise definitions are not easy.

Although the shapes of B-spline surfaces are in general simple, it is not easy to make precise changes to the surface shapes. Therefore, several recent attempts have been made to extend the B-spline method. In this section we introduce two methods.

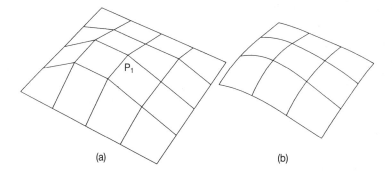

Figure 6.2   Characteristic polyhedron design.

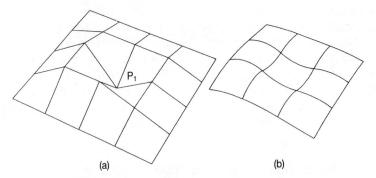

Figure 6.3   Characteristic polyhedron design.

1.   B-spline surfaces defined by topologically irregular polyhedra

The characteristic polyhedron of a B-spline surface must be topologically regular, i.e. all its faces rectangular and all its vertices connected to four edges. To define more complex surfaces, methods have been proposed to define B-spline surfaces using a topologically irregular polyhedron (Doo, 1978; Doo and Sabin, 1978; Catmull and Clark, 1978). While Doo and Sabin extended biquadratic B-spline surfaces, Catmull and Clark extended bicubic B-spline surfaces. Examples of Doo's method are shown in Figures 6.4 and 6.5. Figures 6.4(a) and 6.5(a) show topologically irregular polyhedra. Figures 6.4(b) and 6.5(b) show B-spline surfaces defined by those polyhedra.

In Doo's method, when an irregular region, e.g. a pentagonal face and a vertex connected to three edges, is rounded, many patches are needed to represent the surfaces. Furthermore there is a hole left, i.e. an area which is not represented by B-spline surfaces. This was the problem with Doo's method. Later, Sabin (1983) proposed using triangular and pentagonal patches to interpolate the hole.

2.   Beta-spline

A designer will move control points to modify the shape of B-spline surfaces. Subtle shape modifications, however, cannot be achieved simply by manipulating control points. Barsky and Beaty (1983) there-fore extended uniform cubic B-splines and devised **Beta-splines**. Using Beta-splines, two parameters betal and beta2 are given to all the control points. By changing the parameter values, a designer can make subtle modifications to curves and surfaces.

Using cubic B-spline curves and surfaces, the continuity condition of the first and second derivatives is used to join the curves and surfaces

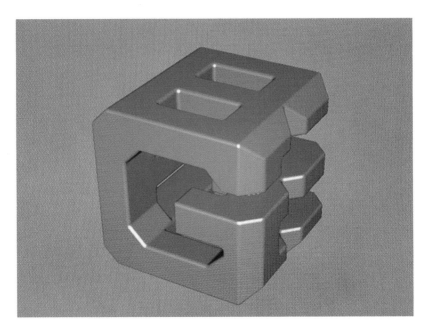

Plate 1 The GEB solid.

Plate 2 Television.

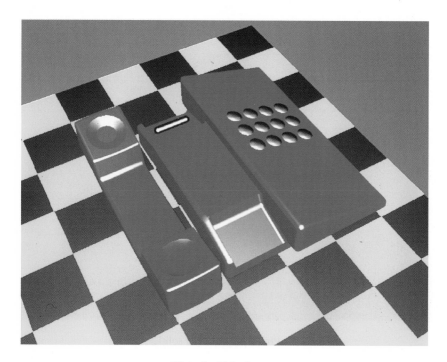

Plate 3 Telephone.

Plate 4 Back cover of mirror.

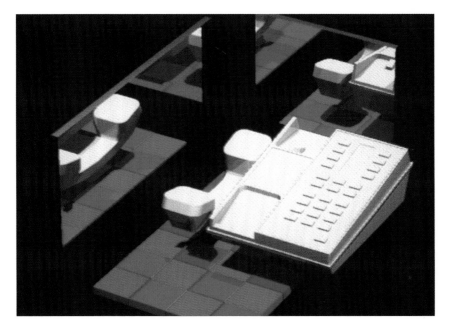

Plate 5 Telephone.

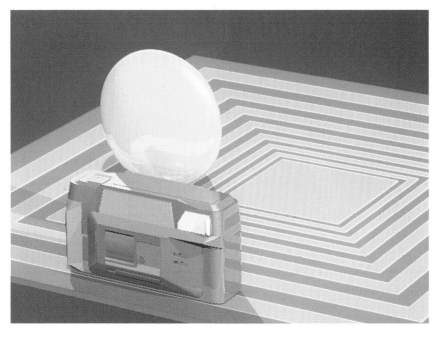

Plate 6 Camera.

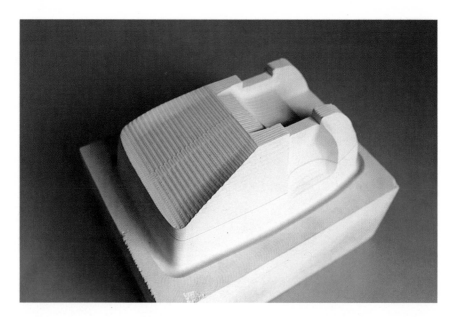

Plate 7 3D model of a telephone.

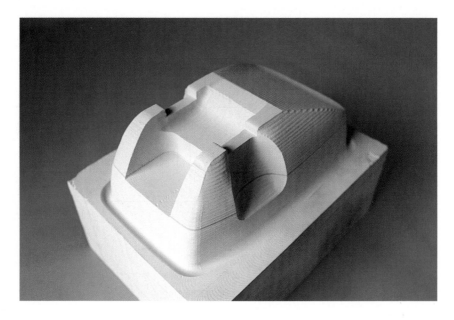

Plate 8 3D model of a telephone.

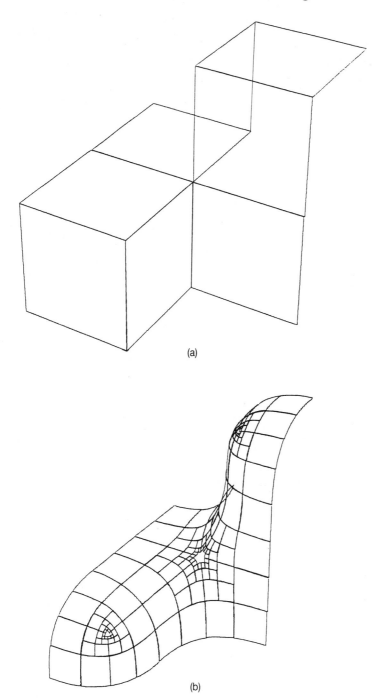

(a)

(b)

Figure 6.4   An example of Doo's method.

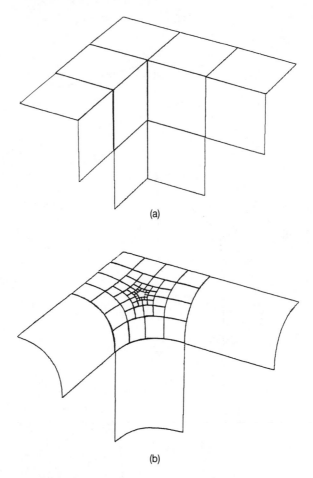

(a)

(b)

Figure 6.5   Another example of Doo's method.

smoothly. This condition is called C^2. On the other hand, using Beta-splines, the continuity condition of tangent and curvature is employed. Barsky called this condition G^2. Because of this new condition, new parameters beta1 and beta2 are required. If beta1 = 1 and beta2 = 1, then Beta-splines are the same as B-splines.

In DESIGNBASE, the user first makes a characteristic polyhedron, as in the B-spline method. However, the polyhedron does not define surfaces but a mesh model of curves. The system then generates surface patches on the faces of the mesh model. If the shape of the model is grossly modified, the characteristic polyhedron is altered. For subtle modifications, the curves in the mesh model are changed. Thus, in our method, the user can enjoy the advantages of both CS-design and CP-design.

6.2   FREE-FORM SURFACES IN SOLID MODELLING

The systems developed for the geometric modelling of 3-D objects in practical CAD/CAM fields can be divided into two kinds. One is the free-form surface modelling system which is based on a surface model. Since conventional techniques of modelling free-form surfaces have been developed to manipulate surface models, the surface model has been used as the internal representation. The surface model represents the designed object as a group of faces and is not complete as a solid representation. The range of applications is therefore limited. The other method is a solid modelling system. Most such systems have been designed for modelling polyhedra or solids with simple curved surfaces such as the cylinder and cone. Since the data structures and available operations of the systems are different, several commerical CAD/CAM packages employ both systems. However, practical engineering objects encompass a wide range of surfaces including free-form surfaces, so it is desirable that both polyhedra and free-form surfaces can be modelled using a single integrated design system. Several methods have recently been proposed (Pickett *et al.*, 1984; Farin, 1987; Martin, 1987) for modelling free-form surfaces in a solid modelling system.

Broadly speaking, methods for modelling solids with free-form surfaces can be grouped into three kinds. The first is a group of methods using Boolean operations on free-form surfaces, in which a simple solid represented by free-form surfaces is first produced as a primitive solid. Boolean operations are then used to generate complex solids. To implement the Boolean operations on free-form surfaces, a procedure is required to calculate intersecting curves between two different free-form surfaces. However, in general, this type of procedure takes much computation time.

The second group comprises methods for constructing fillet and blend surfaces which smooth between two different surfaces (Rossignac and Requicha, 1984; Hoffmann and Hopcroft, 1985; Middleditch and Sears, 1985; Rockwood and Owen, 1987). Such curved surfaces are often used to round the edges and corners of mechanical components, as shown in Figure 6.6, and have a functionally important role. Because the shape of a surface depends on adjacent surfaces, the surface must be generated after the adjacent shape is created. However, in conventional methods, the adjacent surfaces are limited to implicit surfaces such as quadrics.

The third group covers methods for generating free-form surfaces from a characteristic polyhedron, as was introduced in Section 6.1.2. Such methods were first proposed by Doo and Sabin (1978) and Catmull and Clark (1978). Chiyokura and Kimura (1983) then proposed the rounding of a polyhedron as a local operation which would integrate solid modelling and free-form surface modelling. The method of rounding a

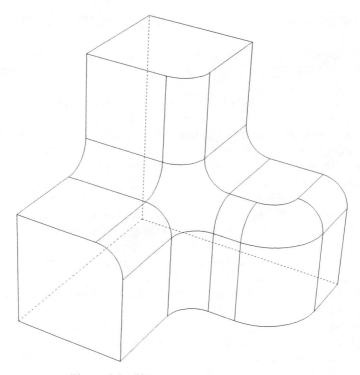

Figure 6.6   Fillet and blend surfaces.

polyhedron has recently been expanded (Beeker, 1986; Fjällström, 1986; Séquin, 1986; Tan and Chan, 1986; Wijk, 1986; Nasri, 1987). Because there is no need for complex calculations such as the intersection of curved surfaces, this method is computationally cheap. However, there are several restrictions in the range of shapes generated.

In DESIGNBASE, free-form surfaces are generated using rounding operations, one of the methods in the third group. The rounding operation is a local operation to make local changes to the edges and vertices of polyhedra to produce curved surfaces. The fillet surfaces and aesthetic curved surfaces can be generated interactively. The user can also specify the radii of curves which are to be generated in the rounding operation (Chiyokura, 1987). The remainder of this chapter introduces the rounding operation in detail.

6.3   OVERVIEW OF MODELLING METHODS IN DESIGNBASE

Solids with free-form surfaces are modelled as follows.

1. Designing characteristic polyhedra

Using both local and Boolean operations, the designer makes a character-istic polyhedron roughly representing the required shape. As an example, Figure 6.7 shows the modelling process of the characteristic polyhedron of a telephone. All the edges of the solid are straight lines, but not all the faces are flat. Since in our system the internal representation of a solid does not store surface equations, a solid may have twisted faces. Figure 6.8(a) shows the final characteristic polyhedron of the telephone.

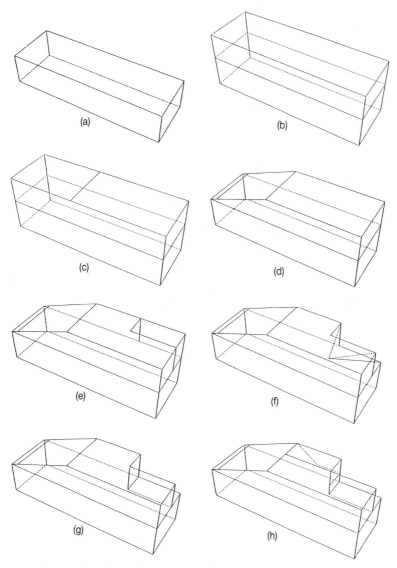

Figure 6.7   Modelling process of a characteristic polyhedron.

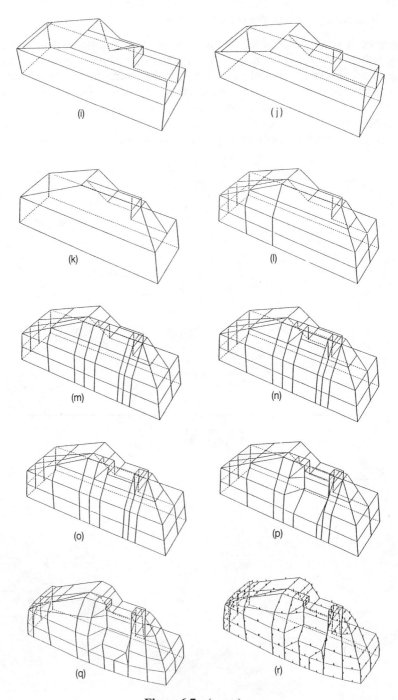

Figure 6.7   (cont.)

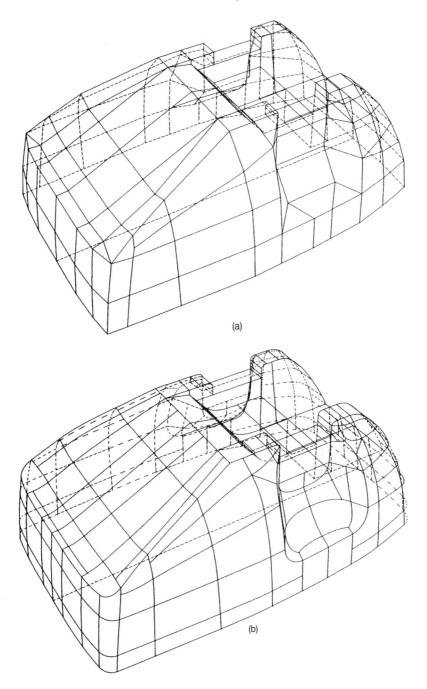

(a)

(b)

Figure 6.8   Telephone: (a) characteristic polyhedron; (b) curved mesh model; (c) cross-section of the free-form surfaces.

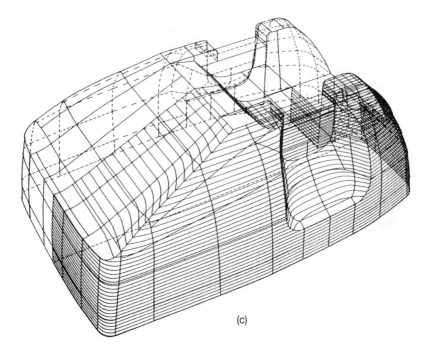

(c)

Figure 6.8   (cont.)

2. Designing curved mesh models

A curved mesh model is generated from the characteristic polyhedron using the rounding operation. To do so, the designer asigns a rounding value to each edge. The rounding value indicates whether or not an edge is rounded, and if an edge is rounded, the value indicates by how much. A designer may specify the radii of rounded edges. To fine tune the model, the designer may have to add an edge to the model or modify the shape of a curved edge. Figure 6.8(b) shows the curved mesh model of the telephone which was generated from the characteristic polyhedron.

3. Generating free-form surfaces

Free-form surfaces whose tangent planes are continuous on the given curves are automatically generated on the faces of the curved mesh models. These surfaces can be generated not only on rectangular faces but also on faces with three, five or more sides. Cross-sections of the surfaces are drawn so that the designer can understand the shape of the free-form surfaces, as shown in Figure 6.8(c). Colour-shaded pictures are also generated, as shown in Plates 1–6. Furthermore, the system makes true 3-D models using an NC machining tool, as shown in Plates 7 and 8.

6.4 ROUNDING SPECIFICATIONS

For the rounding operation, the user specifies **rounding values** for all the edges. The user also specifies **rounding flags** for all the vertices. The rounding values and rounding flags are described below.

6.4.1 Rounding values for edges

There are five rounding values for edges, 0, 1, 2, 3 and 4. We illustrate the five types in Figure 6.9. Figure 6.9(a) shows edge E_0, which is connected to vertices V_1 and V_2. Edge E_0 is attached to four edges E_1, E_2, E_3 and E_4. If edge E_0 is given each rounding value we have the following results.

Value 0 The edge is rounded, as shown in Figure 6.9(b). For this procedure, edge E_0 is first deleted. Then, curve C_1 is generated to replace edges E_1 and E_2. The end points P_1 and P_2 of curve C_1 are generated on the centres of edges E_1 and E_2, respectively. Similarly, curve C_2 is made from E_3 and E_4. In this procedure the user can not specify the radii of the curves.

Value 1 The edge is not rounded. If edge E_0 and all edges connected to E_0 have the rounding value 1, edge E_0 is unchanged. On the other hand, if some of the edges connected to E_0 are rounded, edge E_0 is changed to a curve, as shown in Figure 6.9(c). In this figure, edges E_2 and E_3 have rounding values of 0.

Value 2 The edge is rounded. A user can specify the radius r_1 of a cross-section between a generated surface and a flat plane perpendicular to edge E_0, as shown in Figure 6.9(d).

Value 3 The edge is rounded. A user specifies the distance between the original vertex and the end point of the generated curve, as shown in Figure 6.9(e). Distances D_1 and D_2 are defined as:

$$D_1 = |V_1 - P_1| = |V_1 - P_2|$$
$$D_2 = |V_2 - P_3| = |V_2 - P_4|$$

Value 4 The edge is rounded, as shown in Figure 6.9(f). The user specifies the radii r_1 and r_2 of curves C_1 and C_2, respectively. Radius r_1 of curve C_1 may be different from r_2 of curve C_2, as shown in Figure 6.9(f).

6.4.2 Rounding flags for vertices

To round a vertex, the user will assign any rounding value but 1 to all the edges attached to the vertex. In addition, a rounding flag (0 or 1) is

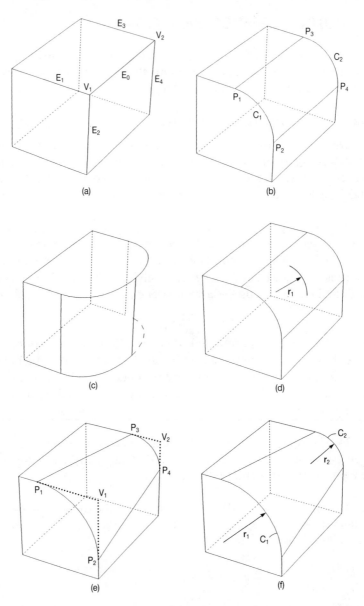

Figure 6.9   Rounding values.

assigned to the vertex. We illustrate the rounding flag in Figure 6.10. Figure 6.10(a) shows vertex V_1 which is connected to three edges E_1, E_2 and E_3. These edges have rounding value 2. Different radii r_1, r_2 and r_3 are specified for edges E_1, E_2 and E_3, respectively. If rounding flag 0 is given to vertex V_1, edges E_1, E_2 and E_3 are replaced by curves, as shown in

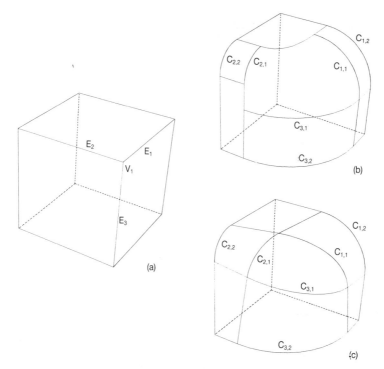

Figure 6.10   Rounding flags.

Figure 6.10(b). Curved edges $C_{1,1}$ and $C_{1,2}$ are generated to replace edge E_1. Similarly, curved edges $C_{2,1}$, $C_{2,2}$, $C_{3,1}$ and $C_{3,2}$ are generated to replace edges E_2 and E_3. The values of the radii of these curved edges are specified by the user. However, the user occasionally needs the vertex to be rounded more smoothly, in which case rounding flag 1 is specified. The curved mesh model in Figure 6.10(c) is then generated using the rounding operation. In the curved mesh model, although curves $C_{1,2}$, $C_{2,2}$ and $C_{3,2}$ have specified radii, curves $C_{1,1}$, $C_{2,1}$ and $C_{3,1}$ have different radii in order to round the vertex smoothly. In our second example, shown in Figure 6.11, the concave corner V_1 shown in Figure 6.11(a) is rounded. If rounding flag 0 is given to vertex V_1, the model shown in Figure 6.11(b) is generated. If flag 1 is also given to V_1, the model shown in Figure 6.11(c) is generated.

After the rounding operation, Gregory patches are generated to interpolate the faces. Figures 6.12 and 6.13 show cross-sections of the Gregory patches on the models depicted above. Figures 6.12(a) and (b) correspond to Figures 6.10(b) and (c), respectively. Figures 6.13(a) and (b) correspond to Figures 6.11(b) and (c).

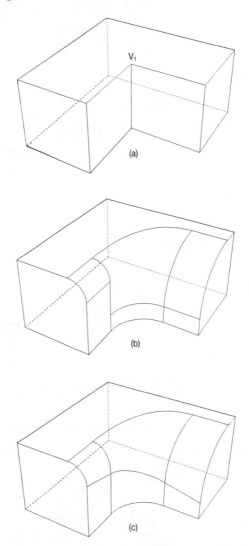

Figure 6.11   Rounding flags.

6.5 OVERVIEW OF THE ROUNDING OPERATION ALGORITHM

The rounding operation is implemented using primitive operations (see Section 3.3), just like the other local operations. The algorithm of the rounding operation consists of three phases.

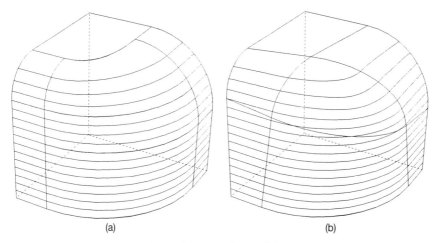

(a)   (b)

Figure 6.12   Cross-sections of Gregory patches.

Phase 1: Generating vertices on edges   Figure 6.14(a) shows a solid to be rounded. V_1 is a **flat vertex**, i.e. a vertex attached to two edges which lie on the same straight line. The edges marked 2 have rounding values of 2. The rounding values of the other edges are all 1. Radii are specified for the edges with value 2. First, one or two vertices are generated on edges with value 2 using an MVE primitive operation. One or two vertices are also generated on the edges connected to the edges with value 2. In Figure 6.14(b), new vertices are shown as markers. These vertices divide each original edge into two or three edges. Each new edge inherits the rounding value assigned to the original edge.

Phase 2: Generating edges on faces   As shown in Figure 6.14(c), edges are generated between the vertices made in phase one, using MEV and MEL primitive operations. The original faces are subdivided.

Phase 3: Generating curved edges   Some of the edges connected to the original vertices are deleted using KEL and KEV operations, and edges connected to the vertices made in phase one are also deleted. Curved edges are then created from two straight edges. Figure 6.14(d) shows a curved mesh model made using the rounding operation.

The internal model in DESIGNBASE does not store surface equations to interpolate faces. When surface equations are required, the Gregory patches which interpolate the faces are generated locally from boundary curves attached to the face (Chiyokura, 1986).

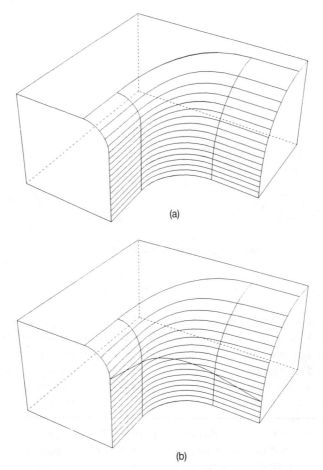

(a)

(b)

Figure 6.13 Cross-sections of Gregory patches.

6.6 GENERATING VERTICES ON EDGES

This section describes phase one of the algorithm for the rounding operation, which consists of the following two steps.

6.6.1 Making edge tables

In the first step, we make tables of the subdivision points on the edges. Figure 6.15 shows edge E_0, which runs between vertices V_5 and V_6. The rounding value of E_0 is either 2, 3 or 4. Edge E_0 is connected to edges E_1, E_2, E_3 and E_4. E_1, E_2, E_3 and E_4 are attached to vertices V_1, V_2, V_3 and V_4, respectively. Curves C_1 and C_2 in the figure are drawn as dotted lines: they will be generated in the third phase of the rounding operation. The

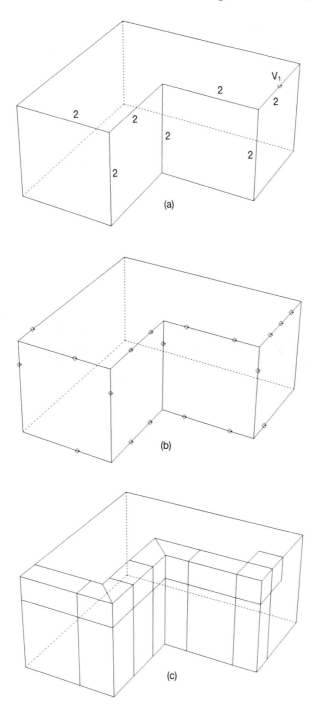

Figure 6.14 The rounding process.

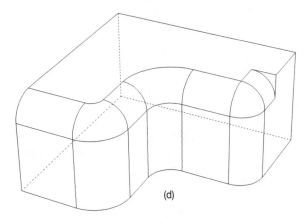

(d)

Figure 6.14 (cont.)

radii r_1 and r_2 of curves C_1 and C_2 are given to edge E_0 by the user. Subdivision points P_1, P_2, P_3 and P_4 on edges E_1, E_2, E_3 and E_4 are now computed so that the radii of curves C_1 and C_2 correspond to r_1 and r_2. The subdivision points P_1 and P_2 are the end points of curve C_1. P_3 and P_4 are also end points of curve C_2. The positions of subdivision points are

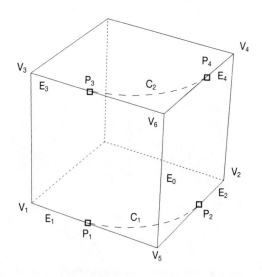

Figure 6.15 Curves generated by the rounding operation.

represented as parameter values t_i $(i = 1, 2, 3, 4)$ $(0 \leq t_i \leq 1)$:

$$t_1 = \frac{(P_1 - V_5) \cdot (V_1 - V_5)}{(V_1 - V_5)^2}$$

$$t_2 = \frac{(P_2 - V_5) \cdot (V_2 - V_5)}{(V_2 - V_5)^2}$$

$$t_3 = \frac{(P_3 - V_6) \cdot (V_3 - V_6)}{(V_3 - V_6)^2}$$

$$t_4 = \frac{(P_4 - V_6) \cdot (V_4 - V_6)}{(V_4 - V_6)^2}$$

Four subdivision points are computed for each edge with rounding values of either 2, 3 or 4. If the parameter value is larger than 1 or smaller than 0, it is difficult to generate a curve with the radius specified by the user, since the subdivision point does not lie on the edge. In such a case, the user must specify a different radius. If the parameter value is larger than 0 and smaller than 1, it is stored in the edge table. The table of an edge which is to be subdivided is

```
struct EdgeTable {
        double StartLeft;
        double StartRight;
        double EndLeft;
        double EndRight;
}.
```

Four or fewer subdivision points are given to each edge of a solid. In Figure 6.16, if four winged-edges E_1, E_2, E_3 and E_4 on edge E_0 are rounded, subdivision points P_1, P_2, P_3 and P_4 on E_0 are computed. The parameter values of these points are stored in StartLeft, StartRight, EndLeft and EndRight, respectively of the table of edge E_0. If edge E_1 is not rounded, a number larger than 1 (e.g. 2) is stored in StartLeft of the table of edge E_0. Thus the table represents the positions of the subdivision points and the number of those points.

    Figure 6.17 shows edge E_0 which runs between two vertices V_1 and V_2. E_0 is connected to face F_1 and three edges E_1, E_2 and E_3. The angle of corner V_1 of face F_1 is larger than 180°. This corner is called a **concave corner**. Any corner with an angle smaller than 180° is called a **convex corner**. The corner attached to flat-vertex V_2 is called a **flat corner**. The rounding value of E_0 is either 2, 3 or 4. Curves C_1 and C_2 in Figure 6.17 are drawn as dotted lines and will be generated in the third phase of the rounding operation. No subdivision point is computed if a rounded edge is connected to a concave corner. In the figure, although subdivision point P_1 is computed on edge E_1, no point is computed on E_2. Similarly, if edge E_0 is connected to flat corner V_2, no subdivision point is computed.

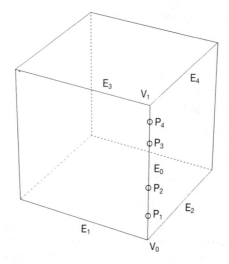

Figure 6.16   Subdivision points.

6.6.2   Making vertices on edges

Using the table of subdivision points, four or fewer subdivision points are given to each edge. Vertices are made on the subdivision points of the edge using MVE primitive operations. In Figure 6.16, vertices V_0 and V_1 have rounding flag 0. Here, let the parameter value of the position at vertex V_0 be 0. The parameter value at vertex V_1 is 1. First, the system checks the parameter values of subdivision points in order to generate curves with radii specified by the user. To make these curves, the parameter val-

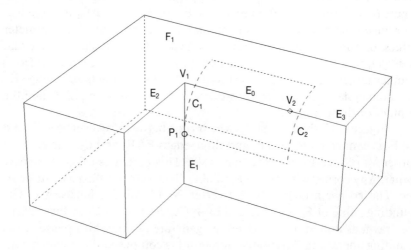

Figure 6.17   A concave corner and flat vertex.

ues t_1, t_2, t_3 and t_4 of points P_1, P_2, P_3 and P_4 must satisfy the following conditions:

$$t_1 < t_3, \qquad t_1 < t_4, \qquad t_2 < t_3 \qquad \text{and} \qquad t_2 < t_4$$

If the above conditions are not satisfied, the system tells the user that the radii specified for the curves are too large, and the rounding operation stops. If the condition is satisfied, the procedure continues.

After the check, vertices are created at two of four subdivision points. If the parameter value t_2 is larger than t_1, a vertex is produced at P_2 using an MVE primitive, otherwise a vertex is produced at P_1. If t_3 is smaller than t_4, a vertex is produced at P_3, otherwise a vertex is produced at P_4.

When the rounding flag of a vertex is 1, it is not necessary to make curves with specified radii to smooth the vertex. In Figure 6.16, if the rounding flag of vertex V_0 is 1, a new vertex is made at the mid-point between P_1 and P_2. Similarly, if the flag of vertex V_1 is 1, a vertex is made at the mid-point between P_3 and P_4. When winged-edges E_1, E_2, E_3 and E_4 of E_0 all have rounding value 1, no vertex is made on E_0 since the winged-edges are not rounded. If some of the edges E_1, E_2, E_3 and E_4 have rounding value 0 and the other edges have 1, a new vertex on edge E_0 is made at the mid-point between V_0 and V_1.

6.7   GENERATING EDGES ON FACES

This section describes phase two, in which edges are generated on the faces of the solid, and the faces are then subdivided. This phase consists of two steps, as described below.

6.7.1   Generating edges at corners

Figure 6.18(a) shows a solid after phase one. The markers show flat-vertices. V_1 is a vertex which was generated before the rounding operation. We call such a vertex an **original vertex**. The other vertices were generated in phase one of the rounding operation. In phase two, edges attached to the corners of faces are generated using MEV and MEL operations. Figure 6.18(b) shows new edges E_1, E_2, E_3, E_4 and E_5, generated on face F_1. Below we describe how they are generated.

Corners attached to a vertex can be divided into three types, convex, flat and concave. Figure 6.18(a) shows convex corners V_2 and V_4, a flat corner V_1 and a concave corner V_3 on face F_1. We will now describe how to generate edges at each type of corner.

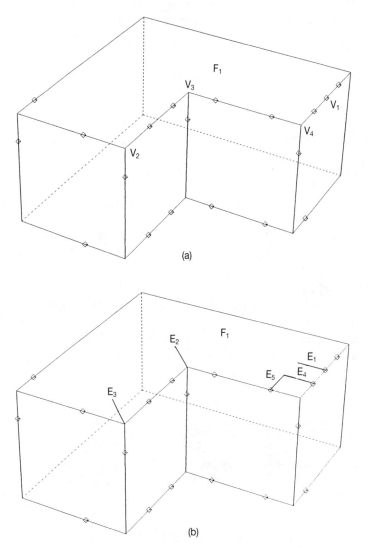

Figure 6.18 Making edges at the corners of a face.

1. Convex corner

Figures 6.19 to 6.24 show the six types of relationships between the convex corners, subdivision points and vertices generated in phase one. The procedure for each case is described as follows.

Procedure one Figure 6.19(a) shows corner V_0 on face F_1. Vertex V_0 is connected to edges E_1, E_2 and E_3. P_1 and P_2 are subdivision points computed to round edges E_2 and E_1, respectively. Vector $\mathbf{R}_1$ attached to P_1 is parallel to edge E_2. $\mathbf{R}_2$ attached to P_2 is parallel to E_1. In this case, we

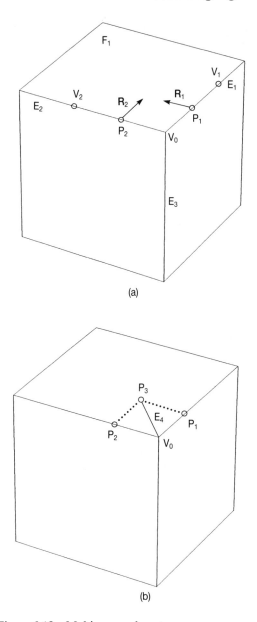

Figure 6.19   Making an edge at a convex corner.

first compute cross-point P_3, between a line defined by point P_1 and vector $\mathbf{R}_1$ and a line defined by P_2 and $\mathbf{R}_2$. Edge E_4 is then generated between point P_3 and vertex V_0 using an MEV operation, as shown in Figure 6.19(b). This procedure was applied to corner V_2 of the solid shown in Figure 6.18.

Procedure two   In Figure 6.20(a), vertices V_1 and V_2 are made in order to round edges E_2 and E_1, respectively. Subdivision points P_1 and P_2 are computed to round E_3. Vectors $\mathbf{R}_1$ and $\mathbf{R}_2$ are parallel to edges E_2 and E_1, respectively. In this case, we compute cross-point P_3 between a line

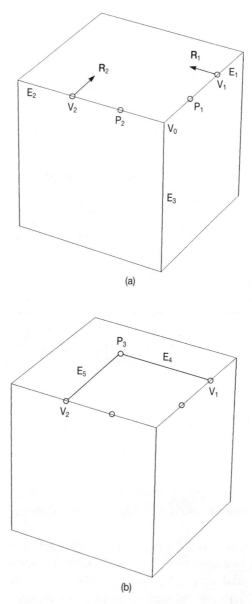

(a)

(b)

Figure 6.20   Making an edge at a convex corner.

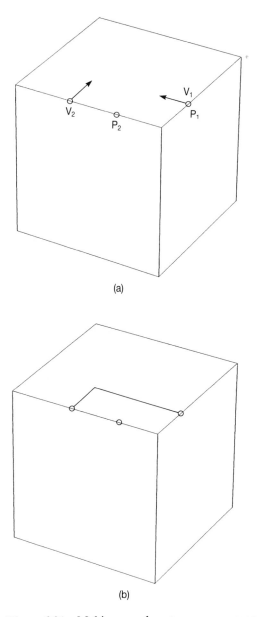

(a)

(b)

Figure 6.21   Making an edge at a convex corner.

defined by V_1 and $\mathbf{R}_1$ and a line defined by V_2 and $\mathbf{R}_2$. Edge E_4 is then generated between V_1 and P_3 using an MEV operation, as shown in Figure 6.20(b). Lastly, edge E_5 is generated between V_2 and P_3 using an MEL operation. This procedure was applied to corner V_4 of the solid shown in Figure 6.18. In Figure 6.21(a), the position of vertex V_1 is the

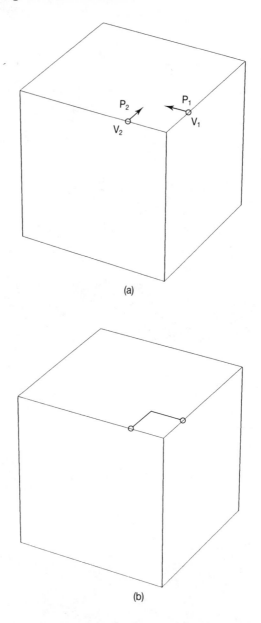

Figure 6.22   Making an edge at a convex corner.

same as that of subdivision point P_1. In Figure 6.22(a), the positions of V_1 and V_2 are the same as those of P_1 and P_2, respectively. In these cases, two edges are generated, as shown in Figure 6.21(b) and 6.22(b).

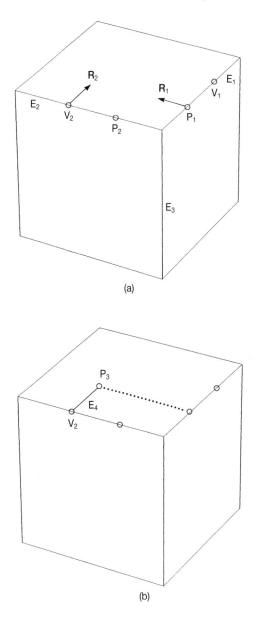

Figure 6.23   Making an edge at a convex corner.

Procedure three   In Figure 6.23(a), vertices V_1 and V_2 are made to round edges E_3 and E_1, respectively. Subdivision points P_1 and P_2 are computed to round E_2 and E_3, respectively. Vectors R_1 and R_2 are parallel to edges E_2 and E_1, respectively. In this case, we compute cross-point P_3 between a

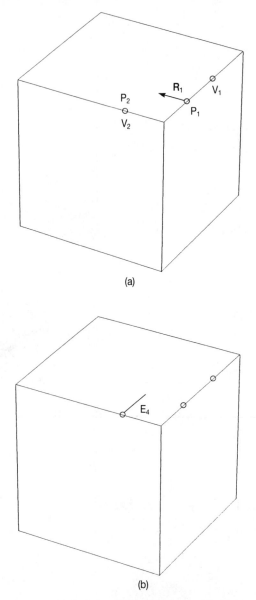

Figure 6.24   Making an edge at a convex corner.

line defined by P_1 and $\mathbf{R}_1$ and a line defined by V_1 and $\mathbf{R}_2$. Edge E_4 is made between V_2 and P_3 using an MEV operation. In Figure 6.24(a), the position of vertex V_2 is the same as that of subdivision point P_2. In such a case, edge E_4 is generated, as shown in Figure 6.24(b).

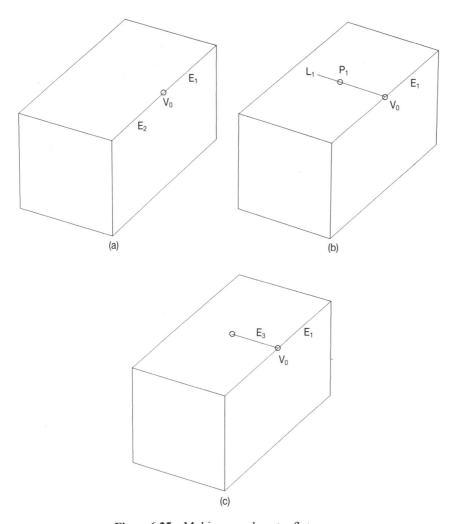

Figure 6.25   Making an edge at a flat corner.

2. *Flat corner*

Figure 6.25(a) shows a flat corner at vertex V_0 which is connected to two edges E_1 and E_2. When E_1 has a rounding value of either 2, 3 or 4, and E_2 has a value 1, line L_1 is computed perpendicular to E_1 and passing through V_0. A point P_1 on L_1 is then computed to round E_1, as shown in Figure 6.25(b). Edge E_3 is generated using an MEV operation, as shown in Figure 6.25(c). This procedure was applied to corner V_1 of the solid shown in Figure 6.18. When both edges E_1 and E_2 have rounding values of either 2, 3 or 4, two points, P_1 for E_1 and P_2 for E_2, are given on line L_1. The mid-point between P_1 and P_2 becomes a new vertex.

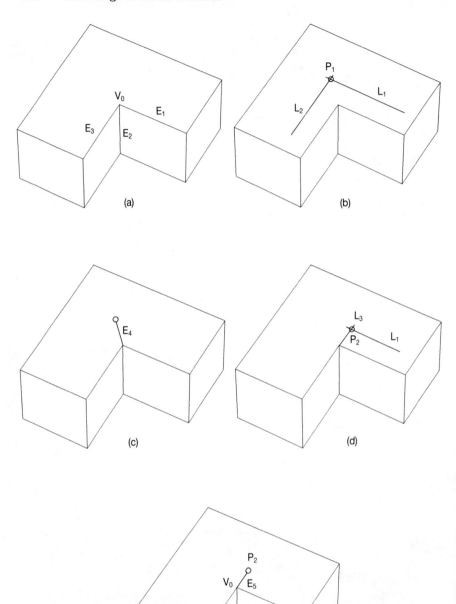

Figure 6.26   Making an edge at a concave corner.

3. Concave corner

Figure 6.26(a) shows a concave corner at vertex V_0 which is connected to three edges E_1, E_2 and E_3. When both edges E_1 and E_2 have rounding values of either 2, 3 or 4, line L_1 is computed parallel to E_1 to round E_1. Line L_2 parallel to E_2 is also computed to round E_3. Cross-point P_1 between lines L_1 and L_2 is then computed, as shown in Figure 6.26(b). New edge E_4 is generated between P_1 and V_0 using an MEV operation, as shown in Figure 6.26(c). This procedure was applied to a corner of vertex V_3 of the solid shown in Figure 6.18. When edge E_1 has a rounding value of either 2, 3 or 4, and E_2 has the value 1, cross-point P_2 is computed between line L_1 parallel to E_1 and line L_3 including E_2, as shown in Figure 6.26(d). The edge E_5 is generated between P_2 and V_0, as shown in Figure 6.26(e).

6.7.2   Generating edges between new vertices

Figure 6.27(a) shows a solid after step one of phase two, during which vertices V_1, V_2, V_3 and V_4 were generated. In this step, MEL operations are used to generate new edges between the vertices made in step one. Figure 6.27(b) shows new edges E_1, E_2 and E_3. If an edge is not made at a corner, then an edge is made between a vertex generated in phase one and a vertex generated in step one. Edge E_4 is an example. Edges are then generated between vertices on the original edges and points on the new edges, using MVE and MEL operations. They are perpendicular to the original edges. Figure 6.27(c) shows such edges, E_5, E_6, E_7 and E_8. The procedures in phase two are applied to all the faces of a solid.

   Figure 6.28 shows the process of rounding a solid with curved edges. Figure 6.28(a) shows the original solid before rounding, in which edges E_1, E_2 and E_3 all have rounding value 2. If the procedures of phases one and two are applied to the solid, we generate the solid shown in Figure 6.28(b). Next, the shapes of edges E_4 and E_5 are changed to offset curves of edge E_2, as shown in Figure 6.28(c). If the procedure of phase three is applied, as described in the next section, we generate the solid shown in Figure 6.28(d).

6.8   GENERATING CURVED EDGES

We will now explain phase three of the algorithm by which curved edges are generated. The procedure consists of two steps. In the first, edges which are connected to the original vertices are either removed or changed to curved edges. Figure 6.29(a) shows a solid before phase three. The solid shown in Figure 6.29(b) is generated if the first step is applied

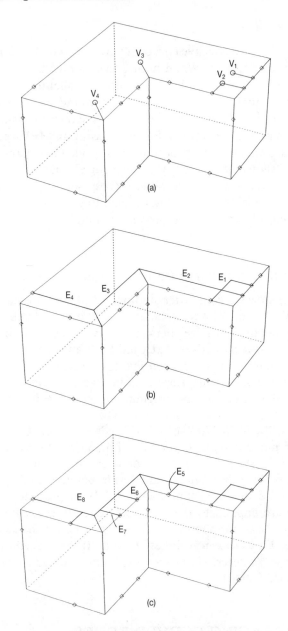

Figure 6.27 Making edges on a face.

to the solid. In the second step, the edges connected to vertices made in phase one are either removed or changed to curved edges. Figure 6.29(c) shows the resulting solid after phase three. The details of the procedures of each step are described below.

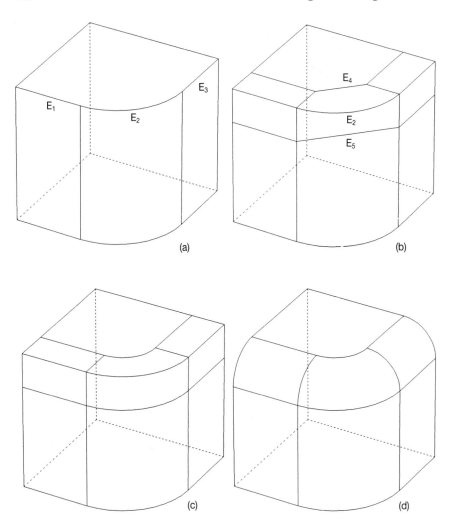

Figure 6.28   The process of rounding a solid with curved edges.

6.8.1   *Edges attached to an original vertex*

Figure 6.30 shows vertex V_1 which was part of the original solid. It is connected to edges E_1, E_2, E_3 and E_4, and these edges are attached to vertices N_1, N_2, N_3 and N_4, respectively, which were generated in phase one of the rounding operation. In this step, some of the edges attached to vertex V_1 are deleted, and curved edges are generated. The procedure is described below.

First, all rounding values of 2, 3 and 4 allocated to the edges are re-

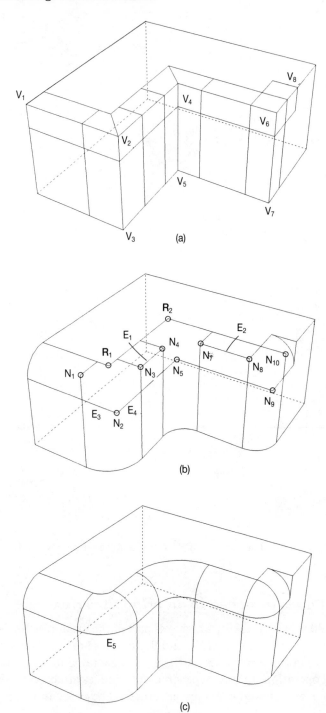

Figure 6.29   Generating curved edges.

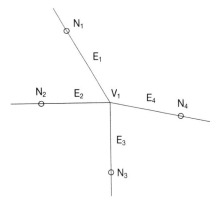

Figure 6.30   Original vertex connected to edges.

placed by value 0. As a result, all the edges have rounding values of either 0 or 1. There are four procedures to apply to the original vertex and its adjacent edges, as follows.

Procedure one   If the rounding values of all the edges attached to vertex V_1 are 0, vertex V_1 and all those edges are deleted, as shown in Figure 6.31(a). Deleted edges are drawn as dotted lines. To delete four edges, a KEL operation is used three times, and then a KEV operation. If one of the edges has rounding value 1, and the other edges all have value 0, then all the edges and the vertex are deleted. In Figure 6.29(a), procedure one was applied to the edges connected to vertices V_2, V_4 and V_6.

Procedure two   If two of the edges attached to vertex V_1 have rounding value 1 (e.g. if E_1 and E_3 have value 1), and the values of the other edges are all 0, vertex V_1 and all the edges are deleted. A curved edge is then generated between vertices N_1 and N_3, as shown in Figure 6.31(b). The tangents of this curve at end points N_1 and N_3 are lines $\overline{N_1V_1}$ and $\overline{N_3V_1}$, respectively. First edges E_2 and E_4 are deleted using KEL. Then vertex V_1 is deleted using KVE. Lastly, the straight edge is changed to a curve using a CLB operation. In Figure 6.29, procedure two was applied to the edges connected to vertices V_1, V_3, V_5 and V_7.

Procedure three   If one of the edges has rounding value 0 (e.g. if edge E_2 has 0), and the values of all the other edges are 1, the edge with value 0 is deleted. A curved edge is then generated between vertices N_1 and N_3, as shown in Figure 6.31(c). The tangents of this curve at end points N_1 and N_3 are lines $\overline{N_1V_1}$ and $\overline{N_3V_1}$, respectively. First edge E_2 is deleted by

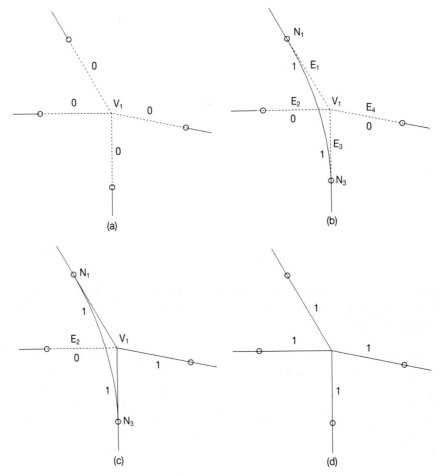

Figure 6.31 Procedures at a vertex.

KEL. A new edge is then created between vertices N_1 and N_3 using MEL. Lastly the edge is changed to a curve using a CLB operation. In Figure 6.29, procedure three was applied to the edges connected to vertex V_8.

Procedure four As shown in Figure 6.31(d), no action is taken if the rounding values of all the edges are 1.

6.8.2 Edges attached to a vertex generated in phase one

In Figure 6.29(b), N_i ($i = 1, \ldots ,10$) are the vertices generated in phase one. If they are connected either to the original edges or to the edges generated in phase one, those edges are deleted. In Figure 6.29(b), edges E_1 and E_2 are deleted using KEL operations. Next a vertex made in phase one and two edges attached to that vertex are deleted, and a curved edge is generated. For example, vertex N_2 and edges E_3 and E_4 shown in Figure 6.29(b) are replaced by curved edge E_5 shown in Figure 6.29(c). KVE and CLB operations are used for this procedure. Lastly, if there remain vertices connected to two edges, like vertices R_1 and R_2 in Figure 6.29(b), they are replaced by curved edges. Figure 6.29(c) shows the resulting solid generated using all the procedures in the rounding operation.

6.9 GENERATING CURVES

When a curve is generated in the rounding operation, three points P_0, P_1 and P_2 are always given to define the curve, as shown in Figure 6.32. P_0 and P_2 are the end points of the curve. The tangents of the curve at P_0 and P_2 are $\overline{P_0P_1}$ and $\overline{P_1P_2}$, respectively. A quadratic Bézier curve defined by points P_0, P_1 and P_2 can satisfy such requirements. However, a designer will not be satisfied with the shape of a quadratic Bézier curve. Figure 6.33(a) shows a square and a circle touching the square internally. Figure 6.3.3(b) shows the same square and four Bézier quadratic curves touching the square internally. Each Bézier curve is defined by the centres of the square edges and a vertex. From a designer's point of view, the circle is much more desirable then a quadratic Bézier curve. However, a circle can not satisfy the requirements expressed by the three points when $\overline{P_0P_1}$ is a different length from $\overline{P_1P_2}$. We therefore

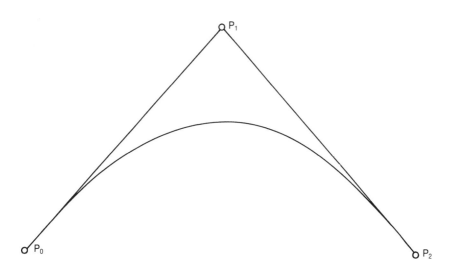

Figure 6.32 Condition for generating a curve.

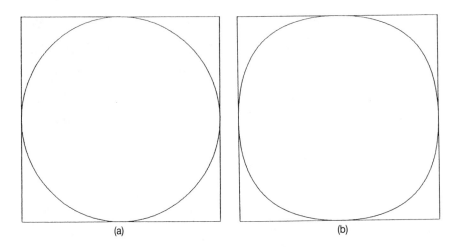

Figure 6.33   Rectangle and curves.

described how to generate a cubic Bézier curve which can both satisfy the requirements of the three points and is similar to a circle.

Figure 6.34 shows three points P_0, P_1 and P_2, defining a curve. First, an arc is defined with end points at P_0 and P_2, and tangent $\overline{P_0P_1}$ at P_0. A cubic Bézier curve $C_1(t)$ $(0 \leq t \leq 1)$ is then generated which approximates the arc. To generate the cubic curve, the end points P_0 and P_2, tangents t_0

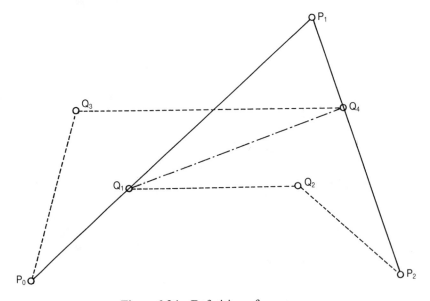

Figure 6.34   Definition of a curve.

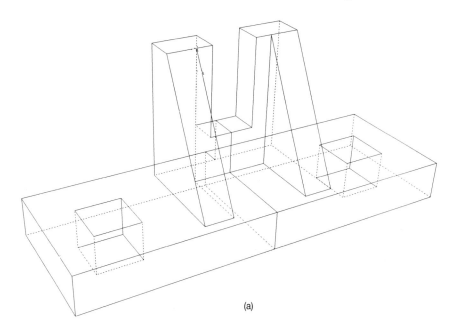

(a)

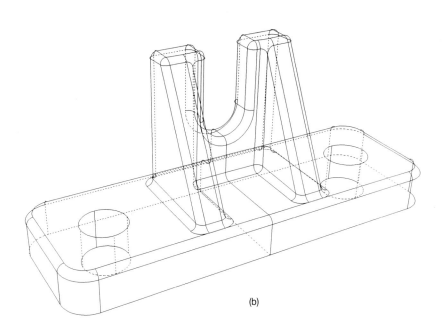

(b)

Figure 6.35   A mechanical part.

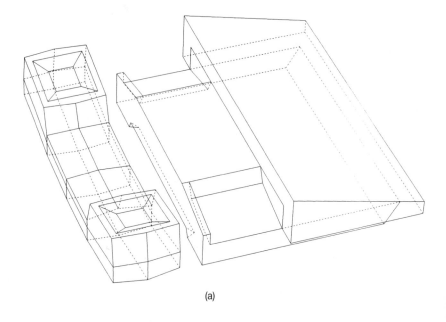

(a)

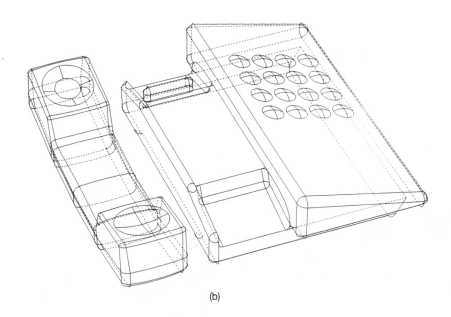

(b)

Figure 6.36 A telephone.

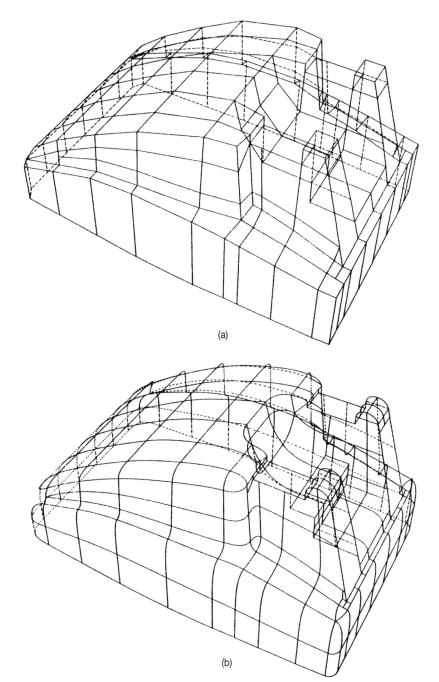

(a)

(b)

Figure 6.37   A telephone.

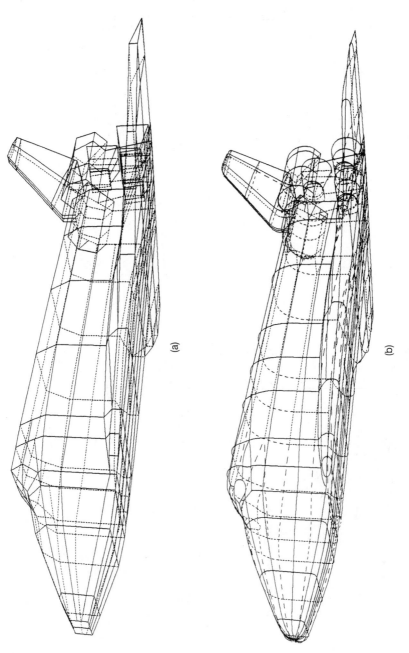

(a)

(b)

Figure 6.38   The Space Shuttle.

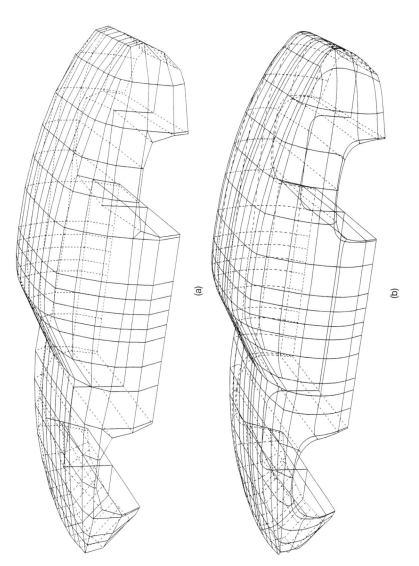

(a)

(b)

Figure 6.39   A car body.

and t_2 at the end points and a point corresponding to $t = 0.5$ are given. Figure 6.34 shows control points Q_1 and Q_2 of the Bézier curve $C_1(t)$. Next, from the end points P_0 and P_2 and a tangent $\overline{P_1P_2}$ at P_1, a cubic Bézier curve $C_2(t)$ approximating the arc is generated. Q_3 and Q_4 are control points of the Bézier curve $C_2(t)$. Lastly, we define a cubic Bézier curve $C_3(t)$ using points P_0, Q_1, Q_4 and P_2. Curve $C_3(t)$ can satisfy the requirements of the three points. When $\overline{P_0P_1}$ is the same length as $\overline{P_1P_2}$, the resulting curve approximates the arc.

6.10 EXAMPLES

Figures 6.35 to 6.39 show examples of models which are made using the DESIGNBASE rounding operation. Part (a) of each figure shows the characteristic polyhedron, and part (b) of each figure shows the final model after the rounding operation.

Chapter 7

Free-form Surface Patches

This chapter introduces several free-form surface patches which have been widely used in CAD/CAM. The method of interpolating curved meshes using Bézier patches is then described.

7.1   THE BICUBIC PARAMETRIC PATCH

Many engineering objects such as car bodies and mechanical components have complex free-form surfaces. Since it is difficult to represent these surfaces by a single mathematical equation, they have been represented by composite surfaces composed of many patches. Although until recently, many kinds of surface patch equations have been used, the most popular is the bicubic parametric patch which is used to interpolate a rectangular boundary. The boundary curves of the patch are represented by cubic polynomials. The coordinates (x, y, z) of a point $\mathbf{P}$ on patch $\mathbf{S}$ is defined by two parameters u and w, as shown in Figure 7.1. The two parameters u and w have values in the interval 0 to 1. The formulation of the

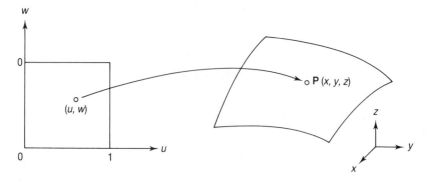

Figure 7.1   A parametric surface patch.

bicubic patch is expressed as

$$S(u, w) = [1 \; u \; u^2 \; u^3] \begin{bmatrix} V_{0,0} & V_{0,1} & V_{0,2} & V_{0,3} \\ V_{1,0} & V_{1,1} & V_{1,2} & V_{1,3} \\ V_{2,0} & V_{2,1} & V_{2,2} & V_{2,3} \\ V_{3,0} & V_{3,1} & V_{3,2} & V_{3,3} \end{bmatrix} \begin{bmatrix} 1 \\ w \\ w^2 \\ w^3 \end{bmatrix}$$

where $V_{i,j}$ ($i = 0, \ldots, 3, j = 0, \ldots, 3$) are vectors that consist of x, y and z values. From the above equation, it is understood that the bicubic patch is defined by 16 vectors. However, because the relationship between the 16 vectors and the shape of the patch is not clear, it is difficult for a designer to specify the 16 vectors to define a particular shape. To be able to define and modify the shape of a patch easily, bicubic patches have been expressed by other formulations, Coons, Bézier and B-spline patches being the most famous.

7.2   THE COONS PATCH

A bicubic Coons (1967) patch $S(u, w)$ is expressed as

$$S(u, w) = [1 \; u \; u^2 \; u^3] \, M_C \, C \, M_C{}^T [1 \; w \; w^2 \; w^3]^T$$
$$0 \le u, w \le 1$$

$$M_C = \begin{bmatrix} 1 & 0 & 0 & 0 \\ 0 & 0 & 1 & 0 \\ -3 & 3 & -2 & -1 \\ 2 & -2 & 1 & 1 \end{bmatrix}$$

[ ]^T transpose matrix

$$C = \begin{bmatrix} S(0,0) & S(0,1) & S_w(0,0) & S_w(0,1) \\ S(1,0) & S(1,1) & S_w(1,0) & S_w(1,1) \\ S_u(0,0) & S_u(0,1) & S_{uw}(0,0) & S_{uw}(0,1) \\ S_u(1,0) & S_u(1,1) & S_{uw}(1,0) & S_{uw}(1,1) \end{bmatrix}$$

where

$$S_u(a,b) = \frac{\partial S(u,w)}{\partial u}\bigg|_{u=a,\,w=b}$$

$$S_w(a,b) = \frac{\partial S(u,w)}{\partial w}\bigg|_{u=a,\,w=b}$$

$$S_{uw}(a,b) = \frac{\partial^2 S(u,w)}{\partial u\,\partial w}\bigg|_{u=a,\,w=b}$$

A Coons patch is defined by position vector $S(u, w)$, derivative vectors $S_u(u, w)$, $S_w(u, w)$ and $S_{uw}(u, w)$ at the four corners of the patch boundary. Figure 7.2 shows a patch boundary and these vectors. Using blending

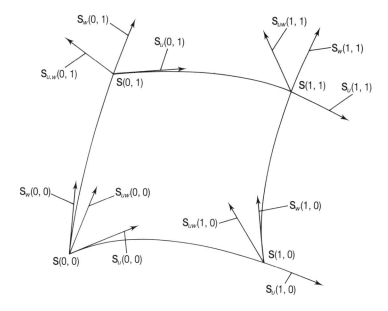

Figure 7.2   A Coons patch.

functions $h_i(u)$ $(i = 0, \ldots, 3)$, the Coons patch is given by

$$\mathbf{S}(u, w) = [h_0(u)\ h_1(u)\ h_2(u)\ h_3(u)]\ \mathbf{C} \begin{bmatrix} h_0(w) \\ h_1(w) \\ h_2(w) \\ h_3(w) \end{bmatrix}$$

where

$$h_0(u) = 1 - 3u^2 + 2u^3$$
$$h_1(u) = u^2(-2u + 3)$$
$$h_2(u) = (1-u)^2 u$$
$$h_3(u) = u^2(u - 1)$$

Figure 7.3 shows the four boundary curves $\mathbf{S}(u, 0)$, $\mathbf{S}(u, 1)$, $\mathbf{S}(0, w)$ and $\mathbf{S}(1, w)$ of the Coons patch and the normal derivatives $\mathbf{S}_w(u, 0)$, $\mathbf{S}_w(u, 1)$, $\mathbf{S}_u(0, w)$ and $\mathbf{S}_u(1, w)$ along the boundary curves. These are all expressed by cubic polynomials. The boundary curves are expressed as

$$\mathbf{S}(u, 0) = [h_0(u)\ h_1(u)\ h_2(u)\ h_3(u)] \begin{bmatrix} \mathbf{S}(0, 0) \\ \mathbf{S}(1, 0) \\ \mathbf{S}_u(0, 0) \\ \mathbf{S}_u(1, 0) \end{bmatrix}$$

$$\mathbf{S}(u, 1) = [h_0(u)\ h_1(u)\ h_2(u)\ h_3(u)] \begin{bmatrix} \mathbf{S}(0, 1) \\ \mathbf{S}(1, 1) \\ \mathbf{S}_u(0, 1) \\ \mathbf{S}_u(1, 1) \end{bmatrix}$$

$$\mathbf{S}(0, w) = [h_0(w)\ h_1(w)\ h_2(w)\ h_3(w)] \begin{bmatrix} \mathbf{S}(0, 0) \\ \mathbf{S}(0, 1) \\ \mathbf{S}_w(0, 0) \\ \mathbf{S}_w(0, 1) \end{bmatrix}$$

$$\mathbf{S}(1, w) = [h_0(w)\ h_1(w)\ h_2(w)\ h_3(w)] \begin{bmatrix} \mathbf{S}(1, 0) \\ \mathbf{S}(1, 1) \\ \mathbf{S}_w(1, 0) \\ \mathbf{S}_w(1, 1) \end{bmatrix}$$

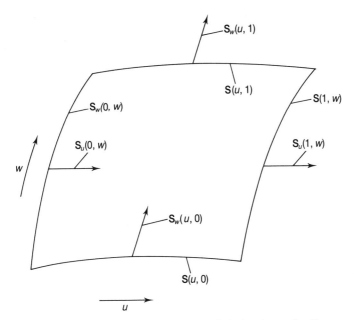

Figure 7.3   The boundary curves and normal derivatives of a Coons patch.

The normal derivatives are expressed as

$$
\mathbf{S}_w(u, 0) = [h_0(u)\ h_1(u)\ h_2(u)\ h_3(u)] \begin{bmatrix} \mathbf{S}_w(0, 0) \\ \mathbf{S}_w(1, 0) \\ \mathbf{S}_{uw}(0, 0) \\ \mathbf{S}_{uw}(1, 0) \end{bmatrix}
$$

$$
\mathbf{S}_w(u, 1) = [h_0(u)\ h_1(u)\ h_2(u)\ h_3(u)] \begin{bmatrix} \mathbf{S}_w(0, 1) \\ \mathbf{S}_w(1, 1) \\ \mathbf{S}_{uw}(0, 1) \\ \mathbf{S}_{uw}(1, 1) \end{bmatrix}
$$

$$
\mathbf{S}_u(0, w) = [h_0(w)\ h_1(w)\ h_2(w)\ h_3(w)] \begin{bmatrix} \mathbf{S}_u(0, 0) \\ \mathbf{S}_u(0, 1) \\ \mathbf{S}_{uw}(0, 0) \\ \mathbf{S}_{uw}(0, 1) \end{bmatrix}
$$

$$
\mathbf{S}_u(1, w) = [h_0(w)\ h_1(w)\ h_2(w)\ h_3(w)] \begin{bmatrix} \mathbf{S}_u(1, 0) \\ \mathbf{S}_u(1, 1) \\ \mathbf{S}_{uw}(1, 0) \\ \mathbf{S}_{uw}(1, 1) \end{bmatrix}
$$

If a designer specifies the four boundary curves of a Coons patch, this determines the position vectors $\mathbf{S}(u, w)$ and derivative vectors $\mathbf{S}_u(u, w)$ and $\mathbf{S}_w(u, w)$ at the corners. In this way it is easy for a designer to specify these vectors. On the other hand, it is difficult for a designer to specify the derivative vector $\mathbf{S}_{uw}(u, w)$ because the relationship between the derivative vector and the patch shape is not obvious. The derivative vector $\mathbf{S}_{uw}(u, w)$ at a corner is called a **twist vector**. For practical use, the twist vector has conventionally been given the value 0. This method occasionally gives undesirable results (see Section 7.6.3).

7.3   THE BÉZIER PATCH

A bicubic Bézier (1972) patch $\mathbf{S}(u, w)$ can be formulated using matrices as

$$\mathbf{S}(u, w) = [1 \; u \; u^2 \; u^3]\mathbf{M}_B \, \mathbf{B} \, \mathbf{M}_B{}^T [1 \; w \; w^2 \; w^3]^T$$

$$0 \le u, \, w \le 1$$

$$\mathbf{M}_B = \begin{bmatrix} 1 & 0 & 0 & 0 \\ -3 & 3 & 0 & 0 \\ 3 & -6 & 3 & 0 \\ -1 & 3 & -3 & 1 \end{bmatrix}$$

$$\mathbf{B} = \begin{bmatrix} \mathbf{P}_{00} & \mathbf{P}_{01} & \mathbf{P}_{02} & \mathbf{P}_{03} \\ \mathbf{P}_{10} & \mathbf{P}_{11} & \mathbf{P}_{12} & \mathbf{P}_{13} \\ \mathbf{P}_{20} & \mathbf{P}_{21} & \mathbf{P}_{22} & \mathbf{P}_{23} \\ \mathbf{P}_{30} & \mathbf{P}_{31} & \mathbf{P}_{32} & \mathbf{P}_{33} \end{bmatrix}$$

Using binomial coefficients as weights for the control points, the formula can also be expressed as

$$\mathbf{S}(u, w) = \sum_{i=0}^{3} \sum_{j=0}^{3} B_{3,i}(u) B_{3,j}(w) \mathbf{P}_{ij}$$

where

$$B_{n,i}(u) = \binom{n}{i} u^i (1-u)^{n-i}$$

The bicubic Bézier patch is defined by the 16 control points $\mathbf{P}_{ij}$ $(i = 0, \ldots, 3, j = 0, \ldots, 3)$ of a characteristic polyhedron, as shown in

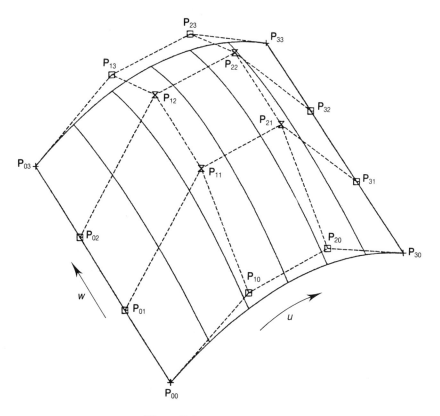

Figure 7.4 A Bézier patch.

Figure 7.4. The figure also shows the cross-section lines between the patch and planes. The boundary curves of a Bézier patch are expressed as Bézier curves. The boundaries are given by

$$\mathbf{S}(u, 0) = \sum_{i=0}^{3} B_{3,i}(u)\mathbf{P}_{i0}$$

$$\mathbf{S}(u, 1) = \sum_{i=0}^{3} B_{3,i}(u)\mathbf{P}_{i3}$$

$$\mathbf{S}(0, w) = \sum_{j=0}^{3} B_{3,j}(w)\mathbf{P}_{0j}$$

$$\mathbf{S}(1, w) = \sum_{j=0}^{3} B_{3,j}(w)\mathbf{P}_{3j}$$

The normal derivatives along the boundaries are given by

$$S_w(u, 0) = \sum_{i=0}^{3} 3B_{3,i}(u)(P_{i1} - P_{i0})$$

$$S_w(u, 1) = \sum_{i=0}^{3} 3B_{3,i}(u)(P_{i3} - P_{i2})$$

$$S_u(0, w) = \sum_{j=0}^{3} 3B_{3,j}(w)(P_{1j} - P_{0j})$$

$$S_u(1, w) = \sum_{j=0}^{3} 3B_{3,j}(w)(P_{3j} - P_{2j})$$

The Bézier patch has similar advantages to the Bézier curve.

1. Convex hull property

Any point on a given Bézier patch is included in a convex hull defined by 16 control points. This is used to advantage in the interference check on two Bézier patches. We can quickly find the case when two Bézier patches do not intersect.

2. Relationship between a polyhedron and a patch

The characteristic polyhedron is approximately the same shape as the patch. In addition, the shape of the patch is smoother than the characteristic polyhedron. The designer can therefore easily understand the relationship between the two, and define or modify the shape of the patch by manipulating the control points.

3. Relationship between a polyhedron and derivative vectors

The derivative vectors at the four corners of a patch can be defined by control points:

$$S_u(0, 0) = 3(P_{10} - P_{00}) = 3a$$
$$S_w(0, 0) = 3(P_{01} - P_{00}) = 3b$$
$$S_{uw}(0, 0) = 9(P_{11} - (P_{00} + a + b))$$
$$S_u(1, 0) = 3(P_{30} - P_{20}) = 3c$$
$$S_w(1, 0) = 3(P_{31} - P_{30}) = 3d$$

$$\mathbf{S}_{uw}(1, 0) = 9((\mathbf{P}_{30} - \mathbf{c} + \mathbf{d}) - \mathbf{P}_{21})$$

$$\mathbf{S}_{u}(0, 1) = 3(\mathbf{P}_{13} - \mathbf{P}_{03}) = 3\mathbf{e}$$

$$\mathbf{S}_{w}(0, 1) = 3(\mathbf{P}_{03} - \mathbf{P}_{02}) = 3\mathbf{f}$$

$$\mathbf{S}_{uw}(0, 1) = 9((\mathbf{P}_{03} + \mathbf{e} - \mathbf{f}) - \mathbf{P}_{12})$$

$$\mathbf{S}_{u}(1, 1) = 3(\mathbf{P}_{33} - \mathbf{P}_{23}) = 3\mathbf{g}$$

$$\mathbf{S}_{w}(1, 1) = 3(\mathbf{P}_{33} - \mathbf{P}_{32}) = 3\mathbf{h}$$

$$\mathbf{S}_{uw}(1, 1) = 9(\mathbf{P}_{22} - (\mathbf{P}_{00} - \mathbf{g} - \mathbf{h})) \tag{7.1}$$

Figure 7.5 lists the program to compute a coordinate of a point on a Bézier patch. The programs to compute the first derivatives with respect to parameters u and w are shown in Figure 7.6.

7.4   THE B-SPLINE PATCH

One of the famous parametric surfaces is the B-spline surface, proposed by Riesenfeld (1973) as surface forms in computer-aided geometric design. B-spline surfaces can be divided into three classes: the uniform, the non-uniform and the rational (Tiller, 1983). This section introduces only the uniform B-spline which is most easily computed. Using matrices, the formulation of a uniform bicubic B-spline patch $\mathbf{S}(u, w)$ is

$$\mathbf{S}(u, w) = [1 \; u \; u^2 \; u^3] \mathbf{M}_A \mathbf{A} \mathbf{M}_A^T [1 \; w \; w^2 \; w^3]^T$$

$$0 \leq u, w \leq 1$$

$$\mathbf{M}_A = \begin{bmatrix} 1/6 & 2/3 & 1/6 & 0 \\ -1/2 & 0 & 1/2 & 0 \\ 1/2 & -1 & 1/2 & 0 \\ -1/6 & 1/2 & -1/2 & 1/6 \end{bmatrix}$$

$$\mathbf{A} = \begin{bmatrix} \mathbf{P}_{00} & \mathbf{P}_{01} & \mathbf{P}_{02} & \mathbf{P}_{03} \\ \mathbf{P}_{10} & \mathbf{P}_{11} & \mathbf{P}_{12} & \mathbf{P}_{13} \\ \mathbf{P}_{20} & \mathbf{P}_{21} & \mathbf{P}_{22} & \mathbf{P}_{23} \\ \mathbf{P}_{30} & \mathbf{P}_{31} & \mathbf{P}_{32} & \mathbf{P}_{33} \end{bmatrix}$$

The bicubic B-spline patch is defined by a characteristic polyhedron of 16 control points $\mathbf{P}_{ij}$ ($i = 0, \ldots, 3, j = 0, \ldots, 3$), like the Bézier patch. Figure 7.7 shows the polyhedron and the patch boundary. Similarly, a quadratic B-spline patch $\mathbf{S}(u, w)$ is defined by nine control points $\mathbf{P}_{ij}$

Figure 7.5 A FORTRAN program for calculating a point on a bicubic Bézier patch. To use the program, the user must specify 16 control points for the Bézier patch and the values of two parameters *u* and *w* for a specific point on the patch. The correspondence between the control points and a number indicating an element of the array is as follows:

$P_{0,0}$...(1) $P_{1,0}$...(2) $P_{2,0}$...(3) $P_{3,0}$...(4)

$P_{0,1}$...(5) $P_{1,1}$...(6) $P_{2,1}$...(7) $P_{3,1}$...(8)

$P_{0,2}$...(9) $P_{1,2}$...(10) $P_{2,2}$...(11) $P_{3,2}$...(12)

$P_{0,3}$...(13) $P_{1,3}$...(14) $P_{2,3}$...(15) $P_{3,3}$...(16)

```
C------------------------------------------------------------
C
C     >> A POINT ON A BEZIER PATCH <<
C
      SUBROUTINE MPTZP(BZ, U, W, PT)
      DIMENSION BZ(3, 16), PT(3)
C
C     /I/ BZ : CONTROL POINTS OF A BEZIER PATCH
C     /I/ U, W : PARAMETERS
C     /O/ PT : A POINT
C
      DIMENSION AU(4), AW(4)
C
      AU(1)=(1.0-U)**3
      AU(2)=3.0*(1.0-U)**2 *U
      AU(3)=3.0*(1.0-U)*U**2
      AU(4)=U**3
C
      AW(1)=(1.0-W)**3
      AW(2)=3.0*(1.0-W)**2 *W
      AW(3)=3.0*(1.0-W)*W**2
      AW(4)=W**3
C
      DO 100 L=1, 3
        IZ=1
        PT(L)=0.0
        DO 110 IW=1, 4
          DO 120 IU=1, 4
            PT(L)=PT(L)+BZ(L, IZ)*AU(IU)*AW(IW)
            IZ=IZ+1
120       CONTINUE
110     CONTINUE
100   CONTINUE
      RETURN
      END
C
C------------------------------------------------------------
```

Figure 7.6 Programs for computing the first derivatives of a point on a Bézier patch with respect to parameters *u* and *w*.

```
C-----------------------------------------------------------
C
C      >> FIRST DERIVATIVE VECTOR ABOUT U
C         ON A BEZIER PATCH <<
C
       SUBROUTINE MDUZP(BZ, U, W, PT)
       DIMENSION BZ(3, 16), PT(3)
C
C      /I/ BZ : CONTROL POINTS OF A BEZIER PATCH
C      /I/ U, W, : PARAMETERS
C      /O/ PT : A POINT
       DIMENSION DU(4), AW(4)
C
       DU(1)=-3.0*(1.0-U)**2
       DU(2)=3.0*((3.0*U-4.0)*U+1.0)
       DU(3)=3.0*U*(2.0-3.0*U)
       DU(4)=3.0*U**2
C
       AW(1)=(1.0-W)**3
       AW(2)=3.0*(1.0-W)**2 *W
       AW(3)=3.0*(1.0-W)*W**2
       AW(4)=W**3
C
       DO 100 L=1, 3
         IZ=1
         PT(L)=0.0
         DO 110 IW=1, 4
           DO 120 IU=1, 4
             PT(L)=PT(L)+BZ(L, IZ)*DU(IU)*AW(IW)
             IZ=IZ+1
120        CONTINUE
110      CONTINUE
100    CONTINUE
       RETURN
       END
C
C-----------------------------------------------------------
C
C      >> FIRST DERIVATIVE VECTOR ABOUT W
C         ON A BEZIER PATCH <<
C
       SUBROUTINE MDWZP(BZ, U, W, PT)
       DIMENSION BZ(3, 16), PT(3)
C
C      /I/ BZ : CONTROL POINTS OF A BEZIER PATCH
```

Figure 7.6   (cont.)

```
C       /I/ U, W : PARAMETERS
C       /0/ PT : A POINT
C
        DIMENSION AU(4), DW(4)
C
        AU(1)=(1.0-U)**3
        AU(2)=3.0*(1.0-U)**2 *U
        AU(3)=3.0*(1.0-U)*U**2
        AU(4)=U**3
C
        DW(1)=-3.0*(1.0-W)**2
        DW(2)=3.0*((3.0*W-4.0)*W+1.0)
        DW(3)=3.0*W*(2.0-3.0*W)
        DW(4)=3.0*W**2
C
        DO 100 L=1, 3
          IZ=1
          PT(L)=0.0
          DO 110 IW=1, 4
            DO 120 IU=1, 4
              T(L)=PT(L)+BZ(L, IZ)*AU(IU)*DW(IW)
              IZ=IZ+1
120         CONTINUE
110       CONTINUE
100     CONTINUE
        RETURN
        END
C
C---------------------------------------------------------------
```

$(i = 0, 1, 2, j = 0, 1, 2)$, as shown in Figure 7.8. The formulation is

$$S(u, w) = [1\ u\ u^2]\mathbf{M'}_A \mathbf{A'}\ \mathbf{M'}_A{}^T[1\ w\ w^2]^T$$

$$0 \le u, w \le 1$$

$$\mathbf{M'}_A = \begin{bmatrix} 1/2 & 1/2 & 0 \\ -1 & 1 & 0 \\ 1/2 & -1 & 1/2 \end{bmatrix}$$

$$\mathbf{A'} = \begin{bmatrix} \mathbf{P}_{00} & \mathbf{P}_{01} & \mathbf{P}_{02} \\ \mathbf{P}_{10} & \mathbf{P}_{11} & \mathbf{P}_{12} \\ \mathbf{P}_{20} & \mathbf{P}_{21} & \mathbf{P}_{22} \end{bmatrix}$$

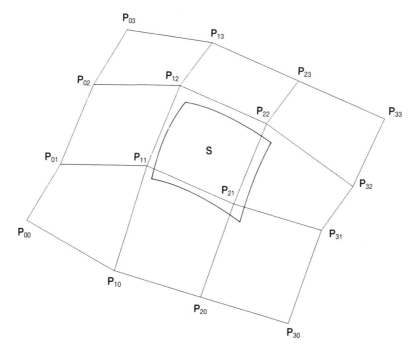

Figure 7.7 A bicubic B-spline patch.

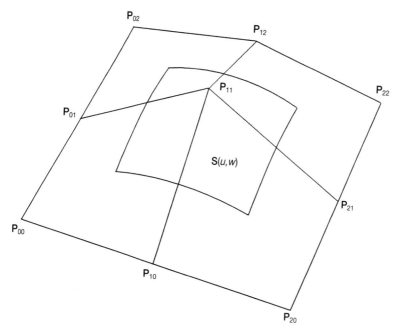

Figure 7.8 A biquadratic B-spline patch.

The B-spline patch has the following advantages.

1. Smooth joins

Since the derivatives on the boundaries of joined B-spline patches are defined by the common control points, a procedure to join B-spline patches with derivative continuity is not required: the continuity of the derivative is implicitly represented in the formulation of B-splines. If bicubic B-spline patches are used, the first and second derivatives of the patches are continuous on the boundary. For quadratic patches, the first derivative is continuous. Figure 7.9 shows a mesh of control points $\mathbf{P}_{ij}$ $(i = 0, \ldots, n, j = 0, \ldots, m)$ given by the designer, and bicubic B-spline patches $\mathbf{S}_{ij}$ $(i = 0, \ldots, n-2, j = 0, \ldots, m-2)$ defined by the mesh.

2. Local control

The designer can make local changes to the shape of the surface patch by manipulating control points. If one control point of a bicubic patch is moved, the shapes of only nine patches are changed. In the case of a quadratic patch, four patches are changed when one control point is changed.

Using the matrix expressions of Coons, Bézier and B-spline patches, we can easily transform one patch expression to another. As an

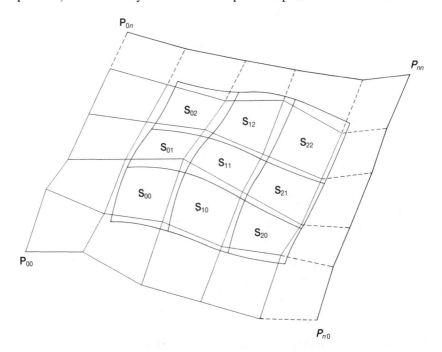

Figure 7.9   Bicubic B-spline patches.

example, we will convert the control points of a bicubic B-spline patch to those of a Bézier patch. Let $\mathbf{A}$ and $\mathbf{B}$ be 4×4 matrices of the control points defining B-spline and Bézier patches, respectively. $\mathbf{M}_A$ and $\mathbf{M}_B$ are the coefficient matrices of a B-spline patch and Bézier patch, respectively. The relationship of two matrices $\mathbf{A}$ and $\mathbf{B}$ is expressed as

$$\mathbf{M}_B \, \mathbf{B} \, \mathbf{M}_B{}^T = \mathbf{M}_A \, \mathbf{A} \, \mathbf{M}_A{}^T$$

An equation for converting $\mathbf{A}$ to $\mathbf{B}$ is then given by

$$\mathbf{B} = \mathbf{M}_B{}^{-1} \, \mathbf{M}_A \, \mathbf{A} \, \mathbf{M}_A{}^T (\mathbf{M}_B{}^T)^{-1}$$

7.5   THE GENERALIZED COONS PATCH

The boundary curves $S(u, 0)$, $S(u, 1)$, $S(0, w)$ and $S(1, w)$ of the bicubic patch described in Sections 7.1 to 7.4 are cubic. The normal derivatives $S_w(u, 0)$, $S_w(u, 1)$, $S_u(0, w)$ and $S_u(1, w)$ along the boundary of the patch are also cubic. A generalized Coons patch (Forrest, 1972) can interpolate the boundaries and normal derivatives which are specified as general functions. For example, we can specify $S(0, w) = \cos(w)$ and $S_u(0, w) = \sin(w)$. The formulation of the patch $S(u, w)$ is given by

$$S(u, w) = [S(u, 0) \; S(u, 1) \; S_w(u, 0) \; S_w(u, 1)] \begin{bmatrix} h_0(w) \\ h_1(w) \\ h_2(w) \\ h_3(w) \end{bmatrix}$$

$$+ [h_0(u) \; h_1(u) \; h_2(u) \; h_3(u)] \begin{bmatrix} S(0, w) \\ S(1, w) \\ S_u(0, w) \\ S_u(1, w) \end{bmatrix}$$

$$- [h_0(u) \; h_1(u) \; h_2(u) \; h_3(u)] \times$$

$$\begin{bmatrix} S(0,0) & S(0,1) & S_w(0,0) & S_w(0,1) \\ S(1,0) & S(1,1) & S_w(1,0) & S_w(1,1) \\ S_u(0,0) & S_u(0,1) & \boxed{S_{uw}(0,0) \quad S_{uw}(0,1)} \\ S_u(1,0) & S_u(1,1) & \boxed{S_{uw}(1,0) \quad S_{uw}(1,1)} \end{bmatrix} \begin{bmatrix} h_0(w) \\ h_1(w) \\ h_2(w) \\ h_3(w) \end{bmatrix}$$

└── Twist vector partition

where

$$h_0(u) = (1 - u^2)(2u + 1)$$
$$h_1(u) = u^2(-2u + 3)$$
$$h_2(u) = (1 - u)^2 u$$
$$h_3(u) = u^2(u - 1)$$

In this formulation, the first term represents a surface interpolating two boundaries $S(u, 0)$ and $S(u, 1)$ and normal derivatives $S_w(u, 0)$ and $S_w(u, 1)$. Similarly, the second term represents a surface interpolating two boundaries $S(0, w)$ and $S(1, w)$ and normal derivatives $S_u(0, w)$ and $S_u(1, w)$. In the equation for the generalized Coons patch, two surfaces are added, and the unwanted third term is then subtracted.

When a generalized Coons patch is defined, a designer can not independently specify four normal derivatives on the boundary. They have to be specified satisfying the following constraint:

$$\left.\frac{\partial S_w(u, 0)}{\partial u}\right|_{u=0} = \left.\frac{\partial S_u(0, w)}{\partial w}\right|_{w=0} = S_{uw}(0, 0)$$

$$\left.\frac{\partial S_w(u, 0)}{\partial u}\right|_{u=1} = \left.\frac{\partial S_u(1, w)}{\partial w}\right|_{w=0} = S_{uw}(1, 0)$$

$$\left.\frac{\partial S_w(u, 1)}{\partial u}\right|_{u=0} = \left.\frac{\partial S_u(1, w)}{\partial w}\right|_{w=1} = S_{uw}(1, 1)$$

$$\left.\frac{\partial S_w(u, 1)}{\partial u}\right|_{u=0} = \left.\frac{\partial S_u(0, w)}{\partial w}\right|_{w=1} = S_{uw}(0, 1)$$

This is called the **compatibility condition** (Barnhill *et al.*, 1978). In the first step to define a generalized Coons patch, the four boundary curves $S(u, 0)$, $S(1, w)$, $S(u, 1)$ and $S(0, w)$ and the four twist vectors $S_{uw}(0, 0)$, $S_{uw}(1, 0)$, $S_{uw}(0, 1)$ and $S_{uw}(1, 1)$ are usually specified. The designer then specifies four normal derivatives $S_w(u, 0)$, $S_u(1, w)$, $S_w(u, 1)$ and $S_u(0, w)$ which satisfy the compatibility condition. However, it is difficult for the designer to guess the twist vectors since their relationship with the patch shape is not clear. Gregory (1974) extended the generalized Coons patch so that four normal derivatives can be specified without restrictions. In his equation, the twist vector partition of a Coons patch is modified as follows:

$$\frac{\left(w\dfrac{\partial \mathbf{S}_w(0, 0)}{\partial u} + u\dfrac{\partial \mathbf{S}_u(0, 0)}{\partial w} \right)}{u + w} \qquad \frac{\left(-u\dfrac{\partial \mathbf{S}_u(0, 1)}{\partial w} + (w - 1)\dfrac{\partial \mathbf{S}_w(0, 1)}{\partial u} \right)}{-u + w - 1}$$

$$\frac{\left((1 - u)\dfrac{\partial \mathbf{S}_u(1, 0)}{\partial w} + w\dfrac{\partial \mathbf{S}_w(1, 0)}{\partial u} \right)}{1 - u + w} \qquad \frac{\left((u - 1)\dfrac{\partial \mathbf{S}_u(1, 1)}{\partial w} + (w - 1)\dfrac{\partial \mathbf{S}_w(1, 1)}{\partial u} \right)}{u - 1 + w - 1}$$

This extension is called the **compatibility correction**.

7.6   INTERPOLATING CURVED MESHES USING BÉZIER PATCHES

In this section we first describe how bicubic Bézier patches are joined with tangent plane continuity. Methods for interpolating curved meshes using Bézier patches are then discussed.

7.6.1   Regular mesh

One of the most popular methods for modelling free-form surfaces is **cross-sectional design**, in which the designer first defines the cross-sections of the shape required and then produces a mesh composed of curves, as shown in Figure 7.10. All the faces of this mesh are in general rectangular and each node is connected to four faces; all the curves of the mesh are cubic. We call such a mesh a **regular mesh**. After the mesh is produced, smooth free-form surfaces are generated on the faces of the mesh.

To interpolate the face of the mesh, bicubic Coons patches and Bézier patches are used as free-form surfaces. Their use makes it possible to generate surfaces whose tangent planes are continuous on the boundary curves. Tangent plane continuity is the most simple condition for joining patches to generate a smooth composite surface. However, to achieve continuity the designer must produce a mesh which satisfies a certain restriction (Faux and Pratt, 1979; Mortenson, 1985).

Figure 7.11 illustrates this restriction. The cubic curves of the mesh in the figure are expressed as

$$\mathbf{C}_{i,j,k}(t)\,(i = 1, \ldots, n-1, j = 1, \ldots, m-1, k = 0,1) \quad 0 \le t \le 1$$

where t is a parameter. These curves are connected to nodes $N_{i,j}$ $(i = 1, \ldots, n, j = 1, \ldots, m)$. Let $\mathbf{C}_{i,j,0}(0)$ and $\mathbf{C}_{i,j,0}(1)$ be the first derivatives of curve $\mathbf{C}_{i,j,0}$ at two nodes $N_{i,j}$ and N_{i+1j}, respectively. Similarly, the first derivatives of curve $\mathbf{C}_{i,j,1}$ at nodes $N_{i,j}$ and $N_{i,j+1}$ are $\mathbf{C}_{i,j,1}(0)$ and $\mathbf{C}_{i,j,1}(1)$. Because the tangents of the curves joined at the nodes are continuous, we can express this as

$$\dot{\mathbf{C}}_{i+1,j,0}(0) = k_{i,j,0} \times \dot{\mathbf{C}}_{i,j,0}(1)$$
$$\dot{\mathbf{C}}_{i,j+1,1}(0) = k_{i,j,1} \times \dot{\mathbf{C}}_{i,j,1}(1)$$

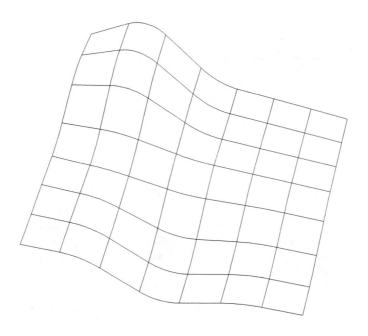

Figure 7.10   A regular mesh.

where $k_{i,j,k}$ $(k = 0, 1)$ are scale factors of the lengths of the first derivatives. To generate surface patches with tangent plane continuity, $k_{i,j,0}$ $(i = 1, \ldots, n)$ and $k_{i,j,1}$ $(j = 1, \ldots, m)$ must be constant. Figure 7.12 shows a parameter space defining a composite surface which satisfies the restriction of the scale factor. This space is called a **tartan grid** (Forrest, 1982).

7.6.2 Joining Bézier patches

Figure 7.13 shows four Bézier patches $\mathbf{S}^i(u, w)$ $(i = 0, \ldots, 3)$ which are to be joined under the condition of tangent plane continuity. The boundary curves of the four patches are already given. The tangents of the joined curves are continuous. The restriction of scale factors described above is imposed on the boundary curves. Let $\mathbf{P}^i_{jk}$ $(i = 0, \ldots, 3, j = 0, \ldots, 3, k = 0, \ldots, 3)$ be the control points of the patches $\mathbf{S}^i$. Consider the joining of two patches $\mathbf{S}^0$ and $\mathbf{S}^1$ which meet at boundary curve C_1. For the tangent planes to be continuous, the normal derivatives of $\mathbf{S}^0$ and $\mathbf{S}^1$

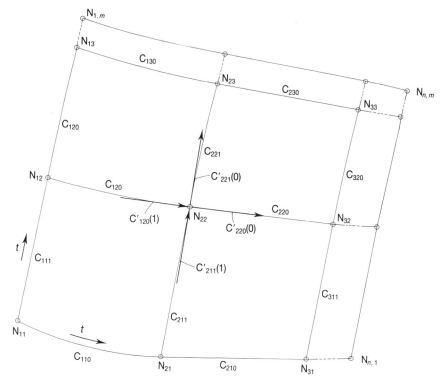

Figure 7.11 A regular mesh.

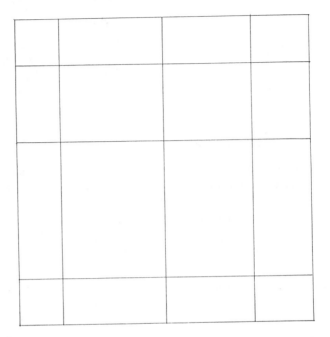

Figure 7.12   A parameter space defining a composite surface.

along curve C_1 must satisfy the following equation:

$$S^0_u(1, w) = k_0 S^1_u(0, w)$$

where k_0 is a scale factor. Using this equation, the relationship between the control points is given by

$$\mathbf{P}^0_{3i} - \mathbf{P}^0_{2i} = k_0(\mathbf{P}^1_{1i} - \mathbf{P}^1_{0i})\ (i = 0, \ldots, 3) \tag{7.2}$$

So if we define control points $\mathbf{P}^0_{21}$ and $\mathbf{P}^0_{22}$ of patch S^0, points $\mathbf{P}^1_{11}$ and $\mathbf{P}^1_{12}$ of patch S^1 are also determined. Similarly, for tangent plane continuity the relationship between the control points of patches S^0 and S^2 which meet on curve C_4 is given by

$$\mathbf{P}^0_{i3} - \mathbf{P}^0_{i2} = k_1(\mathbf{P}^2_{i1} - \mathbf{P}^2_{i0})\ (i = 0, \ldots, 3) \tag{7.3}$$

where k_1 is a scale factor.

    If control point $\mathbf{P}^0_{22}$ is specified, two control points $\mathbf{P}^1_{12}$ and $\mathbf{P}^2_{21}$ are determined. In addition, control point $\mathbf{P}^3_{11}$ is given twice by the relationships of the control points on curves C_2 and C_3. When the restriction of scale factors is imposed, the two given positions of point

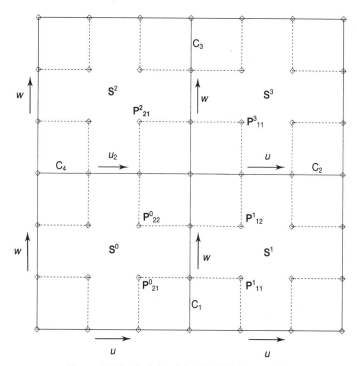

Figure 7.13   Joining bicubic Bézier patches.

$\mathbf{P}^3_{11}$ are the same since equations (7.2) and (7.3) can be applied. However, when the scale factors are not constant, it is difficult to make two coordinates of point $\mathbf{P}^3_{11}$ the same. We therefore impose the restriction on the boundary curves when using bicubic Bézier patches as free-form surfaces to interpolate the mesh.

7.6.3 Defining Bézier patches on the faces of a mesh

Figure 7.14 shows a regular mesh which is to be interpolated. The mesh is composed of nodes N_{ij} ($i = 0, 1, 2, j = 0, 1, 2$) and curves. All the curves are represented by cubic Bézier curves. The tangents of the curves connected at the nodes are continuous. Faces F_i ($i = 0, \ldots, 3$) on the mesh have four sides. Let $\mathbf{S}^i(u_i, w_i)$ ($i = 0, \ldots, 3$) be bicubic Bézier patches generated on faces F_i ($i = 0, \ldots, 3$), respectively. The control points of patches $\mathbf{S}^i$ ($i = 0, \ldots, 3$) are $\mathbf{P}^i_{jk}$ ($i = 0, \ldots, 3, j = 0, \ldots, 3, k = 0, \ldots, 3$). Because the boundary curves of the Bézier patches are given, the control points, except for $\mathbf{P}^i_{jk}$ ($i = 0, \ldots, 3, j = 1, 2, k = 1, 2$), are already determined. To define the Bézier patches it is necessary to specify control points $\mathbf{P}^i_{jk}$ ($i = 0, \ldots, 3, j = 1, 2, k = 1, 2$). Below we describe two methods of determining these control points.

1. Zero twist vectors

To determine the four control points $\mathbf{P}^i_{jk}$ ($i = 0, \ldots, 3, j = 1, 2, k = 1, 2$) for all four patches, we give the value zero to the four twist vectors $\mathbf{S}^i_{uw}(0, 0)$, $\mathbf{S}^i_{uw}(0, 1)$, $\mathbf{S}^i_{uw}(1, 0)$ and $\mathbf{S}^i_{uw}(1, 1)$ ($i = 0, \ldots, 3$). This method has been widely used because of its simplicity. Using equations (7.1), the four control points are given by

$$\mathbf{P}^i_{00} = \mathbf{P}^i_{10} + \mathbf{P}^i_{01} - \mathbf{P}^i_{00}$$
$$\mathbf{P}^i_{21} = \mathbf{P}^i_{20} + \mathbf{P}^i_{31} - \mathbf{P}^i_{30}$$
$$\mathbf{P}^i_{12} = \mathbf{P}^i_{02} + \mathbf{P}^i_{13} - \mathbf{P}^i_{03}$$
$$\mathbf{P}^i_{22} = \mathbf{P}^i_{23} + \mathbf{P}^i_{32} - \mathbf{P}^i_{33}$$

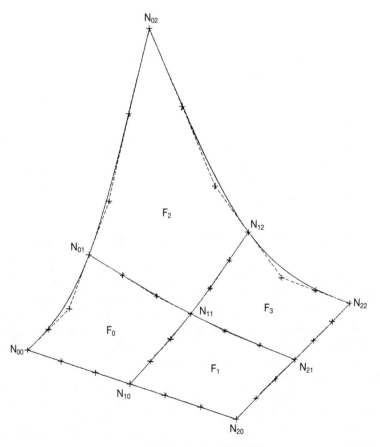

Figure 7.14   A regular mesh.

Figure 7.15 shows the control points defining the bicubic Bézier patches generated on the mesh. Figure 7.16 shows the cross-sections of these patches. The net of control points is fairly wavy. And it can be seen that the shapes of the patches are also wavy. This demonstrates that the zero twist vector method occasionally gives undesirable results.

2. Smoothing normal derivatives

In Figure 7.15 the normal derivatives $S^2_w(u, 0)$ and $S^2_u(0, w)$ of patch S^2 are defined, respectively, by the following four vectors:

$$\mathbf{a}_i = \mathbf{P}^2_{i1} - \mathbf{P}^2_{i0} \quad (i = 0, \ldots, 3)$$
$$\mathbf{b}_i = \mathbf{P}^2_{3i} - \mathbf{P}^2_{2i} \quad (i = 0, \ldots, 3)$$

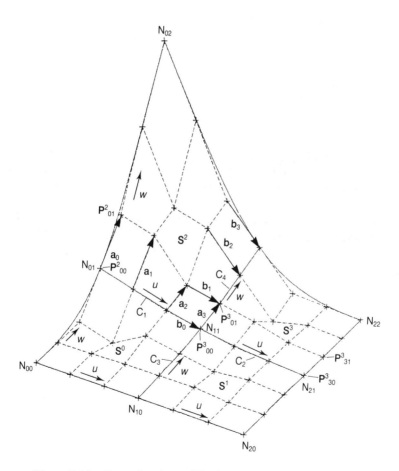

Figure 7.15   Control points of Bézier patches with zero twist.

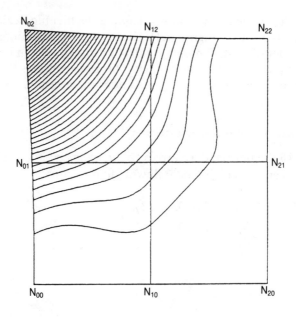

Figure 7.16 Cross-sections of Bézier patches with zero twist.

From the vectors in the figure we can guess the normal derivatives are not smooth, which is why the patch is wavy. We therefore now describe a simple method of defining normal derivatives to generate smooth patches.

In Figure 7.15, C_1, C_2, C_3 and C_4 are boundary curves connected to node N_{11}. To define smooth normal derivatives along C_1 and C_2, we let the first and second derivatives of the normal derivatives be continuous. To do this, we use the algorithm for generating Bézier curves which pass through given points (see Section 5.2). If three vectors

$$\overrightarrow{P^2_{00}P^2_{01}}, \qquad \overrightarrow{P^3_{00}P^3_{01}} \qquad \text{and} \qquad \overrightarrow{P^3_{30}P^3_{31}}$$

are given, the two normal derivatives which interpolate these vectors are defined as cubic Bézier functions. Control points P^2_{11}, P^2_{21}, P^3_{11} and P^3_{21} are then determined, as are control points P^1_{12}, P^1_{22}, P^1_{12} and P^1_{22}. Next, the above procedure is applied to the normal derivatives along curves C_3 and C_4. As a result, control points P^0_{22}, P^1_{12}, P^2_{21} and P^3_{11} are defined twice, so the average of the coordinates of each point is adopted. Figure 7.17 shows the control points of patches defined using the method described above. Figure 7.18 shows the cross-sections of the patches.

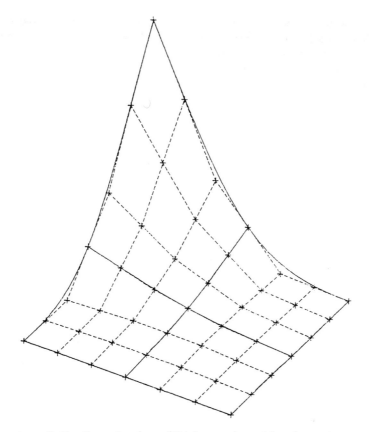

Figure 7.17 Control points of Bézier patches with twist vectors.

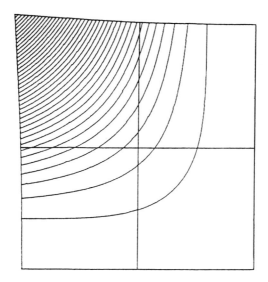

Figure 7.18 Cross-sections of Bézier patches with twist vectors.

From these figures we can see that the patch shape is very smooth. This method does not always give good results, however, because the method of averaging points is adopted without theoretical reason. However, this example illustrates that the control points are good tools with which to handle patch shapes.

Chapter 8

Surface Interpolation of Irregular Curved Meshes

When a designer designs the characteristics of complex free-form surfaces using curved meshes, he or she wishes to produce and modify curves in the mesh without restriction. For example, the designer will freely add or delete curves, or move the Bézier points of curves to change their shapes. As a result, the mesh becomes topologically irregular and does not satisfy the scale factor constraint described in Section 7.6.1. This chapter describes a method of generating free-form surfaces on the faces of such an irregular mesh, as applied in DESIGNBASE.

8.1   IRREGULAR MESHES

There are four types of irregular meshes.

1.   *Meshes where scale factors are not constant*

Figure 8.1 shows an irregular mesh which is topologically the same as a regular mesh. $C_{1,1}$, $C_{2,1}$, $C_{1,2}$, $C_{2,2}$, $C_{1,3}$ and $C_{2,3}$ are cubic curves, and N_1, N_2 and N_3 are where the curves join. The tangents of curves $C_{1,1}$ and $C_{2,1}$ are continuous, the scale factor of the lengths of the derivative vectors at node N_1 is k_1. Similarly, the scale factors at N_2 and N_3 are k_2

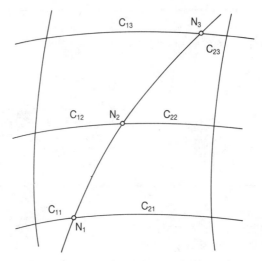

Figure 8.1   An irregular mesh (type 1).

and k_3, respectively. The scale factors k_1, k_2 and k_3 in this mesh are not the same, and the scale factor constraint described in Section 7.6.1 is not satisfied.

2.   *Meshes with three or more than four faces meeting at the same node*

Figures 8.2 shows one example of a mesh where three faces meet at the same node; node N_1 is connected to three curves C_1, C_2 and C_1. Although

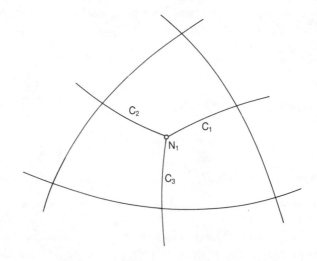

Figure 8.2   An irregular mesh (type 2).

the tangents of the three curves are not continuous at node N_1, they lie on the same plane.

3. Meshes including non-rectangular faces

Figures 8.3(a), (b) and (c) show meshes containing three-sided, five-sided and six-sided non-rectangular faces, respectively. Similar faces are often used to represent the corners of engineering objects.

4. Meshes including T-nodes

Figure 8.4 shows a mesh where node N_1 is connected to three curves C_1, C_2 and C_3. The tangents of curves C_1 and C_2 are continuous. Node N_1 is called a **T-node**. T-nodes often appear in meshes of curves representing the characteristics of free-form surfaces. Figure 8.5 shows one example of a mesh with T-nodes N_i *(i* = 1, . . ., 4). To change the shape of a face in a mesh, a designer adds a new curve on the face, and then changes the shape of the curve. Figure 8.6 shows such a case; nodes N_1 and N_2 are T-nodes.

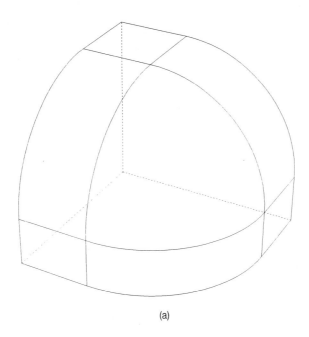

(a)

Figure 8.3   An irregular mesh (type 3).

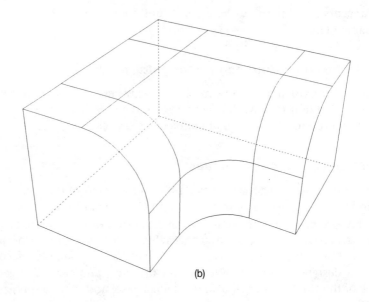

(b)

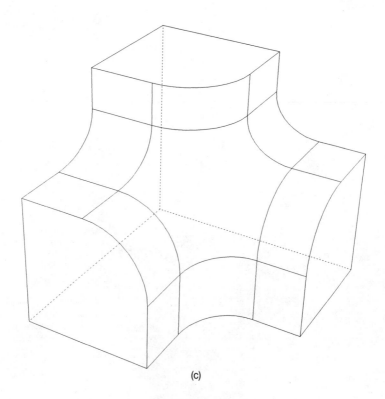

(c)

Figure 8.3   (cont.)

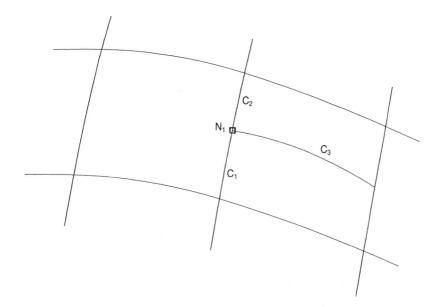

Figure 8.4 An irregular mesh (type 4).

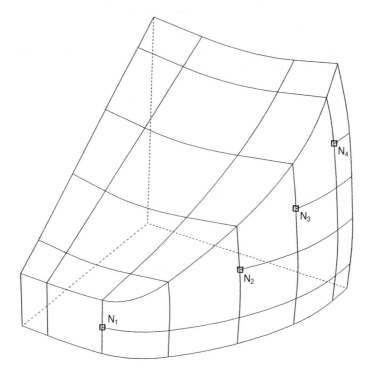

Figure 8.5 A mesh with T-nodes.

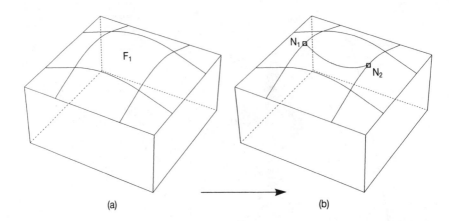

Figure 8.6   A mesh with T-nodes.

This chapter describes the **localized surface interpolation method** which is suitable for the irregular meshes discussed above. When face F_1 of the mesh shown in Figure 8.7 is interpolated, a Gregory patch is generated from the boundary curves attached to the face. In this figure, the referenced edges are marked with *. This localized interpolation method has the following advantages:

1.   The procedure for generating surfaces is simple because only local information is referenced.

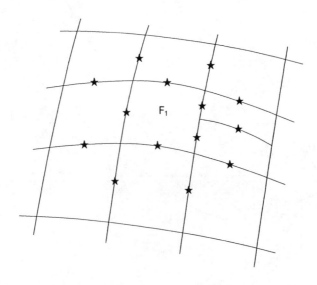

Figure 8.7   An interpolated face in a mesh.

2. Since a designed object's internal representation in the system need
    not include surface equations, because the surface of a face can be
    quickly generated, the internal representation does not use a large
    memory space.

8.2 THE GREGORY PATCH

Gregory (1974) extended the Coons patch so that the normal derivatives
along the boundary of the patch can be independently specified.
Chiyokura and Kimura (1983, 1984) applied the same extension to a
bicubic Bézier patch, and devised a rectangular patch with twenty control
points. This patch is called a **Gregory patch**. In our interpolation method,
Gregory patches are generated on a mesh of arbitrary topology which
represents a free-form surface. As a preparatory step in describing the
interpolation method itself, we explain the properties of Gregory patches
and describe a technique for joining Gregory patches with tangent plane
continuity.

8.2.1 Properties of a Gregory patch

As shown in Figure 8.8, a Gregory patch is defined by a set of twenty control points $P_{i,j,k}$ ($i = 0, \ldots, 3, j = 0, \ldots, 3, k = 0, 1$). Although a bicubic
Bézier patch has four interior control points, each point is split into two
in the expression of a Gregory patch. The formulation of a Gregory patch
is given by

$$S(u, w) = \sum_{i=0}^{3} \sum_{j=0}^{3} B_{3,i}(u) B_{3,j}(w) Q_{ij}(u, w)$$

$$0 \leq u, w \leq 1$$

where

$$B_{n,i}(u) = \binom{n}{i} u^i (1-u)^{n-i}$$

$$Q_{ij}(u, w) = P_{ij0} = P_{ij1} \qquad \text{(except for } Q_{11}, Q_{21}, Q_{12} \text{ and } Q_{22})$$

$$Q_{11}(u, w) = \frac{u P_{110} + w P_{111}}{u + w}$$

$$Q_{21}(u, w) = \frac{(1-u) P_{210} + w P_{211}}{1 - u + w}$$

$$Q_{12}(u, w) = \frac{u P_{120} + (1-w) P_{121}}{u + 1 - w}$$

$$Q_{22}(u, w) = \frac{(1-u)P_{220} + (1-w)P_{221}}{1 - u + 1 - w}$$

Figure 8.9 lists a program for computing the coordinate of a point on a Gregory patch. Any point on a Gregory patch is defined by a sum of sixteen points Q_{ij} ($i = 0, \ldots, 3, j = 0, \ldots, 3$) to which weights are given. While the sixteen control points on a Bézier patch are fixed, the four points Q_{ij} ($i = 1, 2, j = 1, 2$) on a Gregory patch move in a line between two points according to the values of parameters u and w. For example, Q_{11} moves between P_{110} and P_{111}. If $u = 0$, then $Q_{11} = P_{111}$. If $w = 0$, then $Q_{11} = P_{110}$. The Gregory patch has the following properties:

1. Convex hull property

The Gregory patch has a similar convex hull property to that of the Bézier patch, i.e. any point on a patch is always contained in a convex hull defined by twenty control points. This property is useful in making a rough check on interference.

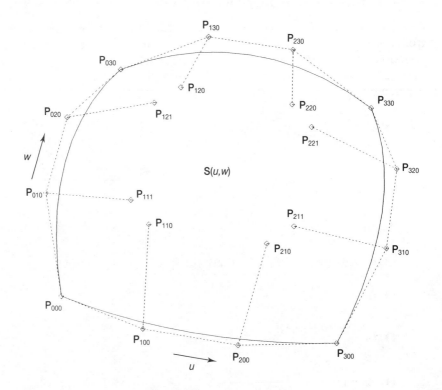

Figure 8.8   A Gregory patch.

Figure 8.9 Programs for calculating a coordinate of a point on a Gregory patch. The subroutines in these programs are those for a Bézier patch, as shown in Figure 7.8. To use the program, the user defines 20 control points of a Gregory patch and the values of two parameters u and w for specifying a point on the patch. The control points are given in an array. The correspondence between the control points and a number indicating each element in the array is as follows:

$P_{0,0,0}$...(1) $P_{1,0,0}$...(2) $P_{2,0,0}$...(3) $P_{3,0,0}$...(4)

$P_{0,1,0}$...(5) $P_{1,1,1}$...(6) $P_{2,1,1}$...(7) $P_{3,1,0}$...(8)

$P_{0,2,0}$...(9) $P_{1,2,1}$...(10) $P_{2,2,1}$...(11) $P_{3,2,0}$...(12)

$P_{0,3,0}$...(13) $P_{1,3,0}$...(14) $P_{2,3,0}$...(15) $P_{3,3,0}$...(16)

$P_{1,1,0}$...(17) $P_{2,1,0}$...(18) $P_{1,2,0}$...(19) $P_{2,2,0}$...(20)

```
C-------------------------------------------------------------
C
C     >> A POINT ON A GREGORY PATCH <<
C
      SUBROUTINE MPTGP(GP, U, W, PT)
      DIMENSION GP(3, 20), PT(3), ZP(3, 16)
C
C     /I/  GP : A GREGORY PATCH
C     /I/  U, W : PARAMETERS
C     /I/  PT : A POINT
C
      DATA ACC/1.0E-5/
C
C     - AT CORNERS -
C
      IF(ABS(U+W).LT.ACC) GOTO 100
      IF(ABS(1.0-U+W).LT.ACC) GOTO 100
      IF(ABS(1.0+U-W).LT.ACC) GOTO 100
      IF(ABS(2.0-U-W).LT.ACC) GOTO 100
      GOTO 110
100   CONTINUE
      CALL MPTZP(GP, U, W, PT)
      RETURN
110   CONTINUE
C
      CALL MPTGP1(GP, ZP, U, W)
      CALL MPTZP(ZP, U, W, PT)
      RETURN
      END
C
C-------------------------------------------------------------
```

Figure 8.9 (cont.)

```
C
C      >> GP TO ZP <<
C
       SUBROUTINE MPTGP1(GP, ZP, U, W)
       DIMENSION GP(3, 20), ZP(3, 16)
C
       DO 200 IZ=1, 16
         DO 210 L=1, 3
           ZP(L, IZ)=GP(L, IZ)
210      CONTINUE
200    CONTINUE
C
       DO 220 L=1, 3
         ZP(L, 6)=(W*GP(L, 6)+U*GP(L, 17))/(U+W)
         ZP(L, 7)=(W*GP(L, 7)+(1.0-U)*GP(L, 18))
      1          /(1.0-U+W)
         ZP(L, 10)=((1.0-W)*GP(L, 10)+U*GP(L, 19))
      1          /(U+1.0-W)
         ZP(L, 11)=((1.0-W)*GP(L, 11)+(1.0-U)*GP(L,20))
      1          /(2.0-U-W)
220    CONTINUE
       RETURN
       END
C
C-------------------------------------------------------------
```

2. Relationship between a Bézier patch and a Gregory patch

When all the eight interior control points of a Gregory patch are placed so that equations $P_{ij0} = P_{ij1}$ ($i = 1, 2, j = 1, 2$) are satisfied, the Gregory patch $S(u, w)$ degenerates to a bicubic Bézier patch, and $S_{uw}(u, w) = S_{wu}(u, w)$ at the four corners of the patch.

3. Independence of normal derivatives

Each normal derivative along the boundary of the patch can be independently specified as a cubic. These derivatives can be defined by control points as follows:

$$S_w(u, 0) = 3\sum_{i=0}^{3} B_{3,i}(u)(P_{i10} - P_{i00})$$

$$S_w(u, 1) = 3\sum_{i=0}^{3} B_{3,i}(u)(P_{i30} - P_{i20})$$

$$\mathbf{S}_u(0, w) = 3 \sum_{i=0}^{3} B_{3,i}(w)(\mathbf{P}_{1i1} - \mathbf{P}_{0i0})$$

$$\mathbf{S}_u(1, w) = 3 \sum_{i=0}^{3} B_{3,i}(w)(\mathbf{P}_{3i0} - \mathbf{P}_{2i1})$$

This property makes our localized interpolation method possible, in which Gregory patches are locally generated to interpolate a face from the edges attached to it.

8.2.2   The first derivative of a Gregory patch

Various applications using surface patches often require a normal vector at a given point on a patch. For example, when a colour-shaded picture is generated, the normal vectors are used to calculate the shade levels of points on the patches. The normal vector on patch $\mathbf{S}(u, w)$ is given by a cross product of the partial derivatives with respect to parameters u and w:

$$\frac{\partial \mathbf{S}(u, w)}{\partial u} \times \frac{\partial \mathbf{S}(u, w)}{\partial w}$$

The first derivative with respect to parameter u is given by

$$\frac{\partial \mathbf{S}(u, w)}{\partial u} = \sum_{i=0}^{3} \sum_{j=0}^{3} \frac{\mathrm{d}B_{3,i}(u)}{\mathrm{d}u} B_{3,j}(w)\mathbf{Q}_{ij}(u, w)$$

$$+ \sum_{i=0}^{3} \sum_{j=0}^{3} B_{3,i}(u)B_{3,j}(w)\frac{\partial \mathbf{Q}_{ij}(u, w)}{\partial u} \qquad (8.1)$$

where

$$\frac{\partial \mathbf{Q}_{ij}(u, w)}{\partial u} = 0 \qquad (\text{except for } \mathbf{Q}_{11}, \mathbf{Q}_{21}, \mathbf{Q}_{12} \text{ and } \mathbf{Q}_{22})$$

$$\frac{\partial \mathbf{Q}_{11}(u, w)}{\partial u} = \frac{w(\mathbf{P}_{110} - \mathbf{P}_{111})}{(u + w)^2}$$

$$\frac{\partial \mathbf{Q}_{21}(u, w)}{\partial u} = \frac{w(\mathbf{P}_{210} - \mathbf{P}_{211})}{(1 - u + w)^2}$$

$$\frac{\partial \mathbf{Q}_{12}(u, w)}{\partial u} = \frac{(1-w)(\mathbf{P}_{120} - \mathbf{P}_{121})}{(u + ! - w)^2}$$

$$\frac{\partial \mathbf{Q}_{22}(u, w)}{\partial u} = \frac{(1-w)(\mathbf{P}_{220} - \mathbf{P}_{221})}{(1 - u + 1 - w)^2}$$

In equation (8.1), the first term is similar to that used to find the first derivative of a Bézier patch. The second term is also similar to that used to calculate a point on a Bézier patch. Thus if programs for calculating both the position and the first derivative of a Bézier patch are given, it is easy to implement a program to find the first derivative of a Gregory patch, as shown in Figure 8.10.

Figure 8.10 Programs for computing the first derivatives of a point on a Gregory patch with respect to parameters u and w.

```
C--------------------------------------------------------------
C
C     >> A FIRST DERIVATIVE OF A POINT ON A GREGORY PATCH
C        WITH RESPECT TO PARAMETER U <<
C
      SUBROUTINE MDUGP(GP, U, W, PT)
      DIMENSION GP(3, 20), PT(3)
C
C     /I/ GP : A GREGORY PATCH
C     /I/ U, W : TWO PARAMETERS
C     /O/ PT : A DERIVATIVE
C
      DIMENSION ZP(3, 16), QT(3)
      DATA ACC/1.0E-5/
C
C     - AT CORNERS -
C
C     IF(ABS(U+W).LT.ACC) GOTO 100
      IF(ABS(1.0-U+W).LT.ACC) GOTO 100
      IF(ABS(U+1.0-W).LT.ACC) GOTO 100
      IF(ABS(2.0-U-W).LT.ACC) GOTO 100
      GOTO 110
100   CONTINUE
      CALL MDUZP(GP, U, W, PT)
      RETURN
110   CONTINUE
C
C     - DERIVATIVE -
C
      CALL MPTGP1(GP, ZP, U, W)
      CALL MDUZP(ZP, U, W, PT)
C
      DO 200 I=1, 16
        DO 210 L=1, 3
          ZP(L, I)=0.0
210     CONTINUE
200   CONTINUE
```

Figure 8.10   (cont.)

```
C
      DO 220 L=1, 3
        ZP(L, 6)=W*(GP(L, 17)-GP(L, 6))/(U+W)**2
        ZP(L, 7)=W*(GP(L, 7)-GP(L, 18))/(1.0-U+W)**2
        ZP(L, 10)=(1.0-W)*(GP(L, 19)-GP(L, 10))/
     1        (U+1.0-W)**2
        ZP(L, 11)=(1.0-W)*(GP(L, 11)-GP(L, 20))/
     1        (2.0-U-W)**2
220   CONTINUE
C
      CALL MPTZP(ZP, U, W, QT)
C
      DO 230 L=1, 3
        PT(L)=PT(L)+QT(L)
230   CONTINUE
      RETURN
      END
C
C------------------------------------------------------------
C
C     >> A FIRST DERIVATIVE OF A POINT ON A GREGORY PATCH
C        WITH RESPECT TO PARAMETER W <<
C
      SUBROUTINE MDWGP(GP, U, W, PT)
      DIMENSION GP(3, 20), PT(3)
C
C     /I/ GP : A GREGORY PATCH
C     /I/ U, W : TWO PARAMETERS
C     /I/ PT : A DERIVATIVE
C
      DIMENSION ZP(3, 16), QT(3)
      DATA ACC/1.0E-5/
C
C     - AT CORNERS -
C
      IF(ABS(U+W).LT.ACC) GOTO 100
      IF(ABS(1.0-U+W).LT.ACC) GOTO 100
      IF(ABS(U+1.0-W).LT.ACC) GOTO 100
      IF(ABS(2.0-U-W).LT.ACC) GOTO 100
      GOTO 110
100   CONTINUE
      CALL MDWZP(GP, U, W, PT)
      RETURN
110   CONTINUE
C
C     - DERIVATIVE -
C
      CALL MPTGP1(GP, ZP, U, W)
```

Figure 8.10 (cont.)

```
      CALL MDWZP(ZP, U, W, PT)
C
      DO 200 I=1, 16
        DO 210 L=1, 3
          ZP(L,I)=0.0
210     CONTINUE
200   CONTINUE
C
      DO 220 L=1, 3
        ZP(L, 6)=U*(GP(L, 6)-GP(L, 17))/(U+W)**2
        ZP(L, 7)=(1.0-U)*(GP(L, 7)-GP(L, 18))/
     1        (1.0-U+W)**2
        ZP(L, 10)=U*(GP(L, 19)-GP(L, 10))/
     1        (U+1.0-W)**2
        ZP(L, 11)=(1.0-U)*(GP(L, 20)-GP(L, 11))/
     1        (2.0-U-W)**2
220   CONTINUE
C
      CALL MPTZP(ZP, U, W, QT)
C
      DO 230 L=1, 3
        PT(L)=PT(L)+QT(L)
230   CONTINUE
      RETURN
      END
C
C------------------------------------------------------------
```

Consider the second term of equation (8.1). If we assume that the second term represents a bicubic Bézier patch, the coordinate of the boundary of the Bézier patch always becomes zero, since the values of the twelve control points which define the boundary of the patch are all zero. Thus when a point on the boundary of a Gregory patch is specified by parameters u and w, the second term of equation (8.1) is zero. This means that the normal derivative on the boundary is defined only by the first term of equation (8.1). We can then see how the four normal derivatives given as arbitrary cubic polynomials can be interpolated by a Gregory patch.

The derivative with respect to parameter w is given by

$$\frac{\partial S(u, w)}{\partial w} = \sum_{i=0}^{3} \sum_{j=0}^{3} B_{3,i}(u) \frac{d B_{3,j}(w)}{dw} Q_{ij}(u, w)$$

$$+ \sum_{i=0}^{3} \sum_{j=0}^{3} B_{3,i}(u) B_{3,j}(w) \frac{\partial Q_{ij}(u, w)}{\partial w}$$

where

$$\frac{\partial Q_{ij}(u, w)}{\partial w} = 0 \qquad (\text{except for } Q_{11}, Q_{21}, Q_{12} \text{ and } Q_{22})$$

$$\frac{\partial Q_{11}(u, w)}{\partial w} = \frac{u(P_{110} - P_{111})}{(u + w)^2}$$

$$\frac{\partial Q_{21}(u, w)}{\partial w} = \frac{(1-u)(P_{210} - P_{211})}{(1 - u + w)^2}$$

$$\frac{\partial Q_{12}(u, w)}{\partial w} = \frac{u(P_{120} - P_{121})}{(u + 1 - w)^2}$$

$$\frac{\partial Q_{22}(u, w)}{\partial w} = \frac{(1-u)(P_{220} - P_{221})}{(1 - u + 1 - w)^2}$$

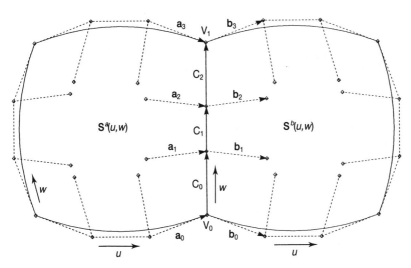

Figure 8.11   Joining Gregory patches.

8.2.3   Joining Gregory patches

This section describes how two Gregory patches are joined with their tangent planes continuous on the common boundary. Figure 8.11 shows the two Gregory patches $S^a(u, w)$ and $S^b(u, w)$ to be joined. The vectors between the control points, $\mathbf{a}_i$ $(i = 0, \ldots, 3)$, $\mathbf{b}_i$ $(i = 0, \ldots, 3)$ and $\mathbf{c}_i$ $(i = 0, \ldots, 2)$ are given by

$$\mathbf{a}_i = \mathbf{P}^a_{3,i,1} - \mathbf{P}^a_{2,i,0}$$
$$\mathbf{b}_i = \mathbf{P}^b_{1,i,1} - \mathbf{P}^b_{0,i,0}$$
$$\mathbf{c}_i = \mathbf{P}^a_{3,i+1,0} - \mathbf{P}^a_{3,i,0} = \mathbf{P}^b_{0,i+1,0} - \mathbf{P}^b_{0,i,0}$$

where $\mathbf{P}^a_{i,j,k}$ and $\mathbf{P}^b_{i,j,k}$ are the control points of patches $S^a(u, w)$ and $S^b(u, w)$, respectively. Using vectors $\mathbf{a}_i$, $\mathbf{b}_i$ and $\mathbf{c}_i$, the first derivatives of the patches on the common boundary are expressed as

$$S^a_u(1, w) = 3 \sum_{i=0}^{3} B_{3,i}(w)\mathbf{a}_i$$

$$S^b_u(0, w) = 3 \sum_{i=0}^{3} B_{3,i}(w)\mathbf{b}_i$$

$$S^a_w(1, w) = S^b_w(0, w) = 3 \sum_{i=0}^{2} B_{2,i}(w)\mathbf{c}_i$$

where

$$B_{n,i}(w) = \binom{n}{i} w^i (1-w)^{n-i}$$

To achieve tangent plane continuity, three derivatives $S^a_u(1, w)$, $S^a_w(1, w)$ and $S^b_u(0, w)$ of any point on the boundary curve have to lie on the same plane. This is expressed as

$$S^b_u(0, w) = k(w)S^a_u(1, w) + h(w)S^a_w(1, w) \qquad (8.2)$$

where $k(w)$ and $h(w)$ are scalar functions. Similarly, the given vectors $\mathbf{a}_0$, $\mathbf{b}_0$ and $\mathbf{c}_0$ connected to patch corner V_0 have to lie on the same plane, and vectors $\mathbf{a}_3$, $\mathbf{b}_3$ and $\mathbf{c}_2$ connected to corner V_1 also lie on the same plane. The relationship between these vectors is

$$\mathbf{b}_0 = k_0 \mathbf{a}_0 + h_0 \mathbf{c}_0 \qquad (8.3)$$
$$\mathbf{b}_3 = k_1 \mathbf{a}_3 + h_1 \mathbf{c}_2$$

where k_0, k_1, h_0 and h_1 are scalar constants, and their values are easily calculated. For simplicity, we assume that $k(w)$ and $h(w)$ are linear functions satisfying equations (8.3):

$$k(w) = (1-w)k_0 + wk_1$$
$$h(w) = (1-w)h_0 + wh_1$$

If these equations are substituted in equation (8.2), the left side of equation (8.2) is cubic, while the order of the right side is four. So that both sides of equation (8.2) are cubic, we have to specify the normal derivative $S^a_u(1, w)$ as a quadratic. Since the quadratic Bézier expression is defined by vectors a_0, q and a_3, the following restriction is applied to vectors a_1 and a_2:

$$a_1 = \frac{(a_0 + 2q)}{3} \tag{8.4}$$

$$a_2 = \frac{(2q + a_3)}{3}$$

(The relationship between the control points of a cubic curve and those of a quadratic curve is described in Section 5.2.) From the above equations, the relationship between a_i, b_i and c_i is given by

$$b_1 = \frac{(k_1-k_0)a_0}{3} + k_0a_1 + \frac{2h_0c_1}{3} + \frac{h_1c_0}{3} \tag{8.5}$$

$$b_2 = k_1a_2 - \frac{(k_1-k_0)a_3}{3} + \frac{h_0c_2}{3} + \frac{2h_1c_0}{3}$$

Proof Using equation (5.1), the derivatives of patch $S^a(u, w)$ and $S^b(u, w)$ on the common boundary are expressed as

$$S^a_u(1, w) = 3\{a_0, a_1, a_2, a_3\} \tag{8.6}$$
$$S^b_u(0, w) = 3\{b_0, b_1, b_2, b_3\}$$
$$S^a_w(1, w) = S^b_w(0, w) = 3\{c_0, c_1, c_2\}$$

To achieve tangent plane continuity, $S^a_u(1, w)$ is specified as a quadratic polynomial, and is rewritten as

$$S^a_u(1, w) = 3\{a_0, q, a_3\} \tag{8.7}$$

where

$$q = \frac{3a_1 - a_0}{2} = \frac{3a_2 - a_3}{2} \tag{8.8}$$

Substituting equations (8.6) and (8.7) in equation (8.2), we obtain

$$\{\mathbf{b}_0, \mathbf{b}_1, \mathbf{b}_2, \mathbf{b}_3\} = ((1-w)k_0 + wk_1)\{\mathbf{a}_0, \mathbf{q}, \mathbf{a}_3\}$$
$$+ ((1-w)h_0 + wh_1)\{\mathbf{c}_0, \mathbf{c}_1, \mathbf{c}_2\}$$

Using equations (5.2) and (5.3), in this equation w is replaced as follows:

$$\{\mathbf{b}_0, \mathbf{b}_1, \mathbf{b}_2, \mathbf{b}_3\} = k_0\left\{\mathbf{a}_0, \frac{2\mathbf{q}}{3}, \frac{\mathbf{a}_3}{3}, 0\right\} + k_1\left\{0, \frac{\mathbf{a}_0}{3}, \frac{2\mathbf{q}}{3}, \mathbf{a}_3\right\}$$

$$= h_0\left\{\mathbf{c}_0, \frac{2\mathbf{c}_1}{3}, \frac{\mathbf{c}_2}{3}, 0\right\} + h_1\left\{0, \frac{\mathbf{c}_0}{3}, \frac{2\mathbf{c}_1}{3}, \mathbf{c}_2\right\}$$

Then

$$\{\mathbf{b}_0, \mathbf{b}_1, \mathbf{b}_2, \mathbf{b}_3\} = \{k_0\mathbf{a}_0 + h_0\mathbf{c}_0,$$
$$\tfrac{1}{3} \times (2k_0\mathbf{q} + k_1\mathbf{a}_0 + 2h_0\mathbf{c}_1 + h_1\mathbf{c}_0),$$
$$\tfrac{1}{3} \times (k_0\mathbf{a}_3 + 2k_1\mathbf{q} + h_0\mathbf{c}_2 + 2h_1\mathbf{c}_1),$$
$$k_1\mathbf{a}_3 + h_1\mathbf{c}_2\}$$

Consequently, $\mathbf{b}_1$ and $\mathbf{b}_2$ are given by

$$\mathbf{b}_1 = \tfrac{1}{3} \times (2k_0\mathbf{q} + k_1\mathbf{a}_0 + 2h_0\mathbf{c}_1 + h_1\mathbf{c}_0)$$
$$\mathbf{b}_2 = \tfrac{1}{3} \times (k_0\mathbf{a}_3 + 2k_1\mathbf{q} + h_0\mathbf{c}_2 + 2h_1\mathbf{c}_1)$$

Using equation (8.3) in the above equation, $\mathbf{q}$ is replaced and we have equation (8.5). ■

If we specify the normal derivative of one of two joined paths as a quadratic, and the derivative of the other patch is determined using equation (8.5), the tangent planes of the patches become continuous. However, there are two problems with this method.

1. Since the relationship between the normal derivative and the patch shape is not obvious, it is not easy for the designer to specify the derivative.

2. While the derivative of one patch is cubic, that of the other patch is quadratic, and so generated surfaces are always asymmetric.

These problems can be solved by using the **cross-boundary tangent**, as described in the next section.

8.3   THE PROCESS OF GENERATING GREGORY PATCHES

This section gives an overview of the patch generation process in our interpolation method. Although the tangent planes of Gregory patches generated on adjacent faces are continuous, the patches are generated separately. The process consists of three stages.

1.   Defining the cross-boundary tangent

To define the tangent planes on the boundary of the face being interpolated, we first specify the **cross-boundary tangents**. The normal vectors on the tangent planes are given by the cross products of the tangents of the boundary and the cross-boundary tangents. Figure 8.12 shows a face F to be interpolated and the cross-boundary tangents $g_i(t)$ $(0 \leq t \leq 1)$ $(i = 1, \dots, 4)$ along edges E_i $(i = 1, \dots, 5)$ of the face. Across edge E_1, the two cross-boundary tangents $g_1(t)$ and $g'_1(t)$ are defined to interpolate two faces F and F′ which meet at E_1. If the tangent planes of faces F and F′ on the boundary are to be continuous, two cross-boundary tangents along edge E_1 are determined such that $g_1(t) = -g'_1(t)$. Otherwise, the two tangents are independently defined. In this figure, the two edges E_3 and E_4 attached to face F meet at T-node vertex V_1, and can be represented as a single cubic Bézier curve, in which case, a single cross-boundary tangent $g_3(t)$ is defined along edges E_3 and E_4.

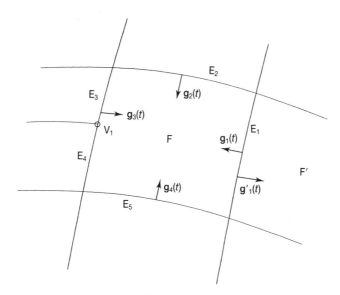

Figure 8.12   Cross-boundary tangents.

2. Determining control points

The cross-boundary tangent $\mathbf{g}(t)$ is given by a quadratic Bézier function defined by three vectors $\mathbf{a}_i$ $(i = 0, 1, 2)$:

$$\mathbf{g}(t) = \sum_{i=0}^{2} \binom{2}{i} t^i (1 - t)^{2-i} \mathbf{a}_i \tag{8.9}$$

Once the three vectors are given, the control points defining the normal derivatives along the boundary of a patch are determined using equations (8.4) and (8.5). The normal derivatives are cubic. If a face is rectangular,

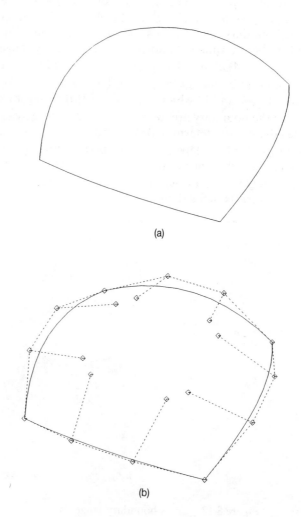

(a)

(b)

Figure 8.13 A rectangular face.

the given control points define it as a Gregory patch, as shown in Figure 8.13. Figure 8.13(a) shows the boundary of a rectangular face, and Figure 8.13(b) shows the control points of a generated Gregory patch.

3.   *Subdividing a non-rectangular face*

When a three- or five-sided face is interpolated, three or five Gregory patches are generated, respectively, as shown in Figures 8.14 and 8.15. For this procedure, control points are given which define the boundary curves and normal derivatives, as shown in Figures 8.14(b) and 8.15(b).

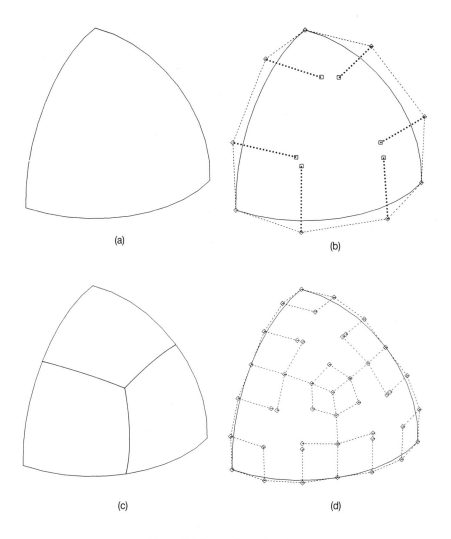

(a)

(b)

(c)

(d)

Figure 8.14   A triangular face.

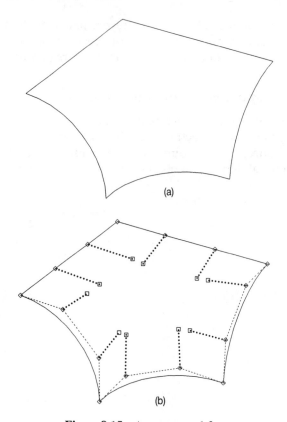

(a)

(b)

Figure 8.15   A pentagonal face.

Internal curves are then automatically generated on the non-four-sided face, and the face is subdivided into rectangular faces, as shown in Figures 8.14(c) and 8.15(c). Lastly, a Gregory patch is generated on each face, as shown in Figures 8.14(d) and 8.15(d). In DESIGNBASE, all faces are interpolated using just the rectangular Gregory patch method.

Alternative methods for interpolating non-rectangular faces use either triangular patches (Barnhill, 1977; Farin, 1986; Longhi, 1985; Shirman, 1986) or pentagonal patches (Sabin, 1983, 1986; Hosaka and Kimura, 1984; Charrot and Gregory, 1984). In all these methods, single patches interpolate non-rectangular faces. Because the mathematical structures of both triangular and pentagonal patches differ from rectangular patches, a specific procedure is required for manipulating each patch. Procedures for displaying the patches and for calculating both cross-sections of the patches and flat planes have to be implemented individually, which increases the implementer's job and enlarges the module size of the system. Therefore in DESIGNBASE, free-form surfaces are represented solely by Gregory patches.

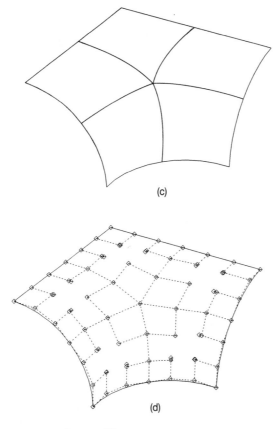

(c)

(d)

Figure 8.15   (cont.)

8.4   DEFINING A CROSS-BOUNDARY TANGENT

We now describe in detail how to define the cross-boundary tangent along the curved boundary of a face which is to be interpolated. If the boundary curve is not connected to any T-nodes, the cross-boundary tangent is given by a linear function. If the curve is connected to one or more T-nodes, the tangent is quadratic. The procedure for each case is given below.

8.4.1   The ordinary case

Figure 8.16 shows edge E_0 at which two faces F_1 and F_2 meet. In this section, we will describe how to define a cross-boundary tangent along edge E_0, which runs between two vertices V_1 and V_2. Z_1 and Z_2 are the control points of a Bézier curve which represents edge E_0. Edges E_1, E_2, E_3 and

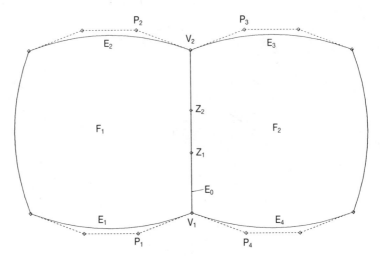

Figure 8.16 Boundary curves.

E_4 are winged-edges of edge E_0. P_1, P_2, P_3 and P_4 are the Bézier control points of edges E_1, E_2, E_3 and E_4, respectively. The process of defining the cross-boundary tangent consists of three steps.

1. Calculating normal vectors

The boundary curves of a mesh implicitly indicate whether or not the tangent planes of surfaces on two faces which meet a common edge are continuous. Our system therefore first checks the continuity of the tangent planes of the two faces. Surface patches are then generated which interpolate the faces from curves of the mesh. In Figure 8.17, the tangent planes of the surfaces on two faces F_1 and F_2 become continuous. On the other hand, the surfaces on faces F_3 and F_4 are independently generated.

To check the continuity of faces F_1 and F_2, in Figure 8.16, the normal vectors $\mathbf{n}_{1,1}$ and $\mathbf{n}_{1,2}$ at corners V_1 and V_2 of face F_1 are calculated using vector cross products:

$$\mathbf{n}_{1,1} = \frac{(\mathbf{V}_1 - \mathbf{P}_1) \times (\mathbf{Z}_1 - \mathbf{V}_1)}{|(\mathbf{V}_1 - \mathbf{P}_1) \times (\mathbf{Z}_1 - \mathbf{V}_1)|}$$

$$\mathbf{n}_{1,2} = \frac{(\mathbf{V}_2 - \mathbf{Z}_2) \times (\mathbf{P}_2 - \mathbf{V}_2)}{|(\mathbf{V}_2 - \mathbf{Z}_2) \times (\mathbf{P}_2 - \mathbf{V}_2)|}$$

$\mathbf{V}_1$, $\mathbf{V}_2$, $\mathbf{P}_1$, $\mathbf{P}_2$, $\mathbf{Z}_1$ and $\mathbf{Z}_2$ are the positions of V_1, V_2, P_1, P_2, Z_1 and Z_2. The normal vectors $\mathbf{n}_{2,1}$ and $\mathbf{n}_{2,2}$ at corners V_1 and V_2 of face F_2 are also calculated:

$$\mathbf{n}_{2,1} = \frac{(\mathbf{V}_1 - \mathbf{Z}_1) \times (\mathbf{P}_4 - \mathbf{V}_1)}{|(\mathbf{V}_1 - \mathbf{Z}_1) \times (\mathbf{P}_4 - \mathbf{V}_1)|}$$

$$\mathbf{n}_{2,2} = \frac{(\mathbf{Z}_2 - \mathbf{V}_2) \times (\mathbf{V}_2 - \mathbf{P}_3)}{|(\mathbf{Z}_2 - \mathbf{V}_2) \times (\mathbf{V}_2 - \mathbf{P}_3)|}$$

$\mathbf{P}_3$ and $\mathbf{P}_4$ are the positions of P_3 and P_4. Vector $\mathbf{n}_{1,1}$ at vertex V_1 is then compared with $\mathbf{n}_{2,1}$. If the vector values are the same, the tangent planes of F_1 and F_2 should be continuous around vertex V_1. Otherwise, the surfaces are independently generated. Vector $\mathbf{n}_{2,1}$ is similarly compared with $\mathbf{n}_{2,2}$ to check the continuity around V_2.

2.   Determining vectors $\mathbf{a}_0$ and $\mathbf{a}_2$

The cross-boundary tangent on edge E_0 is expressed as a quadratic Bézier function defined by three vectors $\mathbf{a}_0$, $\mathbf{a}_1$ and $\mathbf{a}_2$. This section describes how to determine vectors $\mathbf{a}_0$ and $\mathbf{a}_2$ at vertices V_1 and V_2. Although the directions of the tangent vectors have geometric meaning here, their

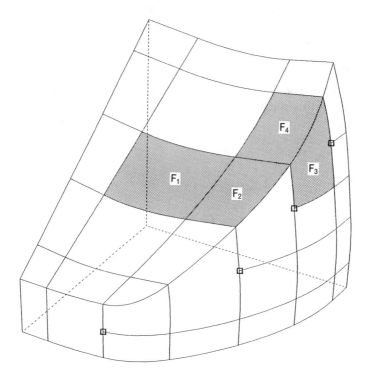

Figure 8.17   A mesh model.

magnitudes have none, so we let vectors $\mathbf{a}_0$ and $\mathbf{a}_2$ be unit vectors. To generate a smooth surface on face F_1 alone, $\mathbf{a}_0$ and $\mathbf{a}_2$ should be parallel to vectors $\overrightarrow{P_1V_1}$ and $\overrightarrow{P_2V_2}$, respectively. If it is not necessary to connect two faces F_1 and F_2 smoothly, $\mathbf{a}_0$ and $\mathbf{a}_2$ are therefore defined as follows:

$$\text{if} \quad \mathbf{n}_{1,1} \neq \mathbf{n}_{1,2} \quad \text{then} \quad \mathbf{a}_0 = \frac{(P_1 - V_1)}{|P_1 - V_1|} \tag{8.10}$$

$$\text{if} \quad \mathbf{n}_{2,1} \neq \mathbf{n}_{2,2} \quad \text{then} \quad \mathbf{a}_2 = \frac{(P_2 - V_2)}{|P_2 - V_2|}$$

On the other hand, when faces F_1 and F_2 are smoothly connected, we give vector $\mathbf{a}_0$ the average value of vectors $\overrightarrow{V_1P_1}$ and $\overrightarrow{P_4V_1}$. Vector $\mathbf{a}_2$ is similarly defined. Vectors $\mathbf{a}_0$ and $\mathbf{a}_2$ are expressed as

$$\text{if} \quad \mathbf{n}_{1,1} = \mathbf{n}_{1,2} \quad \text{then} \quad \mathbf{a}_0 = \frac{(P_1 - P_4)}{|P_1 - P_4|} \tag{8.11}$$

$$\text{if} \quad \mathbf{n}_{2,1} = \mathbf{n}_{2,2} \quad \text{then} \quad \mathbf{a}_2 = \frac{(P_2 - P_3)}{|P_2 - P_3|}$$

3. Determining vector $\mathbf{a}_2$

To generate a smooth surface, the cross-boundary tangent should be smooth. For simplicity, let the tangent be linear. Vector $\mathbf{a}_1$ can then be expressed as

$$\mathbf{a}_1 = \frac{(\mathbf{a}_0 + \mathbf{a}_2)}{2} \tag{8.12}$$

8.4.2 On faces connected to T-nodes

In Figure 8.18, face F_1 is to be interpolated. It is attached to the T-node vertex V_3 and vertices V_1 and V_2. Vertex V_3 is connected to three edges E_1, E_2 and E_3. Edges E_1 and E_2 are joined with tangent continuity, and can be represented by a single cubic Bézier curve. Z_1, Z_2 and Z_3 are the Bézier control points of edges E_1, E_2 and E_3, respectively. P_1, P_2, P_3 and P_4 are also Bézier control points of the edges attached to face F_1. The cross-boundary tangent $\mathbf{g}(t)$ is given to determine the normal derivative of F_1 along edges E_1 and E_2. Since $\mathbf{g}(t)$ is expressed as a quadratic Bézier function defined by three vectors $\mathbf{a}_0$, $\mathbf{a}_1$ and $\mathbf{a}_2$, we now describe a method for obtaining these three vectors.

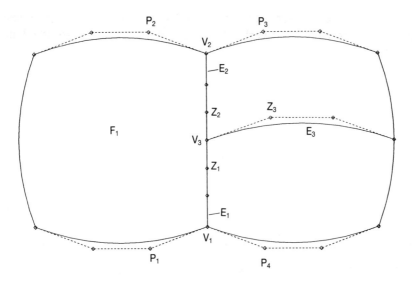

Figure 8.18 Boundary curves with T-nodes.

1. Calculating normal vectors

Normal vectors $\mathbf{n}_{1,1}$ and $\mathbf{n}_{1,2}$ of vertex V_1, and vectors $\mathbf{n}_{2,1}$ and $\mathbf{n}_{2,2}$ of vertex V_2 are computed using the method described in Section 8.4.1, part 1.

2. Determining vectors $\mathbf{a}_0$ and $\mathbf{a}_2$

Tangents $\mathbf{a}_0$ and $\mathbf{a}_2$ are determined using equations (8.10) and (8.11).

3. Determining vector $\mathbf{a}_1$

If $\mathbf{n}_{1,1} \neq \mathbf{n}_{1,2}$ and $\mathbf{n}_{2,1} \neq \mathbf{n}_{2,2}$ it is not necessary to consider whether or not the surfaces are smoothly joined. Vector $\mathbf{a}_1$ is therefore determined using equation (8.12). If $\mathbf{n}_{1,1} = \mathbf{n}_{1,2}$ or $\mathbf{n}_{2,1} = \mathbf{n}_{2,2}$ we define the cross-boundary tangent as a quadratic so that the surface are smoothly joined. A method for defining vector $\mathbf{a}_1$ is described below.

 In a single cubic Bézier curve representing edges E_1 and E_2, let the parameter values at vertices V_1 and V_2 be 0 and 1, respectively. Parameter value t_3 then corresponds to the position of vertex V_3 and is given by

$$t_3 = \frac{|V_3 - Z_1|}{|Z_2 - Z_1|}$$

Next, we let the cross-boundary tangent $\mathbf{g}(t_3)$ at vertex V_3 be the same as the tangent to edge E_3 at vertex V_3. Tangent $\mathbf{g}(t_3)$ is then expressed as

$$\mathbf{g}(t_3) = \frac{(V_3 - Z_3)}{|V_3 - Z_3|}$$

Substituting this equation in equation (8.9), $\mathbf{a}_1$ is given by

$$\mathbf{a}_1 = \frac{\mathbf{g}(t_3) - B_0(t_3)\mathbf{a}_0 + B_2(t_3)\mathbf{a}_2}{B_1(t_3)}$$

Vectors $\mathbf{a}_0$, $\mathbf{a}_1$ and $\mathbf{a}_2$ define the cross-boundary tangent.

8.4.3 Examples of Gregory patches on rectangular faces

We will now look at some examples of Gregory patches generated on rectangular faces. In Figure 8.19, face F_1 is attached to two T-node vertices V_1 and V_2. Figure 8.20 shows the cross-sections of the free-form surfaces generated in the same model. Further, Figures 8.21 and 8.22 show the cross-sections of the free-form surfaces in the models depicted in Figures 8.5 and 8.6, respectively.

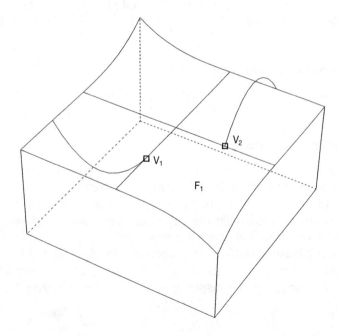

Figure 8.19   A mesh model with T-nodes.

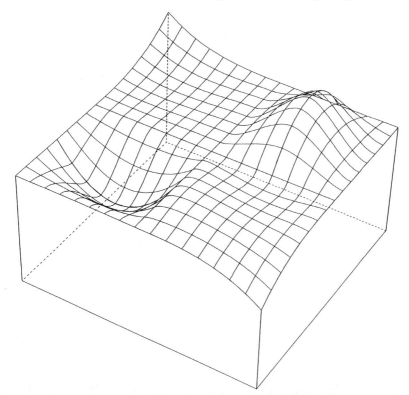

Figure 8.20   Gregory patches.

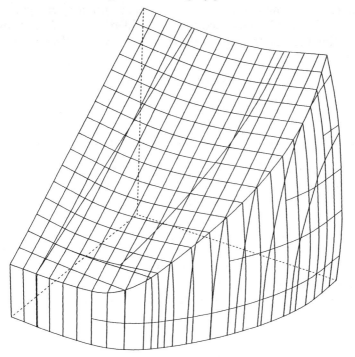

Figure 8.21   Gregory patches.

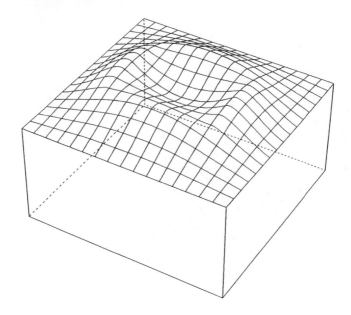

Figure 8.22   Gregory patches.

8.5   INTERPOLATING NON-RECTANGULAR FACES

Our interpolation method fits Gregory patches into non-retangular faces such as three-sided, five-sided and six-sided faces. Details of the interpolation method for each of these types of face are described below.

8.5.1   Interpolating a three-sided face

Three-sided faces are interpolated in three stages.

1.   *Subdividing the boundary curves and normal derivatives*

The face boundaries are given by three cubic Bézier curves and the normal derivatives along the boundaries are also given. Control points R_i ($i = 0, \ldots, 14$) are shown in Figure 8.23, where R_i ($i = 0, \ldots, 8$) are the control points of the Bézier curves, and points R_i ($i = 9, \ldots, 14$) represent the normal derivatives. First, each curve is subdivided into two curves at a point corresponding to parameter value 0.5. Similarly, the normal derivatives are subdivided, and the lengths of the control vectors are halved. Figure 8.24 shows the control points which represent the subdivided curves and normal derivatives. P_1, P_2 and P_3 are the subdivision points.

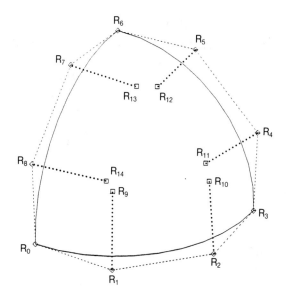

Figure 8.23   A three-sided face.

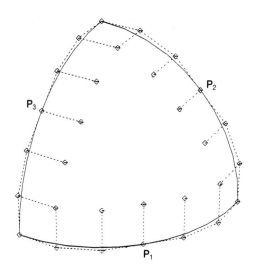

Figure 8.24   Subdivided boundary curves and their normal derivatives.

2.   Generating internal curves

In the second stage, internal curves are generated to subdivide the face into three rectangular faces. Figure 8.25 shows three internal curves C_1, C_2 and C_3 which are to be generated; they are expressed as cubic Bézier curves. P_0 is the point at which the curves meet. $P_{1,1}$, $P_{1,2}$, $P_{2,1}$, $P_{2,2}$, $P_{3,1}$ and $P_{3,2}$ are the control points of the Bézier curves. Of these points, $P_{1,1}$, $P_{2,1}$ and $P_{3,1}$ have already been defined. To specify the internal curves, we therefore have to determine the positions of P_0, $P_{1,2}$ $P_{2,2}$ and $P_{3,2}$.

Many methods can be considered for generating these internal curves. We therefore apply the restriction that limits the internal curves to quadratics. Thus the control points of the quadratic Bézier curves which represent the internal curves are given by

$$Q_i = \frac{3P_{i,1} - P_i}{2} \quad (i = 1, 2, 3)$$

Next, we determine the position of point P_0, as follows:

$$P_0 = \frac{Q_1 + Q_2 + Q_3}{3} \tag{8.13}$$

The reason for using the above equation is described in the next section. From points P_0, Q_1, Q_2 and Q_3, the control points $P_{1,2}$, $P_{2,2}$ and $P_{3,2}$ of the internal curves are given by

$$P_{i,2} = \frac{2Q_i + P_0}{3} \quad (i = 1, 2, 3)$$

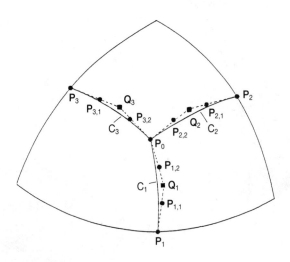

Figure 8.25   Internal curves in a three-sided face.

3. *Generating a Gregory patch*

A Gregory patch is now generated on each rectangular face so that the tangent planes of the generated patches are continuous on the internal curves. Figure 8.26 shows three patches $S^i(u, w)$ $(i = 1, 2, 3)$ which are to be joined. The origin of the uw-parameter coordinates of each patch lies on the corner of the triangular face. $\mathbf{a}_i$, $\mathbf{b}_i$ $(i = 0, \ldots, 3)$ and $\mathbf{c}_i$ $(i = 0, \ldots, 2)$ are the vectors between the control points of patches S^1 and S^2 which meet on curve C_1. These vectors are define as

$$\mathbf{a}_i = \mathbf{P}^1_{3,i,0} - \mathbf{P}^1_{2,i,1}$$

$$\mathbf{b}_i = \mathbf{P}^2_{i,2,0} - \mathbf{P}^2_{i,3,0}$$

$$\mathbf{c}_i = \mathbf{P}^1_{3,i+1,0} - \mathbf{P}^1_{3,i,0}$$

where $\mathbf{P}^1_{i,j,k}$ and $\mathbf{P}^2_{i,j,k}$ are the control points of patches S^1 and S^2, respectively. These vectors define the normal derivatives of patches S^1 and S^2 along curve C_1. The vectors connected to points $\mathbf{P}_0$ and $\mathbf{P}_1$ have the followng relationship:

$$\mathbf{b}_0 = k_0 \mathbf{a}_0$$

$$\mathbf{b}_3 = k_1 \mathbf{a}_3 + h_1 \mathbf{c}_2$$

Here, $k_0 = 1$ since the parameter value corresponding to point $\mathbf{P}_0$ on the original curve is 0.5. Also, $k_1 = 1$ and $h_1 = 1$ since the position of point

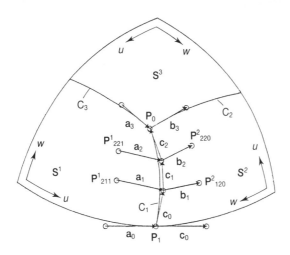

Figure 8.26   Vectors between control points.

$\mathbf{P}_0$ is defined by equation (8.13). If $k_0 \neq k_1$, the degree of the normal derivative of patch $\mathbf{S}^1$ is different from that of $\mathbf{S}^2$ (see Section 8.2.3), so it is desirable that $k_0 = k_1$. This is the reason for using equation (8.13). To achieve tangent plane continuity, equation (8.5) is imposed on the vectors, and the relationship of the vectors is given by

$$\mathbf{b}_1 = \mathbf{a}_1 + \frac{\mathbf{c}_0}{3} \tag{8.14}$$

$$\mathbf{b}_2 = \mathbf{a}_2 + \frac{2\mathbf{c}_1}{3} \tag{8.15}$$

The procedure described above is applied to the vectors connected to the internal curves C_2 and C_3, and the equations for tangent plane continuity on curves C_2 and C_3 are determined.

Furthermore, in order for the shapes of the patches to be smoother, we apply the following restriction to the control points of all the patches:

$$\mathbf{P}^i_{2,2,0} = \mathbf{P}^i_{2,2,1} \qquad (i = 1, 2, 3) \tag{8.16}$$

Control points $\mathbf{P}^i_{2,2,j}$ ($i = 1, 2, 3, j = 0, 1$) are determined using equation (8.15), for all the internal curves, and equation (8.16), for all the patches. Lastly, equation (8.14) is used for all the internal curves, to determine points $\mathbf{P}^i_{2,1,1}$ and $\mathbf{P}^i_{1,2,0}$ ($i = 1, 2, 3$) for all the patches. The program for generating Gregory patches on a three-sided face is listed in Figure 8.27. Figure 8.28(a) shows the control points of Gregory patches generated on a curved mesh which includes a three-sided face. Figure 8.28(b) shows the cross-sections of the patches.

Figure 8.27 The programs for generating Gregory patches to interpolate a triangular face.

```
C----------------------------------------------------------------
C
C      >> GENERATION OF GREGORY PATCHES
C          ON A TRIANGULAR FACE <<
C
       SUBROUTINE MTRGP(ZE, ZG)
       DIMENSION ZE(3, 14), GA(3, 20, 3)
C
C      /I/ ZE : A TRIANGULAR PATCH
C      /O/ ZG : THREE GREGORY PATCHES
C
       DIMENSION T1(3)
```

Figure 8.27   (cont.)

```
C
C        - EDGE -
C
         CALL MTRGP1(3, ZE, ZG)
C
C        - TANGENT -
C
         CALL MTRGP2(3, ZE, ZG)
C
C        - THE CENTER AND INSIDE CURVES -
C
         CALL MTRGP3(3, ZG)
C
C        - CONTINUITY BETWEEN INSIDE PATCHES -
C
         DO 500 I=1, 3
           IG2=I+1
           IF(IG2.EQ.4) IG2=1
           DO 510 L=1, 3
             ZG(L, 20, I)=(4.0*ZG(L, 12, I)-ZG(L, 11, I)
        1      -4.0*ZG(L, 12, IG2)+ZG(L, 11, IG2)
        2         +4.0*ZG(L, 2, I)-ZG(L, 3, I))/3.0
             ZG(L, 13, I)=ZG(L, 20, I)
510      CONTINUE
C
         DO 520 L=1, 3
             T1(L)=ZG(L, 11, I)-ZG(L, 10, I))/6.0
520      CONTINUE
C
           DO 530 L=1, 3
             ZG(L, 19, I)=ZG(L, 18, I)+T1(L)
             ZG(L, 14, IG2)=ZG(L, 15, IG2)+T1(L)
530      CONTINUE
500      CONTINUE
C
         RETURN
         END
C
C-------------------------------------------------------------------
C
C        >> MID POINT AND INSIDE CURVES <<
C
         SUBROUTINE MTRGP3(N, ZG)
         DIMENSION ZG(3, 20, 3)
C
C        /O/ ZG : THREE GREGORY PATCHES (LOOP)
C
```

Figure 8.27   (cont.)

```
C      - THE CENTER -
C
       DO 300 I=1, N
         DO 310 L=1, 3
           ZG(L, 12, I)=(ZG(L, 11, I)*3-ZG(L, 10, I))/2.0
310      CONTINUE
300    CONTINUE
C
       DO 320 L=1, 3
         ZG(L, 1, 1)=ZG(L, 12, 1)
         DO 325 I=2, N
           ZG(L, 1, 1)=ZG(L, 1, 1)/+ZG(L, 12, I)
325      CONTINUE
         ZG(L, 1, 1)=ZG(L, 1, 1)/FLOAT(N)
C
         DO 327 I=2, N
           ZG(L, 1, I)=ZG(L, 1, 1)
327      CONTINUE
320    CONTINUE
C
C      - CONTROL POINTS -
C
       DO 350 I=1, N
         IG2=I+1
         IF(IG2.GT.N) IG2=1
         DO 360 L=1, 3
           ZG(L, 12, I)=(2.0*ZG(L, 12, I)+ZG(L, 1, I))/3.0
           ZG(L, 2, IG2)=ZG(L, 12, I)
360      CONTINUE
350    CONTINUE
       RETURN
       END
C
C-------------------------------------------------------------
C
C
C      >> CONTROL POINTS WHICH REPRESENT TANGENT
C            DERIVATIVE ON BOUNDARY CURVES <<
C
       SUBROUTINE MTRGP2(N, GP, SGP)
       DIMENSION GP(3, 1), SGP(3, 20, 1)
       DIMENSION ZP(3, 8)
C
C      /I/ N : THE NUMBER OF EDGES
C      /I/ GP : A GREGORY PATCH
C      /O/ GP : SUBDIVIDED PATCHES
```

Figure 8.27   (cont.)

```
C
      IB=1
      N3=N*3
      ID=N3+1
      DO 100 IP=1, N
        IB1=IB-1
        IF(IB1.LE.0) IB1=N3
        IB3=IB+3
        IF(IB3.GT.N3) IB3=1
C
      DO 110 L=1, 3
        ZP(L, 1)=GP(L, IB1)-GP(L, IB)
        ZP(L, 2)=GP(L, ID)-GP(L, IB+1)
        ZP(L, 3)=GP(L, ID+1)-GP(L, IB+2)
        ZP(L, 4)=GP(L, IB3+1)-GP(L, IB3)
110     CONTINUE
        IB=IB+3
        ID=ID+2
C
      DO 120 K=1, 4
        DO 130 L=1, 3
        ZP(L, K)=ZP(L, K)/2.0
130       CONTINUE
120   CONTINUE
C
C      - SUB -
C
        CALL CSDCZ(3, ZP, 0.5)
C
C    - SGP -
C
      IP1=IP+1
      IF(IP1.GT.N) IP1=1
      DO 140 L=1, 3
        SGP(L, 17, IP)=SGP(L, 8, IP)+ZP(L, 2)
        SGP(L, 18, IP)=SGP(L, 9, IP)+ZP(L, 3)
        SGP(L, 11, IP)=SGP(L, 10, IP)+ZP(L, 4)
C
        SGP(L, 3, IP1)=SGP(L, 4, IP1)+ZP(L, 5)
        SGP(L, 15, IP1)=SGP(L, 5, IP1)+ZP(L, 6)
        SGP(L, 16, IP1)=SGP(L, 6, IP1)+ZP(L, 7)
140     CONTINUE
100   CONTINUE
      RETURN
      END
C
C-------------------------------------------------------------------------
```

Figure 8.27 (cont.)

```
C
C      >> CONTROL POINTS OF EDGES
C
       SUBROUTINE MTRGP1(N, ZE, ZG)
       DIMENSION ZE(3, 14), ZG(3, 20, 3)
C
C      /I/ N : THE NUMBER OF EDGES
C      /I/ ZE : A TRIANGULAR PATCH (LOOP)
C      /O/ ZG : THREE GREGORY PATCHES (LOOP)
C
       DIMENSION ZT(3, 8)
C
       N3=N*3
       DO 160 I=1, N
         IZE=(I-1)*3+1
         DO 170 K=1, 4
           IF(IZE.GT.N3) IZE=1
           DO 180 L=1, 3
             ZT(L, K)=ZE(L, IZE)
180        CONTINUE
           IZE=IZE+1
170      CONTINUE
         CALL CSDCZ(3, ZT, 0.5)
C
         IG1=I
         IG2=I+1
         IF(IG2.GT.N) IG2=1
C
         IV1=7
         IV2=4
         DO 190 K=1, 4
           DO 200 L=1, 3
             ZG(L, IV1, IG1)=ZT(L, K)
             ZG(L, IV2, IG2)=ZT(L, K+4)
200        CONTINUE
           IV1=IV1+1
           IV2=IV2+1
190      CONTINUE
160    CONTINUE
       RETURN
       END
C
C----------------------------------------------------------------
```

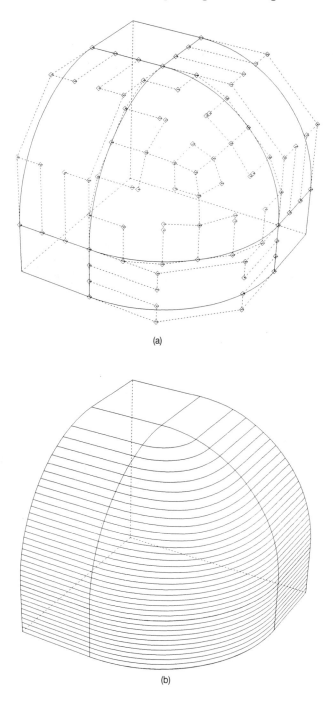

(a)

(b)

Figure 8.28 Gregory patches generated on a curved mesh which includes a three-sided face.

8.5.2 Interpolating a five-sided face

The procedure for interpolating a five-sided face is largely similar to that applied to a three-sided face. There is a difference, however, in generating the internal curves. Five-sided faces are interpolated in three stages.

1. Generating internal curves

To subdivide a five-sided face, five internal curves are generated on the face. To do so, the same method as that used in the case of a three-sided face is applied. Figure 8.29 shows a five-sided face and five internal curves C_i $(i = 1, \ldots, 5)$. P_i $(i = 1, \ldots, 5)$ are the end points of the internal curves, and $P_{i,1}$ and $P_{i,2}$ are the Bézier control points of the curves. P_0 is where all the internal curves meet. Although points $P_{i,2}$ $(i = 1, 2, 3)$ which are generated when interpolating a three-sided face lie on the same plane, points $P_{i,2}$ $(i = 1, \ldots, 5)$ on a five-sided face generally do not. In order that the tangent planes of generated patches be continuous, the points must lie on the same plane. We therefore first define a plane which is close to the five points (see Section 3.3.1). Next, the five points are translated onto the plane. Lastly, point P_0 is determined as the average of $P_{i,2}$ $(i = 1, \ldots, 5)$:

$$P_0 = \frac{1}{5} \times (P_{1,2} + P_{2,2} + P_{3,2} + P_{4,2} + P_{5,2})$$

2. Generating internal curves

In Figure 8.29, θ_i $(i = 1, \ldots, 5)$ is the angle between vectors $\overrightarrow{P_0 P_{i,2}}$ and $\overrightarrow{P_0 P_{i+1,2}}$. So that angles of the normal derivatives of the two patches along the internal curves are the same, let $k_0 = k_1 = 1$ in equations (8.3). The relationship of the angles is then

$$|P_{i+2,2} - P_0| \sin \theta_{i+1} = |P_{i,2} - P_0| \sin \theta_i \qquad (i = 1, \ldots, 5)$$

where $P_{6,2} = P_{1,2}$, $P_{7,2} = P_{2,2}$ and $\theta_6 = \theta_1$. If x_i $(i = 1, \ldots, 5)$ is the length of the vector between points P_0 and $P_{i,2}$, the above equation can be rewritten as

$$x_i = x_{i+2} \times \frac{\sin \theta_{i+1}}{\sin \theta_i} \tag{8.17}$$

So we properly translate point $P_{i,2}$ $(i = 1, \ldots, 5)$ to a line between points P_0 and $P_{i,2}$ $(i = 1, \ldots, 5)$ so that equation (8.17) can be satisfied.

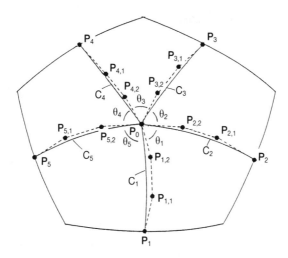

Figure 8.29 Internal curves in a five-sided face.

3. Generating Gregory patches

Figure 8.30 shows how two patches S^1 and S^2 generated on the five-sided face are joined. a_i, b_i and c_i are vectors between the control points of the Gregory patches. These points define the normal derivatives of patches S^1 and S^2 along the internal curve C_1. The vectors connected to points P_0 and P_1 satisfy equation (8.3). In this equation, $k_0 = k_1 = 1$ because the positions of the control points were determined through equation (8.17).

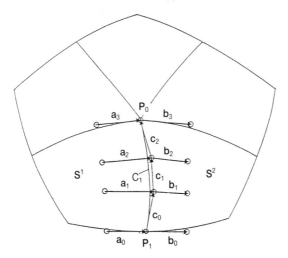

Figure 8.30 Vectors between control points.

Scalar constant h_1 can be easily calculated. From equation (8.17), we obtain

$$\mathbf{b}_1 = \mathbf{a}_1 + \frac{h_1 \mathbf{c}_0}{3} \tag{8.18}$$

$$\mathbf{b}_2 = \mathbf{a}_2 + \frac{2h_1 \mathbf{c}_1}{3}$$

The procedure described above is applied to the vectors connected to the other internal curves C_i $(i = 2, \ldots, 5)$. Using equations (8.18) for all internal curves and equations (8.16) for all the patches, we can determine the control points of the five Gregory patches. This method can be used to interpolate n-sided faces (where $n > 4$ and n is odd). Figure 8.31 lists the programs for obtaining Gregory patches to interpolate faces with n odd sides. Figures 8.32 and 8.33 show two examples of Gregory patches generated on five-sided faces.

Figure 8.31   Programs for generating Gregory patches on any odd-sided face.

```
C--------------------------------------------------------------------
C
C     >> GENERATION OF GREGORY PATCHES ON
C         A FACE WITH N ODD SIDES <<
C
      SUBROUTINE MDDGP(NG, ZE, ZG, WK)
      DIMENSION ZE(3, 1), ZG(3, 20, 1), WK(1)
C     DIMENSION ZE(3, NG*3), ZG(3, 20, NG), WK(1)
C
C     /I/ NG : NUMBER OF EDGES
C     /I/ ZE : BEZIER POINTS OF EDGES
C     /O/ ZG : GREGORY PATCHES
C     /W/ WK : WORK AREA (NG*(16*NG+24))
C
      IW2=1+16*NG*NG
      IW3=IW2+12*NG
      NG4=NG*4
      CALL MDDGP1(NG, NG4, ZE, ZG, WK, WK(IW2), WK(IW3))
      RETURN
      END
C
      SUBROUTINE MDDGP1(NG, NG4, ZE, ZG, AM, XX, BV)
      DIMENSION ZE(3, 1), ZG(3, 20, 1)
     1        , AM(NG4, 1), XX(3, 1), BV(3, 1)
C     DIMENSION ZE(3, NG*3), ZG(3, 20, NG)
C    1        , AM(4*NG, 4*NG), XX(3, 4*NG), BV(3, 4*NG)
```

Figure 8.31   (cont.)

```
C
C     /I/ ZE : EDGE OF PATCH
C     /O/ ZG : N GREGORY PATCHES
C
      DIMENSION
     1    , AA0(3), AA3(3), BB0(3), BB3(3)
     2    , CC0(3), CC1(3), CC2(3)
C
C     - EDGE -
C
      CALL MTRGP1(NG, ZE, ZG)
C
C     - TANGENT -
C
      CALL MTRGP2(NG, ZE, ZG)
C
C     - THE CENTER -
C
      CALL MTRGP3(NG, ZG)
C
C     - NORMAL VECTOR -
C
      CALL MDDGP3(NG, ZG)
C
C     - MOVE P.12 AND SET K=1 -
C
      IF(MOD(NG, 2).EQ.1) CALL MDDGP2(NG, ZG, AM, BV, XX)
C
C     - CONTINUITY BETWEEN INSIDE PATCHES -
C
      NG4=NG*4
      DO 520 K=1, NG4
        DO 530 L=1, NG4
          AM(L, K)=0.0
530     CONTINUE
520   CONTINUE
C
      DO 500 I=1, NG
        IM=(I-1)*4
        IG1=I
        IG2=I+1
        IF(IG2.GT.NG) IG2=1
C
        DO 510 L=1, 3
          AA0(L)=ZG(L, 10, IG1)-ZG(L, 9, IG1)
          AA3(L)=ZG(L, 1, IG1)-ZG(L, 2, IG1)
          BB0(L)=ZG(L, 5, IG2)-ZG(L, 4, IG2)
```

Figure 8.31   (cont.)

```
          BB3(L)=ZG(L, 12, IG2)-ZG(L, 1, IG2)
          CC0(L)=ZG(L, 11, IG1)-ZG(L, 10, IG1)
          CC1(L)=ZG(L, 12, IG1)-ZG(L, 11, IG1)
          CC2(L)=ZG(L, 1, IG1)-ZG(L, 12, IG1)
510   CONTINUE
C
      A=CC2(1)**2+CC2(2)**2+CC2(3)**2
      B=(AA3(1)-BB3(1))*CC2(1)
     1  +(AA3(2)-BB3(2))*CC2(2)
     2  +(AA3(3)-BB3(3))*CC2(3)
      AL=-B/A
C
      - AM -
C
        AM(IM+1, IM+1)=1.0
        AM(IM+1, IM+3)=1.0
        AM(IM+2, IM+2)=-1.0
        AM(IM+2, IM+4)=1.0
        AM(IM+3, IM+1)=-1.0
        AM(IM+3, IM+3)=1.0
        AM(IM+4, IM+4)=1.0
        IA2=IM+6
        IF(IA2.GT.NG4) IA2=2
        AM(IM+4, IA2)=1.0
C
C     - BV -
C
      DO 540 L=1, 3
        BV(L, IM+1)=ZG(L, 15, IG2)-ZG(L, 18, IG1)
        BV(L, IM+2)=(2.0*AL*CC1(L))/3.0
        BV(L, IM+3)=(AL*CC0(L))/3.0
        BV(L, IM+4)=CC2(L)+BB3(L)
540     CONTINUE
500   CONTINUE
C
      CALL MGE(AM, BV, XX, NG4, 3, IST)
C
      DO 550 I=1, NG
        IM=(I-1)*4
        IG1=I
        IG2=I+1
        IF(IG2.GT.NG) IG2=1
        DO 560 L=1, 3
          ZG(L, 19, IG1)=ZG(L, 11, IG1)-XX(L, IM+1)
          ZG(L, 20, IG1)=ZG(L, 12, IG1)-XX(L, IM+2)
          ZG(L, 14, IG2)=ZG(L, 3, IG2)-XX(L, IM+3)
          ZG(L, 13, IG2)=ZG(L, 2, IG2)-XX(L, IM+4)
```

Figure 8.31　(cont.)

```
560      CONTINUE
550    CONTINUE
       RETURN
       END
C
C-------------------------------------------------------------
C
C      >> MOVE P.12 AND SET K=1 <<
C
       SUBROUTINE MDDGP2(NG, ZG, TV, SB, XX)
       DIMENSION ZG(3, 20, NG)
       DIMENSION TV(3, NG), SB(NG), XX(NG)
C
C
       AL=0.0
       DO 100 I=1, NG
         A=0.0
         DO 110 L=1, 3
         TV(L, I)=ZG(L, 12, I)-ZG(L, 1, I)
         A=A+TV(L, I)*2
110      CONTINUE
C
         A=SQRT(A)
         AL=AL+A
         DO 120 L=1, 3
           TV(L, I)=TV(L, I)/A
120      CONTINUE
100    CONTINUE
       AL=AL/FLOAT(NG)
C
C      - CB -
C
       DO 200 I=1, NG
         IG=I+1
         IF(IG.GT.NG) IG=1
         CB=0.0
         DO 210 L=1, 3
           CB=CB+TV(L, I)*TV(L, IG)
210      CONTINUE
         SB(I)=SQRT(1.0-CB**2)
200    CONTINUE
C
C      - XX -
C
       XL=0.0
       I=1
```

Figure 8.31   (cont.)

```
      XX(1)=1.0
      DO 300 K=1, NG
        I1=I+1
        IF(I1.GT.NG) I1=1
        I2=I+2
        IF(I2.GT.NG) I2=I2-NG
C
        XX(I2)=SB(I)*XX(I)/SB(I1)
        XL=XL+XX(I2)
        I=I2
300   CONTINUE
      XL=XL/FLOAT(NG)
      AX=AL/XL
C
      DO 310 I=1, NG
        XX(I)=XX(I)*AX
310   CONTINUE
C
C     - ZG -
C
      DO 400 I=1, NG
        IG=I+1
        IF(IG.GT.NG) IG=1
        DO 410 L=1, 3
          ZG(L, 12, I)=ZG(L, 1, I)+TV(L, I)*XX(I)
          ZG(L, 2, IG)=ZG(L, 12, I)
410     CONTINUE
400   CONTINUE
C
      RETURN
      END
C
C------------------------------------------------------------------------
C
C     >>NORMAL VECTOR ON THE CENTER <<
C
      SUBROUTINE MDDGP3(NE, SGP)
      DIMENSION SGP(3, 20, 1)
C
C     /I/ NE : THE NUMBER OF EDGES
C     /O/ SGP : SUBDIVIDED PATCHES
C
      DIMENSION VNR(3), A(3), B(3), C(3)
C
      DO 90 L=1, 3
        VNR(L)=0.0
90    CONTINUE
```

Figure 8.31   (cont.)

```
C
C     - NORMAL VECTOR -
C
      DO 100 IP=1, NE
        DO 110 L=1, 3
          A(L)=SGP(L, 2, IP)-SGP(L, 1, IP)
          B(L)=SGP(L, 12, IP)-SGP(L, 1, IP)
110     CONTINUE
        CALL MCRPR(A, B, C)
        CALL MUNVR(C, IST)
        DO 120 L=1, 3
          VNR(L)=VNR(L)+C(L)
120     CONTINUE
100   CONTINUE
      CALL MUNVR(VNR, IST)
C
C     - MOVE P2 AND P12 -
C
      DO 200 IP=1, NE
        IP1=IP-1
        IF(IP1.LE.0) IP1=NE
C
        D=0.0
        DO 210 L=1, 3
          D=D+(SGP(L, I, IP)-SGP(L, 2, IP))*VNR(L)
210     CONTINUE
        DO 220 L=1, 3
          SGP(L, 2, IP)=SGP(L, 2, IP)+D*VNR(L)
          SGP(L, 12, IP1)=SGP(L, 2, IP)
220     CONTINUE
200   CONTINUE
      RETURN
      END
C
C-------------------------------------------------------------------
```

8.5.3   Interpolating a six-sided face

When a six-sided face is interpolatd, six internal curves are generated first to subdivide the face. Six Gregory patches are then generated on the face. The greater part of the procedure is similar to that used to interpolate five-sided faces. However, we can not impose equation (8.16) on the six patches, since if it is used, the system of equations for obtaining the control points becomes indeterminate. Thus after the six-sided face is subdivided, each four-sided face is interpolated using the method

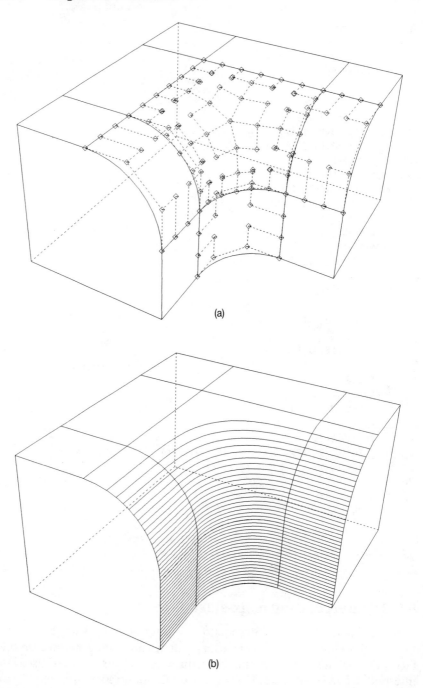

(a)

(b)

Figure 8.32   Gregory patches generated on a curved mesh which includes a five-sided face.

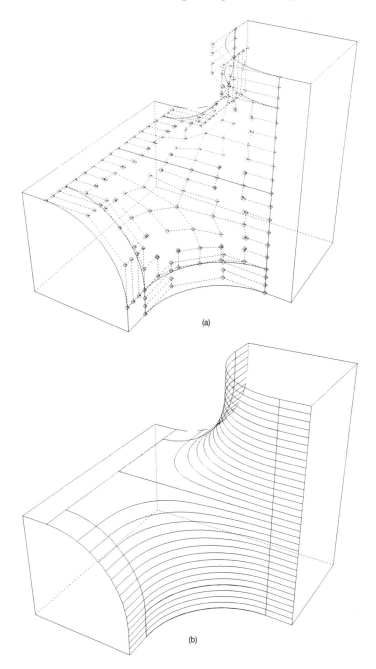

(a)

(b)

Figure 8.33   Gregory patches generated on a curved mesh which includes a five-sided face.

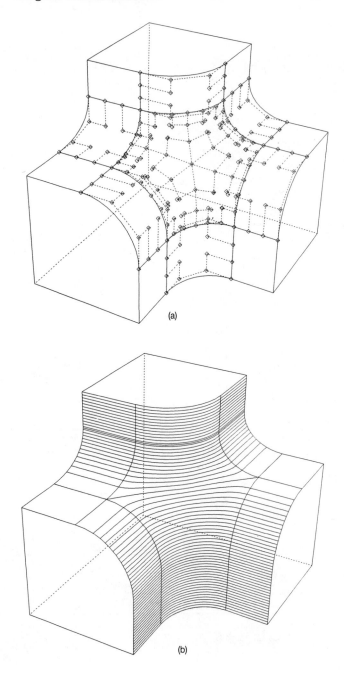

(a)

(b)

Figure 8.34 Gregory patches generated on a curved mesh which includes a six-sided face.

described in Section 8.4.1. An n-sided face (where $n > 5$ and n is even) is interpolated using this method. Figure 8.34 shows Gregory patches generated on a curved mesh which includes a six-sided face.

8.5.4   Problems with non-rectangular faces

When the non-rectangular faces shown in Figures 8.35 and 8.36 are interpolated using the method described above, the surfaces generated are not always smooth. Figure 8.35(a) shows a five-sided face in which the length ratios of the edges are quite different. Figure 8.36(a) shows a face with a corner greater than 180°. If internal curves are generated on these faces using the method described in Section 8.5.2, the curves may be wavy. As a result, the Gregory patches generated may be wavy. In the present version of our system, the designer has to make these faces with proper edges so that smooth surfaces are generated, as shown in Figures 8.35(b) and 8.36(b). Ideally the system should generate these internal curves automatically. The development of this procedure will be the basis of important future research work.

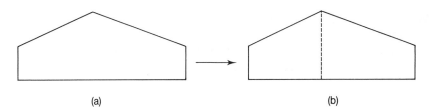

(a)   (b)

Figure 8.35   An internal curve in a face.

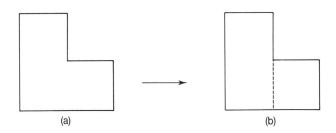

(a)   (b)

Figure 8.36   An internal curve in a face.

Chapter 9

Displaying Solid Models

9.1   Line drawings
9.2   Generating colour-shaded images
9.3   Making three-dimensional models

When 3-D shapes are designed using a solid modelling system, the system has facilities to display the solid models so that the designer can understand the shapes represented in the computer. In this chapter we discuss several techniques of displaying solid models.

9.1   LINE DRAWINGS

The various methods of producing line drawings to represent solid models are introduced below.

9.1.1   Wire-frame drawing

The simplest way of depicting a solid model is by a **wire-frame drawing** as shown in Figure 9.1(a), in which all the edges in the model are drawn. It is particularly easy to generate such a picture from a boundary representation.

To draw a shape in 3-D space, each point on the shape is transferred to the display screen (Newmann and Sproull, 1979). This is done by first converting each point in the **world coordinate** (X_w, Y_w, Z_w) into a point (X_e, Y_e, Z_e) in the eye coordinate. This is called a **viewing transformation**, and is built up from several translations and rotations. Figure 9.2 shows the eye coordinate system, in which the origin is the position of the eye. The Z_e axis points forward from the viewpoint, the X_e axis runs to the right and the Y_e axis lies vertically upwards. Finally, each point in the eye

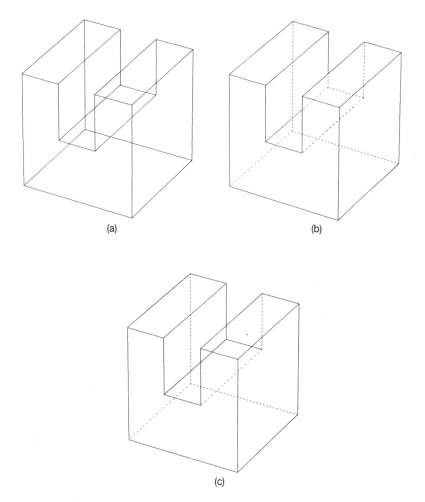

(a)   (b)

(c)

Figure 9.1   A line drawing of a solid model.

coordinate system is projected onto a coordinate point (X_s, Y_s) on the screen. This is called a **perspective translation.**

9.1.2   Localized hidden line removal

The wire-frame drawing described in the previous section does not enable a designer to understand 3-D shapes since it does not include depth information. On the other hand, using the hidden line removal picture shown in Figure 9.1(b), the user can understand 3-D shapes easily, since hidden lines are drawn as dotted lines. Although many algorithms for hidden line removal have been proposed (Sutherland

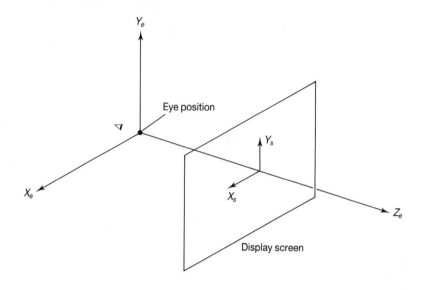

Figure 9.2   The eye coordinate system.

et al., 1974; Newmann and Sproull, 1979; Foley and Van Dam, 1982), these procedures take much computation time if the solid shapes are complex. We therefore propose a system of localized hidden line removal, as shown in Figure 9.1(c). Although this procedure can not be used to remove all hidden lines, it does generate a picture rapidly, and can therefore help the user to understand 3-D shapes in an interactive design environment.

In the first step of the produre, each edge is divided into two edges: a **convex edge** and a **concave edge**, as shown in Figure 9.3. If the angle of faces F_1 and F_2 meeting at edge E is smaller than 180°, E is convex; otherwise, it is concave. To check whether an edge is convex or concave, a vector **f** which is perpendicular to edge E on face F_1 is first obtained. It is computed as the cross product of normal $\mathbf{n}_1$ on F_1 and vector **e** on E. Although **e** has two directions, the direction is selected so that F_1 is the face on the left of **e**. Next, the dot product of **f** and normal $\mathbf{n}_2$ on F_2 is found. The computation described above is expressed as

$$((\mathbf{n}_1 \times \mathbf{e}) \cdot \mathbf{n}_2)$$

If the resulting value is smaller than 0, E is convex; otherwise, it is concave.

In the second step, the visibility of each face is checked. Consider an infinite surface which includes a face. The surface separates a space into two regions: inside and outside. If the eye position lies in the inside,

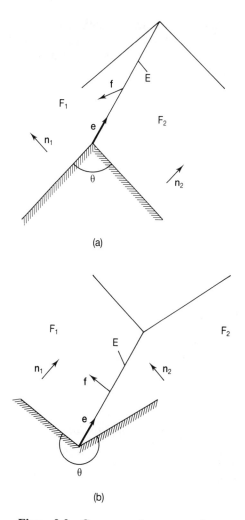

Figure 9.3   Convex and concave edges.

the face is invisible. Otherwise, the face may be visible. The dot product
of normal **n** of the face and a vector from the eye position P_e to any vertex
V on the face is computed, as follows:

$$(\mathbf{n} \cdot (\mathbf{P}_e - \mathbf{V}))$$

where we call $P_e - V$ a **viewing vector**. If the value of the dot product is
larger than 0, the face is invisible; otherwise it may be visible.

Using the information obtained above, we can locally remove
hidden lines. The procedure is applied to each edge independently. First,
both side faces of an edge are given. If the edge is convex, and either side

of the face may be visible, the edge is drawn. The edge is also drawn if it is concave, and both sides of the face are visible, since it is hidden by its adjacent faces. In the other cases, the edge is drawn as a dotted line. The algorithm is shown in Figure 9.4.

Figure 9.4   Algorithm for localized hidden lines.

```
Local__Hidd(body)
int body;
{

        int edge;
        int enumber;
        int fnumber;
        int face1, face2;

        /* get the number of all edges and faces */
        GetEdgeNumber(body, &enumber);
        GetFaceNumber(body, &fnumber);

        /* check the type of all edges */
        CheckEdgeType(body, enumber);

        /* check visibility of all face */
        CheckVisibility(body, fnumber);

        for(edge = 1;  edge <= enumber;  edge++) {

            /* get both side faces */
            GetBothFaces(body, edge, &face1, &face2);

            /* procedure for a convex edge */
            if(edge is a convex edge &&
                (face1 is visible || face2 is visible)) {
                DrawLine(body, edge);
            }

            /* procedure for a concave edge */
            if(edge is a concave edge &&
                (face1 is visible && face2 is visible)) {
                DrawLine(body edge);
            }

            /* draw a hidden line */
            DrawDottedLine(body, edge);
        }
```

9.1.3   Hidden line removal

Many fast hidden line removal algorithms have been proposed for generating a picture on a graphic display. Since most of the algorithms are dependent on the resolution of the display, they are not so effective when using a high-resolution printer. In a CAD/CAM environment, the designer often needs a design drawn on a large sheet of paper. This section introduces a simple hidden line removal procedure for polyhedra which is independent of the display resolution.

First, the visibility check used in localized hidden line removal is performed for all the edges and faces of a solid. As a result, the invisible edges and faces are found first and the remaining edges and faces may then be visible. The invisible edges are either drawn as dotted lines or not at all. The faces and edges which may be visible are stored in the tables for the previous procedure. The system then checks whether or not each edge is hidden by all the faces in the table. The check consists of the following three steps.

1.   *Depth check*

The coordinates of all the vertices in a solid are converted into those in the eye coordinate system. The maximum and minimum Z-values of the edges are stored in the table, as well as the values of the faces. Then the hidden line removal procedure is applied to each edge independently.

Now the faces stored in the table may hide each edge. In this step the Z-value information is used to detect which faces may hide edges. Figure 9.5 shows the relationship between an edge and three faces. Face F_1 never hides edge E_1 because the mimimum Z-value of F_1 is larger than the maximum Z-value of E_1. Such a face is marked $+$. Face F_2 may hide edge E_1 because the maximum Z-value of F_1 is smaller than the minimum

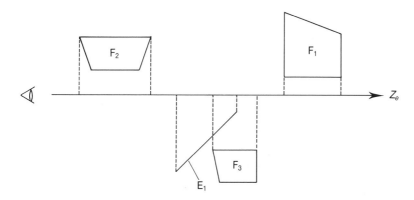

Figure 9.5   An edge and faces which may hide it in the eye coordinate system.

Z-value of E_1. Such a face is marked $-$. Since the relationship between F_3 and E_1 can not be found from the Z-values, such a face is marked 0.

2. Area check

The coordinates of all the vertices in the eye coordinate system are converted into 2-D screen coordinates. Boxes are created using the edge and the faces marked $-$ and 0, and then the boxes are used in the area interference check between the edge and the face. If there is no interference, the mark on the face is changed to $+$.

3. Subdividing line segments

First, a check is made to determine if the edge and the face marked $-$ intersect. If they do, the line of the edge is subdivided by the polygon of the face, as shown in Figure 9.6(a). Line L consists of three segments S_1, S_2 and S_3. Since S_2 lies on the polygon, it is either drawn as a dotted line or not at all. S_1 and S_3 may be visible. This procedure is then applied to the remaining line segment and the other faces marked $-$.

Next, the intersection between the edge and the face marked 0 is checked. If they do intersect, the edge is subdivided by the face, as shown in Figure 9.6(b). Line L is divided into segments S_1, S_2, S_3, S_4 and S_5.

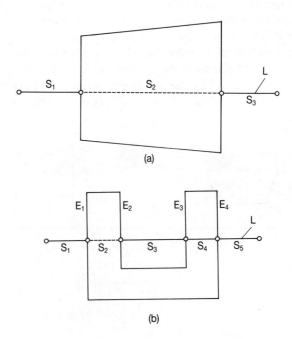

(a)

(b)

Figure 9.6   Line segments and a polygon.

Edges E_1, E_2, E_3 and E_4 intersect with line L. Since S_2 and S_4 lie on the polygon, they may be hidden by it. Here, the relationship between line L and edge E_1 connected to segment S_2 in the polygon is checked. If E_1 is closer to the eye point than line L, S_2 is hidden by the polygon; otherwise, S_2 may be visible. For the procedure, an infinite plane is defined which passes through the two end points of L and one end point of E_1. This plane divides the space into two regions. If the other end point of E_1 and the eye point lie in the same region, E_1 is closer to the eye; otherwise, S_2 is closer. The same procedure is applied to segment S_4 and edge E_4. In the figure, S_2 is a hidden line and S_4 is visible. A similar procedure is then applied to the remaining segments and the other faces marked 0. When the edge and all the faces marked − or 0 have been dealt with, the visible part of the edge is known. This procedure is applied to all edges, and the hidden line removal process is then complete.

To generate a hidden line removal picture of a solid with curved faces, the faces are first approximated by a set of flat polygons, and the method for polyhedra is then applied. Hidden line techniques which deal directly with curved surfaces have been proposed by Griffiths (1978) and Ohno (1981).

9.1.4   Drawing cross-sections and silhouette curves

One effective method of displaying curved surfaces is to draw cross-sections between the surfaces and planes perpendicular to either the X-, Y- or Z-axis, as shown in Figure 6.8. To do so, points on the mesh of a surface patch are first computed, and either the X-, Y- or Z-values of these coordinates are stored in an array $[n, n]$. The intersection points between the boundary of the surface patch and the plane are then found. The intersection curves are followed using the array. Figure 9.7 illustrates how an intersection curve is followed between a surface patch and a plane perpendicular to the Z-axis. The mesh of the patch and the starting point of the intersection line P_0 are shown. P_0 lies on line $\overline{Q_1Q_2}$, which is a side of rectangle $Q_1Q_2Q_3Q_4$. The first procedure is to find on which line ($\overline{Q_2Q_3}$, $\overline{Q_3Q_4}$ or $\overline{Q_4Q_1}$) an intersection point lies. If the point lies on a line, the Z-value of one end point of the line will be larger than the Z-value of the plane, and the Z-value of the other end point is smaller. Thus each line is checked to determine whether or not the point lies on it. Once the line is found, the position of the point is computed. In the figure, P_1 is an intersection point on line $\overline{Q_3Q_4}$. The same procedure is then applied to the other rectangle connected to the line on which the point lies. When the point on the boundary is found, this completes the procedure of following a single intersection line. The result is that the curve is defined as a number of straight line segments. When the precise

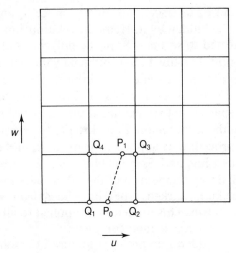

Figure 9.7 Mesh of a surface patch.

shape of a curve is needed, a larger number has to be given to n, although the computation time will become extended.

The method of obtaining the **silhouette curve** of a curved surface is similar to the procedure described above. Figure 9.8 shows an example of

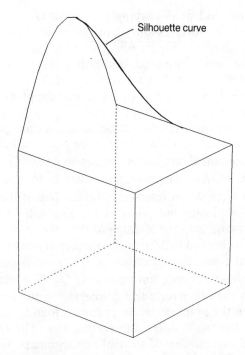

Figure 9.8 Silhouette curve on a curved face.

a silhouette curve on a Gregory patch. To generate such a curve, the coordinates of a point $S(u, w)$ on the surface which corresponds to a node on a mesh and a normal vector $n(u, w)$ on the point are first calculated. Then the dot product of $n(u, w)$ and a unit vector between the eye position P_e and point $S(u, w)$ is computed using:

$$\left(n(u, w) \cdot \frac{P_e - S(u, w)}{|P_e - S(u, w)|} \right)$$

and its value stored in the elements of the array. For silhouette curves of a curved surface, since the normal $n(u, w)$ is always perpendicular to the vector $P_e - S(u, w)$, the value of the dot product is zero. Using this property, silhouette curves can be found from the array.

9.2 GENERATING COLOUR-SHADED IMAGES

To display solid models with curved surfaces realistically, colour-shaded images need to be generated on a raster graphic display. Although there are many methods for generating colour images, this section introduces three types: **polygon sort shading**, **scan line shading** (Lane *et al.*, 1980) and **ray tracing** (Whitted, 1980).

9.2.1 Polygon sort shading

The polygon sort shading method for polyhedra is simple and quick. First, each face is checked for visibility using the dot product of the face normal and the viewing vector. The faces which may be visible are sorted according to their Z-values in the eye coordinate. Finally, these faces are drawn in sorted order. Occasionally the order of faces can not be determined uniquely. Figure 9.9 gives two examples. In Figure 9.9(a), two faces A and B are shown, with face A concave. While part of A hides part of B, the other part of A is hidden by part of B. Figure 9.9(b) shows a case in which the order of faces is cyclic. Polygon sort shading thus does not always generate a complete picture. However, since it is quick and simple, it can help the user to understand the shape of a solid model in an interactive design environment.

The level of shading on each face is determined using a **shading model** (Foley and Van Dam, 1982). The simplest equation for determing the shade level **I** at a point P on a face F is as follows:

$$I = (N \cdot L)$$

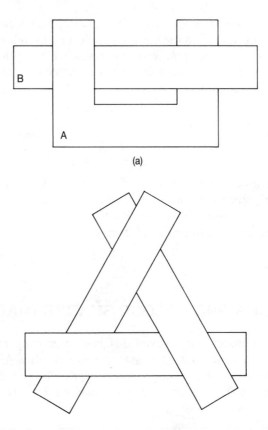

(a)

Figure 9.9   The order of faces drawn using the polygon sort shading method.

where **N** is the normal unit vector on face F, and **L** is the unit vector from point P to a light source, as shown in Figure 9.10. In polygon sort shading, the whole area of each face has the same shade level. When a solid shape has curved faces, each face is subdivided into a number of small polygons, and the same procedure is applied. The disadvantage of polygon sort shading is that curved surfaces are not drawn smoothly.

9.2.2   Scan line shading

The scan line shading method draws a picture for each scan line of a display screen. A **scan line plane** is defined which passes through a scan line and is parallel to the XZ-plane in the eye coordinate, as shown in Figure 9.11. Then the intersection lines of the scan line plane and the faces of the solid are computed. If a face is planar, the intersection is given as a straight line, and its end points and their normal vectors are easily

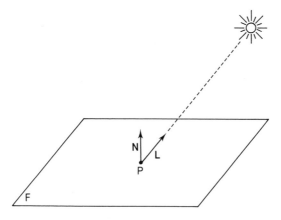

Figure 9.10 Shading model.

computed. If a face is curved and thus represented by a surface patch, the patch is approximated by a mesh polygon, and the intersection points between the lines of the mesh and the plane are computed, as shown in Figure 9.12. The parameter values indicating the point on the surface patch are determined using the information on the intersection points.

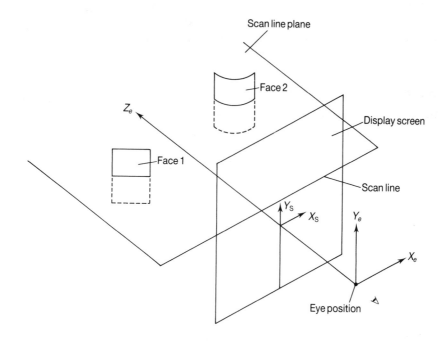

Figure 9.11 Scan line plane in the eye coordinate system.

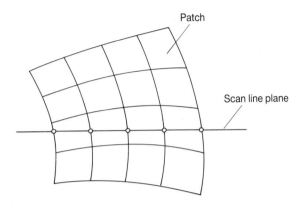

Figure 9.12   Intersection between a scan line plane and a surface patch mesh.

The position and normal vectors on the points are computed using the equation of the surface patch. As a result, the intersection between the plane and the faces is given as many line segments, and each segment has the positions and normal vectors of its end points.

The shade levels at the two end points of the line segment are computed, and the shade levels along the line are linearly interpolated. The intersection lines are sorted according to the Z-value, and the shade levels of the lines are given to the scan line in sorted order. In the scan line method, curved surfaces can be drawn smoothly. Plates 1–4 show shaded images of solid models generated using the scan line method. The solid models are constructed using DESIGNBASE.

9.2.3   Ray tracing

In ray tracing, the shade level of each pixel is determined by tracing a ray of a light in 3-D space. Since this procedure is performed for every pixel in a graphic display, it is expensive. However, ray tracing has the advantage that shadows, reflections and transparency can be realistically displayed. For curved surfaces, the main procedure in ray tracing is to find the intersection point between a surface patch and a ray. Several methods have been proposed (Kajiya, 1982; Toth, 1985). Plates 5 and 6 show colour-shaded images generated using ray tracing.

9.3   MAKING THREE-DIMENSIONAL MODELS

In the final stage of a design process, the designer needs to make very stringent checks on the designed object's shape. This is most effectively done by making true 3-D models, as shown in Plates 7 and 8. This has the obvious advantage that it the model be examined in detail from all

Figure 9.13   An NC machine tool.

Figure 9.14   Machining a 3-D model.

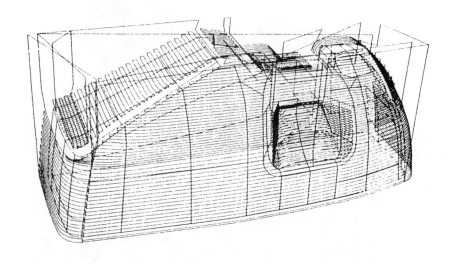

Figure 9.15   The cutter path for machining a solid model.

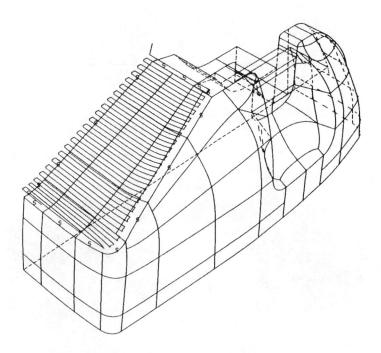

Figure 9.16   The cutter path for machining a face-set.

angles, and there is no ambiguity of interpretation. Such models are made using soft materials such as plastic foam, hard wax and wood, using an NC machine tool, as shown in Figure 9.13. Figure 9.14 illustrates machining in progress. Since a ball-end mill is generally used to machine curved surfaces, the cutting path of the centre of the ball-end is generated by a computer from information on the solid model. Figure 9.15 shows the cutter path data. In this example, the user specifies several of the face-sets of a solid model which do not have sharp edges, and the cutter path for each face-set is generated, as shown in Figure 9.16. All of the cutter paths are then combined so that they become one continuous line. Ideally, the cutter path should be generated automatically so that once designed, the model can be easily made.

Appendix

Reference Functions

A.1   Reference functions of edges
A.2   Reference functions of loops
A.3   Basic reference functions of vertices
A.4   Reference functions of a body

In DESIGNBASE, information about solids is given through the reference functions. The reference functions can be divided to two groups. One is a **basic reference function**. The functions get information directly from the data structure of a boundary representation. The other is an **applied reference function**. These are combinations of basic reference functions, and are not read directly from the data structure of the solid. Reference functions are explained below. In expressing function variables, ↑ and ↓ mean output and input, respectively.

A.1   REFERENCE FUNCTIONS OF EDGES

A.1.1   Basic reference functions of edges

1.   rbEType – *type of an edge shape*

```
            ↓     ↓     ↑     ↑        ↑
    rbEType(body, edge, type, point1, point2)
    int body, edge;
    int *type;
    struct dbCoord {
            double x;
            double y;
            double z;
    } *point1, *point2;
```

This detects the shape of edge in body. If the shape of edge is a straight line, type $= 0$. If the shape of edge is a curve, type $= 1$, and the Bézier points of edge are stored in point1 and point2.

2. rbE Vertex – *vertices attached to an edge*

```
      ↓       ↓      ↑          ↑
rbEVertex(body, edge, vertex1, vertex2)
int body, edge;
int *vertex1, *vertex2;
```

This finds vertex1 and vertex2 which are attached to edge.

3. rbELoop – *loops attached to an edge*

```
      ↓       ↓      ↑       ↑
rbELoop(body, edge, loopL, loopR)
int body, edge;
int *loopL, *loopR;
```

This gets left-side loop loopL and right-side loop loopR of edge.

4. rbEStatus – *status of edge*

```
      ↓       ↓      ↑
rbEStatus(body, edge, flag)
int body, edge;
int *flag;
```

This determines the status of edge. If edge is alive, flag $= 1$; if it is dead, flag $= 0$.

5. rbEExist – *edge attached to two vertices*

```
      ↓        ↓         ↓        ↑
rbEExist(body, vertex1, vertex2, edge)
int body, vertex1, vertex2;
int *edge;
```

This searches edge which runs between vertex1 and vertex2. If such an edge is not found, edge $= 0$.

A.1.2 Applied reference functions of edges

1. raEVertexPosition – *position of vertices attached to an edge*

```
              ↓    ↓    ↑   ↑
raEVertexPosition(body, edge, p1, p2)
int body, edge;
struct dbCoord *p1, *p2;
```

p1 and p2 give the coordinates of two vertices attached to edge.

2. raEParamPosition – *parameter position on an edge*

```
              ↓    ↓    ↑         ↑
raEParamPosition(body, edge, parameter, position)
int body, edge;
real parameter;
struct dbCoord *positon;
```

This determines position on edge which corresponds to parameter ($0 \leq$ parameter ≤ 1).

3. raEWingedEdge – *winged-edges*

```
            ↓    ↓    ↑
raEWingedEdge(body, edge, w-edge)
int body, edge;
int w-edge[4];
```

This finds the four winged-edges w-edge[4] of edge.

A.2 REFERENCE FUNCTIONS OF LOOPS

A.2.1 Basic reference functions of loops

1. rbLType – *type of a loop*

```
        ↓    ↓    ↑
rbLType(body, loop, type)
int body, loop;
int *type;
```

This determines the type of loop. If loop is a P-loop, type $= 0$; if loop is a C-loop, type $= 1$.

2. rbLEdVt – *edges and vertices of a loop*

```
       ↓      ↓     ↓     ↑        ↑
rbLEdVt(body, loop, size, number, pool)
int body, loop;
int size;
int *number;

struct dbEdgeVertex {
      int edge;
      int vertex;
} *pool;
```

This determines the vertices and edges attached to loop. size is the array size of pool. number is the number of edges.

3. rbLEdNm – *the number of edges in a loop*

```
       ↓      ↓     ↑
rbLEdNm(body, loop, number)
int body, loop;
int *number;
```

Number gives the number of edges in loop.

4. rbLPloop – *C-loop belonging to P-loop*

```
       ↓     ↓      ↑
rbLPloop(body, loop, ploop)
int body, loop;
int *ploop;
```

Obtains a P-loop to which loop belongs. If loop is a P-loop, ploop = loop; if loop is a C-loop, ploop = the Ploop Id of loop.

5. rbLCloop – *C-loops*

```
       ↓      ↓     ↓     ↑        ↑
rbLCloop(body, loop, size, number, cloop)
int body, loop;
int size;
int *number;
int cloop[];
```

This finds the C-loops included in loop. size is the array size of cloop. number is the number of C-loops. All C-loops are stored in cloop.

6. rbLC1Nm – *the number of C-loops*

```
              ↓      ↓     ↑
    rbLC1Nm(body, loop, number)
    int body, loop;
    int *number;
```

number gives the number of C-loops which belong to loop.

7. rbLStatus – *status of a loop*

```
              ↓      ↓     ↑
    rbLStatus(body, loop, flag)
    int body, loop;
    int *flag;
```

Determines the status of loop. If loop is alive, flag = 1, if it is dead, flag = 0.

8. rbLEdge – *an edge of a loop*

```
             ↓      ↓    ↑
    rbLEdge(body, loop, edge)
    int body, loop;
    int *edge;
```

edge gives one of the edges attached to loop.

9. rbLVertex – *a vertex of a loop*

```
              ↓      ↓     ↑
    rbLVertex(body, loop, vertex)
    int body, loop;
    int *vertex;
```

vertex gives one of vertices attached to loop.

10. rbLNormal – *normal vector of a loop*

```
               ↓      ↓     ↑
    rbLNormal(body, loop, vector)
    int body, loop;
    struct dbCoord *vector;
```

This calculates a unit normal vertor of loop.

A.2.2 Applied reference functions of loops

1. raLPntLp – *point in a loop*

```
       ↓       ↓      ↓      ↑
raLPntLp(body, loop, point, flag)
int body, loop;
struct dbCoord *point;
int *flag;
```

This tests whether or not point is included in loop. If it is included then, flag = 1. Otherwise, flag = 0. If it lies on the boundary of loop, then flag = 2.

2. raLPntFc – *point in a face*

```
       ↓       ↓      ↓      ↑
raLPntFc(body, loop, point, flag)
int body, loop;
struct dbCoord *point;
int *flag;
```

This tests whether or not point is included in a face defined by loop and its C-loops. If it is included in the face, then flag = 1. Otherwise, flag = 0.

3. raLFlat – *shape of a loop*

```
       ↓      ↓     ↑
raLFlat(body, loop, flag)
int body, loop;
int *flag;
```

This tests if a shape of loop is flat or curved. If it is flat, then flag = 0. Otherwise, flag = 1.

4. raLGregoryPatch – *Gregory patches of a loop*

```
              ↓      ↓     ↓      ↑        ↑
raLGregoryPatch(body, loop, size, number, patch)
int body, loop;
int size;
int *number;
struct dbCoord patch[];
```

This generates Gregory patches interpolating loop. The control points of the patches are given in patch. size is the array size of patch. number is the number of generated patches. The algorithm is described in Sections 7.5 and 7.6.

5.   raLCornerType – *type of a corner*

<pre>
              ↓   ↓   ↓   ↑
     raLCornerType(body, loop, vertex, type)
     int body, loop, vertex;
     int *typeI;
</pre>

This detects an angle of a corner which is attached to vertex and loop. If the angle of the corner is smaller than 180°, type = 0. If the angle is 180°, type = 2. If the angle is larger than 180°, type = 1.

A.3   BASIC REFERENCE FUNCTIONS OF VERTICES

1.   rbVEdLp – *edges and loops attached to a vertex*

<pre>
           ↓   ↓   ↓   ↑   ↑
     rbVedLp(body, vertex, size, edgeno, edgeloop)
     int body, vertex;
     int size;
     int *edgeno;
     struct dbEdgeLoop {
             int edge;
             int loop;
     } *edgeloop;
</pre>

edgeloop gives the edges and loops connected to vertex. size is the array size of edgeloop. The number of edges is given in edgeno.

2.   rbVEdNm – *the number of edges attached to a vertex*

<pre>
            ↓   ↓   ↓
     rbVEdNm(body, vertex, edgeno)
     int body, vertex;
     int *edgeno;
</pre>

edgeno gives the number of edges connected to vertex.

3.   rbVPosition – *position of a vertex*

<pre>
              ↓   ↓   ↑
     rbVPosition(body, vertex, coord)
     int body, vertex;
     struct dbCoord *coord;
</pre>

coord gives the position of vertex.

4. rbVStatus – *status of a vertex*

rbVStatus(body, vertex, flag)
int body, vertex;
int *flag;

If vertex is alive, flag = 1. If vertex is dead, flag = 0.

5. rbVEdge – *edge of a vertex*

rbVEdge(body, vertex, edge)
int body, vertex;
int *edge;

edge gives one of the edges connected to vertex.

A.4   REFERENCE FUNCTIONS OF A BODY

1. rbBInStatus – *status of a body*

rbBInStatus(body, flag)
int body;
int *flag;

If a solid specified by internal name body is alive, flag = 1. If body is dead, flag = 0.

2. rbBExStatus – *status of a body*

rbBExStatus(name, flag)
char *name;
int *flag;

If a solid specified by external name is alive, flag = 1. If the solid is dead, flag = 0.

3. rbBNumber – *the number of solids*

rbBNumber(number)
int *number;

number gives the number of solids defined in DESIGNBASE.

4. rbBEdgeNumber – *the number of edges*

             ↓   ↑
rbBEdgeNumber(body, edgeno)
int body;
int *edgeno;

edgeno gives the number of edges used in body.

5. rbBLoopNumber – *the number of loops*

             ↓   ↑
rbBLoopNumber(body, loopno)
int body;
int *loopno;

loopno gives the number of loops used in body.

6. rbBVertexNumber – *the number of vertices*

             ↓   ↑
rbBVertexNumber(body, vertexno)
int body;
int *vertexno;

vertexno gives the number of vertices used in body.

7. rbBId – *internal name to external one*

             ↓   ↑
rbBId(name, body)
char *name;
int *body;

From the external name of a body, an internal body name is given in body.

8. rbBName – *external name to internal one*

             ↓   ↑
rbBName(body, name)
int body;
char *name;

The internal name of a body is converted to an external name.

Bibliography

Agin, G. J. and Binford, T. O. (1973). 'Computer description of curved objects' *Proceedings of the 3rd International Joint Conference on Artificial Intelligence,* August, 629–640

Archer, Jr, J. E., Conway, R. and Schneider, F. B. (1984). 'User recovery and reversal in interactive systems' *ACM Trans. Programming Languages and Systems,* **6,** 1–19

Armstrong, G. T., Carey, G. C. and de Pennington, A. (1984). 'Numerical code generation from geometric modeling systems' In *Solid Modeling by Computers.* M. S. Pickett and J. W. Boyse, Eds. New York: Plenum Press, 139–158

Baer, A., Eastman, C. M. and Henrion, M. (1980). 'Geometric modelling: a survey, *Computer Aided Design* **11,** 253–272

Barnhill, R. E. (1977). 'Representation and approximation of surfaces' In *Mathematical Software III.* J. Rice, Ed. New York: Academic Press, 69–120

Barnhill, R. E. (1985). 'Surface in computer aided geometric design: a survey with new results' *Computer Aided Geometric Design* **2,** 1–17

Barnhill, R. E., Brown, J. H. and Klucewicz, I. M. (1978). 'A new twist in computer aided geometric design' *Computer Graphics and Image Processing,* **8,** 78–91

Barnhill, R. E., Farin, G., Jordan, M. and Piper, B. R. (1987). 'Surface/surface intersection' *Computer Aided Geometric Design,* **4,** 3–16

Barsky, B. A. and Beatty, J. C. (1983). 'Local control and bias and tension in Beta-spline' *Computer Graphics (SIGGRAPH '83 Proc.),* **17,** 193–218

Baumgart, B. G. (1974). *Geometric modelling for computer vision,* Report STAN-CS-74-463. Stanford University: Stanford Artificial Intelligence Laboratory

Baumgart, B. G. (1975). 'A polyhedron representation for computer vision' *AFIPS Conf. Proc.,* **44,** 589–596

Beeker, E. (1986). 'Smoothing of shapes designed with free-form surfaces', *Computer Aided Design,* **18,** 224–232

Besl, P. J. and Jain, R. C. (1985). 'Three-dimensional object recognition' *ACM Computing Surveys,* **17,** 75–145

Bézier, P. E. (1972). *Numerical Control – Mathematics and Applications,* London: John Wiley

Böhm, W., Farin, G. and Kahmann, J. (1984). 'A survey of curve and surface models in CAGD' *Computer Aided Geometric Design*, **1**, 1–60

Boyse, J. W. (1979). 'Interference detection among solids and surfaces' *Communications of the ACM*, **22**, 3–9

Boyse, J. W. and Gilchrist, J. E. (1982). 'GMSolid: interactive modeling for design and analysis of solids' *IEEE Computer Graphics and Applications*, **2**, 27–40

Braid, I. C. (1975). 'The synthesis of solids bounded by many faces' *Communications of ACM*, **18**, 209–216

Braid, I. C. (1979). *Notes on a geometric modeller*, CAD Group Document No. 101, Computer Laboratory. Cambridge: University of Cambridge

Braid, I. C. and Lang, C. A. (1973). 'Computer-aided design of mechanical components with volume building bricks' In *Computer Languages for Numerical Control*. J. Hatvany, Ed. Amsterdam: North-Holland, 173–184

Braid, I. C., Hillyard, R. C. and Stroud, I. A. (1980). 'Stepwise construction of polyhedra in geometric modelling' In *Mathematical Methods in Computer Graphics and Design*. K. W. Brodlie, Ed. New York: Academic Press, 123–141

Brown, C. M. (1982). 'PADL-2: a technical summary' *IEEE Computer Graphics and Applications*, **2**, 69–84

CAM-I (1981). *TIPS-1 geometric modelling and software*, PS-91-GM-01. Arlington, Texas: Computer Aided Manufacturing – International

Carlbom, I. (1987). 'An algorithm for geometric set operations using cellular subdivision techniques' *IEEE Computer Graphics and Applications*, **7**, 44–55

Carlson, W. E. (1982). 'Advanced techniques for complex 3D objects synthesis using surface intersection' *Computer Graphics (SIGGRAPH '82 Proc.)*, **16**, 255–259

Casale, M. S. (1987). 'Free-form surface modelling with trimmed surface patches' *IEEE Computer Graphics and Applications*, **7**, 33–43

Catmull, E. and Clark, J. (1978). 'Recursively generated B-spline surfaces on arbitrary topological meshes' *Computer Aided Design*, **10**, 350–355

Charrot, P. and Gregory, J. A. (1984). 'A pentagonal surface patch for CAGD' *Computer Aided Geometric Design*, **1**, 87–94

Chiyokura, H. (1980). *A design method of free-form shape for computer aided design* (in Japanese), Master's Thesis. Japan: Keio University, Department of Mathematics

Chiyokura, H. (1983). *A study of modelling solids with free-form surfaces* (in Japanese), Doctor's Thesis. Japan: University of Tokyo, Department of Precision Machinery Engineering

Chiyokura, H. (1985). *Solid Modelling* (in Japanese). Tokyo: Kogyochosakai

Chiyokura, H. (1986). 'Localized surface interpolation for irregular meshes' *Advanced Computer Graphics – Proc. Computer Graphics Tokyo '86*. T. L. Kunii, Ed. Tokyo: Springer-Verlag, 3–19

Chiyokura, H. (1987). 'An extended rounding operation for modelling solids with free-form surfaces' *Computer Graphics 1987 – Proc. CG International '87*. T. L. Kunii, Ed. Tokyo: Springer-Verlag, 249–268

Chiyokura, H. and Kimura, F. (1983). 'Design of solids with free-form surfaces' *Computer Graphics (SIGGRAPH '83 Proc.)*, **17**, 289–298

Chiyokura, H. and Kimura, F. (1984). 'A new surface interpolation method for irregular curve models' *Computer Graphic Forum*, **3**, 209–218

Chiyokura, H. and Kimura, F. (1985). 'A representation of solid design process using basic operations' In *Frontiers in Computer Graphics – Proc. Computer Graphics Tokyo '84*. T. L. Kunii, Ed. Tokyo: Springer-Verlag, 26–43

Chiyokura, H. and Kimura, F. (1985a). 'A method of representing solid design process' *IEEE Computer Graphics and Applications*, **5**, 32–41

Coons, S. A. (1967). *Surfaces for computer aided design of space forms*, MIT Project MAC, TR-41

Courter, S. M. and Brewer, J. A. (1986) 'Automated conversion of curvilinear wire-frame models to surface boundary models: a topological approach' *Computer Graphics (SIGGRAPH '86 Proc.)*, **20**, 171–178

Doo, D. (1978). 'A subdivision algorithm for smoothing down irregular shaped polohedrons' *Proc. Conf. Interactive Technique in CAD*, Bologna, Italy, 157–165

Doo, D. and Sabin, M. A. (1978). 'Behaviour of recursive division near extraordinary points' *Computer Aided Design*, **10**, 356–360

Eastman, C. and Henrion, M. (1977). 'GLIDE: a language for design information systems' *Computer Graphics (SIGGRAPH ' 77 Proc.)*, **11**, 24–33

Farin, G. (1986). 'Triangular Bernstein–Bézier patches' *Computer Aided Geometric Design*, **3**, 83–128

Farin, G. Ed. (1987). *Geometric Modeling*, Philadelphia: SIAM

Farouki, R. (1987). 'Direct surface section evaluation' In *Geometric Modeling*. G. Farin, Ed. Philadelphia: SIAM 319–334

Faux, I. D. and Pratt, M. J. (1979). *Computational Geometry for Design and Manufacture*. London: Ellis Horwood

Fjällström, P. (1986). 'Smoothing of polyhedra models' *Proc. ACM Symposium on Computational Geometry*, Yorktown Heights, New York, 226–235

Foley, J. D. and Van Dam, A. (1982). *Fundamentals of Interactive Computer Graphics*. Reading, MA: Addison-Wesley

Forrest, A. R. (1972). 'Interactive interpolation and approximation by Bézier polynomials' *Computer Journal*, **15**, 71–79

Forrest, A. R. (1972a). 'On Coons and other methods for the representation of curved surfaces' *Computer Graphics and Image Processing*, **1**, 341–359

Forrest, A. R. (1978). 'A unified approach of geometric modelling' *Computer Graphics (SIGGRAPH '78 Proc.)*, **12**, 264–269

Forrest, A. R. (1982). 'User interface for free-form surface design' *Lecture notes for seminar on sculptured surfaces*, ACM SIGGRAPH '82. Boston

Goldfeather, J., Hultquist, J. and Fuchs, H. (1986). 'Fast constructive solid geometry display in the pixel-powers graphics system' *Computer Graphics (SIGGRAPH '86 Proc.)*, **20**, 107–116

Gosling, J. (1982). *Unix Emacs Reference Manual*. Carnegie-Mellon University

Grayer, A. R. (1977). 'The automatic production of machined components starting from a stored geometric description' In *Advanced Computer-Aided Manufacturing*. D. McPherson, Ed. Amsterdam: North-Holland, 137–151

Gregory J. A. (1974). 'Smooth interpolation without twist constraints' In *Computer Aided Geometric Design*. R. E. Barnhill and R. F. Riesenfeld, Ed. New York: Academic Press, 71–87

Gregory J. A. and Charrot, P. (1980). 'A C1 triangular interpolation patch for computer-aided geometric design' *Computer Graphics and Image Processing*, **13**, 80–87

Griffiths, J. G. (1978). 'A surface display algorithm' *Computer Aided Design*, **10**, 65–73

Hatvany, J. Ed. (1973). *Computer Languages for Numerical Control.* Amsterdam: North-Holland

Hanrahan, P. M. (1982). 'Creating volume models from edge-vertex graphs' *Computer Graphics (SIGGRAPH '82 Proc.)*, **16**, 77–84

Hillyard, R. (1982). 'The BUILD group of solid modellers' *IEEE Computer Graphics and Applications*, **2**, 43–52

Hoffmann, C. and Hopcroft, J. (1985). 'Automatic surface generation in computer aided design' *Visual Computer*, **1**, 92–100

Hosaka, M. and Kimura, F. (1977). 'An interactive geometrical design system with handwriting input' *Information Processing '77*. Amsterdam: North-Holland, 167–172

Hosaka, M. and Kimura, F. (1978). 'Synthesis methods of curves and surfaces in interactive CAD' *Proc. Conf. Interactive Technique in CAD*. Bologna, Italy, 151–156

Hosaka, M. and Kimura, F. (1980). 'A method and theory for three-dimensional free-form shape construction' *Journal of Information Processing*, **3**, 140–151

Hosaka, M. and Kimura, F. (1984). 'Non-four sided patch expression with control points' *Computer Aided Geometric Design*, **1**, 75–86

Hosaka, M., Kimura, F. and Kakishita, N. (1974). 'A unified method for processing polyhedra' *Information Processing '74*. Amsterdam: North-Holland, 167–172

Houghton, E. G., Emnett, R. F., Factor, J. D. and Sabharwal, C. L. (1985). 'Implementation of a divide-and-conquer method for intersection of parametric surfaces' *Computer Aided Geometric Design*, **2**, 173–183

Idesawa, M. (1973). 'A system to generate a solid figure from a three view' *Bulletin of the Japan Society of Mechanical Engineering*, **16**, 216–225

Johnson, R. H. (1986). *Solid modeling: a state-of-the-art report*, Chestnut Hill, Massachusetts: CAD/CIM Alert, Management Roundtable, Inc.

Kajiya, J. (1982). 'Ray tracing parametric patches' *Computer Graphics (SIGGRAPH '82 Proc.)*, **16**, 245–254

Lane, J. M., Carpenter, L. C., Whitted, T. and Blinn, J. F. (1980). 'Scan line methods for displaying parametrically defined surfaces' *Communications of ACM*, **23**, 23–24

Lee, Y. T. and Requicha, A. G. (1982). 'Algorithms for computing the volume and other integral properties of solids: I – Known methods and open issues; II – A family of algorithms based on representation conversion and cellular approximation' *Communications of ACM*, **25**, 635–650

Lien, S. and Kajiya, J. T. (1984). 'A symbolic method for calculating the integral properties of arbitrary nonconvex polyhedra' *IEEE Computer Graphics and Applications*, **4**, 35–41

Longhi, L. L. (1985). *Interpolating patches between cubic boundaries*, Master's Thesis. Berkeley: University of California, Computer Science Division

Mäntylä, M. (1983). Computational Topology: A study of Topological Manipulations and Interrogations in Computer Graphics and Geometric *Modeling.* Acta Polytechnica Scandinavica, Mathematics and Computer Science Series No. 37. Helsinki

Mäntylä, M. and Sulonen, R. (1982). 'GWB: a solid modeler with Euler operators' *IEEE Computer Graphics and Applications,* **2**, 17–31

Mäntylä, M. and Tamminen, M. (1983). 'Localized set operations for solid modeling' *Computer Graphics (SIGGRAPH '83 Proc.)* **17**, 279–288

Markowski, G. and Wesley, M. A. (1980). 'Fleshing out wire frame' *IBM Journal of Research and Development,* **24**, 582–597

Martin, R. R. Ed. (1987). *The Mathematics of Surfaces II,* Oxford: Clarendon Press

Meagher, D. J. (1981). 'Geometric modeling using octree encoding' *Computer Graphics and Image Processing,* **19**, 129–147

Middleditch, A. E. and Sears, K. H. (1985). 'Blend surfaces for set theoretic volume modelling' *Computer Graphics (SIGGRAPH '85 Proc.),* **19**, 161–170

Mortenson, M. E. (1985). *Geometric Modeling.* New York: John Wiley

Nasri, A. H. (1987). 'Polyhedral subdivision methods for free-form surfaces' *ACM Transactions on Graphics,* **6**, 29–73

Newmann, W. M. and Sproull, R. F. (1979). *Principles of Interactive Computer Graphics.* New York: McGraw-Hill

Ohno, Y. (1981). *An Experiment on Hidden Line Elimination of Curved Surfaces.* Japan: Keio University, Institute of Information Science

Okino, N., Kakazu, Y. and Kubo, H. (1973). 'TIPS-1: technical information processing system for computer-aided design, drawing and manufacturing' In *Computer Languages for Numerical Control.* J. Hatvany, Ed. Amsterdam: North-Holland, 141–150

Okino, N., Kakazu, Y. and Morimoto, M. (1984). 'Extended depth buffer algorithms for hidden surface visualization' *IEEE Computer Graphics and Applications,* **4**, 79–88

Pickett, M. S. and Boyse, J. W. Eds. (1984). *Solid Modeling by Computers,* New York: Plenum Press

Pickett, M. S., Tilove, R. B. and Shapiro, V. (1984). 'RoboTeach: an off-line robot programming system' In *Solid Modeling by Computers.* M. S. Pickett and J. W. Boyse, Eds. New York: Plenum Press, 159–184

Requicha, A. G. (1980). 'Representation for rigid solids: theory, method and systems' *ACM Computing Surveys,* **12**, 437–464

Requicha, A. G. and Voelcker, H. B. (1982). 'Solid modelling: a historical summary and contemporary assessment' *IEEE Computer Graphics and Applications,* **2**, 9–24

Requicha, A. G. and Voelcker, H. B. (1983). 'Solid modelling: current status and research directions' *IEEE Computer Graphics and Applications,* **3**, 25–37

Riesenfeld, R. F. (1973). *Applications of B-spline approximation to geometric problems of computer aided design.* Ph.D. Thesis, Syracuse University

Riesenfeld, R. F. (1983). 'A view of spline-based solid modelling' *Proc. AUTOFACT 5,* SME

Rockwood, A. P. and Owen, J. C. (1987). 'Blending surfaces in solid modeling' In *Geometric Modeling.* G. Farin, Ed. Philadelphia: SIAM, 367–383

Rogers, D. F. and Adams, J. A. (1976). *Mathematical Elements of Computer Graphics*. New York: McGraw-Hill

Rossignac, T. and Requicha, A. (1984). 'Constant-radius blending in solid modeling' *Computers in Mechanical Engineering*, **3**, 65–73

Sabin, M. A. (1983). 'Non-rectangular surface patches suitable for inclusion in a B-spline surface' In *EUROGRAPHICS '83*. P. ten Hagen, Ed. Amsterdam: North-Holland, 57–69

Sabin, M. A. (1986). 'Some negative results in *N* sided patches' *Computer Aided Design*, **18**, 38–44

Sakurai, H. and Gossard, D. C. (1983). 'Solid model input through orthographic views' *Computer Graphics (SIGGRAPH '83 Proc.)*, **17**, 243–247

Sarraga, R. F. and Waters, W. C. (1984). 'Free-form surfaces in GMsolid: goals and issues' In *Solid Modeling by Computers*. M. S. Pickett and J. W. Boyse, Eds. New York: Plenum Press, 187–209

Satoh, H., *et al.* (1985). 'Fast image generation of constructive solid geometry using array processor' *Computer Graphics (SIGGRAPH '85 Proc.)*, **19**, 95–102

Segal, M. and Séquin, C. H. (1985). 'Consistent calculations for solid modeling' *Proc. of ACM Symposium on Computational Geometry*, Baltimore

Séquin, C. H. (1986). 'Procedural spline interpolation in UNICUBIX' *USENIX Computer Graphics Workshop Proceedings*

Shirman, L. A. (1986). *Symmetric interpolation of triangular and quadrilateral patches between cubic boundaries*, Tech. Report No. UCB/CSD 87/319, Computer Science Division, University of California, Berkeley, California, 1985

Spur, G. and Gausemeier, J. (1975). 'Processing of workpiece information for production engineering drawing' In *Proc. 16th International Machine Tool Design and Research Conf.* Manchester, UK, 17–21

Stacey, T. W. and Middleditch, A. E. (1986). 'The geometry of machining for computer-aided manufacture' *Robotica*, **4**, 83–91

SUN (1985). *Programmer's Reference Manual for SunWindows*. Mountain View, California: Sun Microsystems

Sutherland, I. E., Sproull, R. F. and Schumacker, R. A. (1974). 'A characterization of ten hidden-surface algorithms' *ACM Computing Survey*, **6**.

Tan, S. T. and Chan, K. C. (1986). 'Generation of high order surfaces over arbitrary polyhedral meshes', *Computer Aided Design*, **18**, 441–423

Teitelman, W. (1978). *Interlisp Reference Manual*. Palo Alto: Xerox Research Center

Thibault, W. C. and Naylor, B. F. (1987). 'Set operations on polyhedra using binary space partitioning trees' *Computer Graphics (SIGGRAPH '87 Proc.)*, **21**, 153–162

Thomas, S. W. (1984). *Modelling volumes bounded by B-spline surfaces*. Ph.D. Thesis, University of Utah

Thomas, S. W. (1985). 'The Alpha-1 computer-aided geometric design system in the UNIX environment' *Login*, **10**, 54–64

Thomas, S. W. (1987). 'Modeling with sculptured solids' *Lecture Notes for Seminar on Advanced Solid Modeling*, ACM SIGGRAPH '87, Anaheim

Tiller, W. (1983). 'Rational B-splines for curve and surface representation' *IEEE Computer Graphics and Applications*, **3**, 61–69

Toriya, H., Satoh, T., Ueda, K. and Chiyokura, H. (1986). 'UNDO and REDO operations for solids modeling' *IEEE Computer Graphics and Applications*, **6**, 35–42

Toth, D. L. (1985). 'On ray tracing parametric surfaces' *Computer Graphics (SIGGRAPH '85 Proc.)*, **19**, 171–179

Veenman, P. (1979) 'ROMULUS – the design of a geometric modeller' In *Geometric Modelling Seminar*. W. A. Carter, Ed. CAM-I document P-80-GM-01

Vitter, J. S. (1984) 'US&R: a new framework for redoing' *IEEE Software*, **1**, 39–52

Voelcker, H. B. and Requicha, A. G. (1977). 'Geometric modelling of mechanical parts and processes' *IEEE Computer*, **10**, 48–57

Wang, W. P. and Wang, K. K. (1986). 'Geometric modeling for swept volume of moving solids' *IEEE Computer Graphics and Applications*, **6**, 8–17

Weiler, K. (1985). 'Edge-based data structures for solid modeling in curved-surface environments' *IEEE Computer Graphics and Applications*, **5**, 21–40

Wesley, M. A. and Markowsky, G. (1981). 'Fleshing out Projections' *IBM Journal of Research and Development*, **25**, 938–954

Wesley, M. A., Lazano-Perez, T., Lieberman, L. I., Lavin, M. A. and Grossman, D. D. (1980). 'A geometric modelling system for automated mechanical assembly' *IBM Journal of Research and Development*, **24**, 64–74

Whitted, T. (1980). 'An improved illumination model for shaded display' *Communication of ACM*, **23**, 343–349

Van Wijk, J. J. (1986). 'Bicubic patches for approximating non-rectangular control-point meshes', *Computer Aided Geometric Design*, **3**, 1–13

Wördenweber, B. (1984). 'Finite element mesh generation' *Computer Aided Design*, **16**, 285–291

Woo, T. C. (1977). 'Computer-aided recognition of volumetric design-CARVD' In *Advanced Computer-Aided Manufacturing*. D. McPherson, Ed. Amsterdam: North-Holland, 121–135

Woodwark, J. (1986). *Computing Shape*. London: Butterworths

Yamaguchi, F. and Tokieda, T. (1984). 'A unified algorithm for Boolean shape operations' *IEEE Computer Graphics and Applications*, **4**, 24–37

Index

ancestor solid   56

B-rep   6, 13, 22
B-spline curve   110
B-spline patch   199
B-spline surface   199
Beta-spline   148
Bézier   101, 196
Bézier curve   101
Bézier patch   196, 207
Bézier surface   196
bicubic parametric patch   191
blended surface   151
Boolean operation   8, 79
boundary representation   6, 13, 22
BUILD   13
BUILD2   15, 20, 29

C-loop   30
C-vertex   93
CAD   1
CAD/CAM   1
CAM   1
CAM-I   14
CATIA   12
CBL   53
characteristic polyhedral design   147
characteristic polyhedron   147
CLB   53
closed curve   121
colour shaded image   277
COMPAC   15
compatibility condition   206
compatibility correction   207

compound-solid operation   56
compound-solid tree   59
computer vision   4
concave corner   165
concave edge   270
constricted loop   93
constructive solid geometry   8, 13, 21
constructive solid geometry
    representation   8, 13, 21
control point   101
control vector   114
convex corner   165
convex edge   270
convex hull property   102, 223
Coons patch   192, 205
cross-boundary tangent   235
cross-section   146, 275
cross-sectional design   146, 207
CS   56
CSG   8, 13, 21
CSG-rep   8, 13, 21
CSG-tree   9
curvature   116
curvature radius   139, 142
curvature vector   116
curve   100
curved surface   2
cut operation   73
cutter path   11

DESIGNBASE   12, 19, 20, 25
difference   8, 79
difference operation   8, 79
dual representation   14